THE
WILDFLOWER GARDENER'S GUIDE

Midwest, Great Plains, and Canadian Prairies Edition

HENRY W. ART

Botanical illustrations by Hyla M. Skudder

Garden illustrations by Elayne Sears

Photographs by the author

STOREY

A Garden Way Publishing Book
Storey Communications, Inc.
Pownal, Vermont 05261

Cover photograph of wood lily (Lilium philadelphicum) *by Henry W. Art*
Book design and production by Andrea Gray
Edited by Deborah Burns
Maps rendered by Northern Cartographic, Inc.
Grass illustrations by Henry W. Art

Copyright © 1991 by Storey Communications, Inc.

Printed in the United States by Courier
Second Printing, July 1994

Library of Congress Cataloging-in-Publication Data

Art, Henry Warren.
 The wildflower gardener's guide. Midwest, Great Plains, and
 Canadian prairies edition / Henry W. Art ; botanical illustrations
 by Hyla M. Scudder, garden illustrations by Elayne Sears,
 photographs by the author.
  p. cm.
  Includes bibliographical references and index.
  ISBN 0-88266-669-X — ISBN 0-88266-668-1 (pbk.)
  1. Wild flower gardening—Middle West. 2. Wild flower gardening—
Great Plains. 3. Wild flower gardening—Prairie Provinces.
4. Wild flowers—Middle West. 5. Wild flowers—Great Plains.
6. Wild flowers—Prairie Provinces. I. Title.
SB439.24.M629A77 1991
635.9'676'0977—dc20
                                                    90-55865
                                                      CIP

This book is dedicated to Kay, Jon, Susan, Steven, Emily, Christopher,
and the generations of Native North American prairie children
who preceded them.

Contents

Acknowledgments

The author and illustrator would like to thank the following people and organizations:

The Virginia Native Plant Society and the California Native Plant Society for their assistance in framing the Wildflower Conservation Guidelines published in this volume.

For helpful assistance on botanical issues and scouting sites for wildflower photography: Patty Leslie of the San Antonio Botanical Center; Annie Gillespie, John Averett, and Elizabeth Carmack of the National Wildflower Research Center, Austin, TX; Brian Bader of Prairie Nursery, Westfield, WI; Gayle Weinstein of the Denver Botanic Garden; Rick Brune of the Colorado Native Plant Society; Randy Mock of the Green Hills Foundation/Dallas Nature Center.

Dr. R. Stewart Smith, Director of Agricultural Research & Development, LiphaTech, for information concerning rhizobium strains.

Walter Kittredge, Michael Canoso, and Emily Wood for assistance in the use of the Harvard University Herbaria (the collections of the Gray Herbarium and Arnold Arboretum).

Chris Skudder for moral support and encouragement. Katherine Art for hospitality.

Michael Barrow and Andrew Art for computer assistance and Karen Worley, Sawyer Library, Williams College, for computerized literature searches.

John and Martha Storey and Pam Art, of Storey Communications, for sustained interest in and support of publishing about gardening with wildflowers and native plants.

Deborah Burns for sensitive editing and continued enthusiasm. Andrea Gray and Elayne Sears for design and illustration of this series of books.

Hundreds of people from the botanic gardens, nature centers, arboreta, wildflower seed companies, native plant propagation nurseries, native plant societies, and botanical organizations, who responded to requests for the information contained in the appendices.

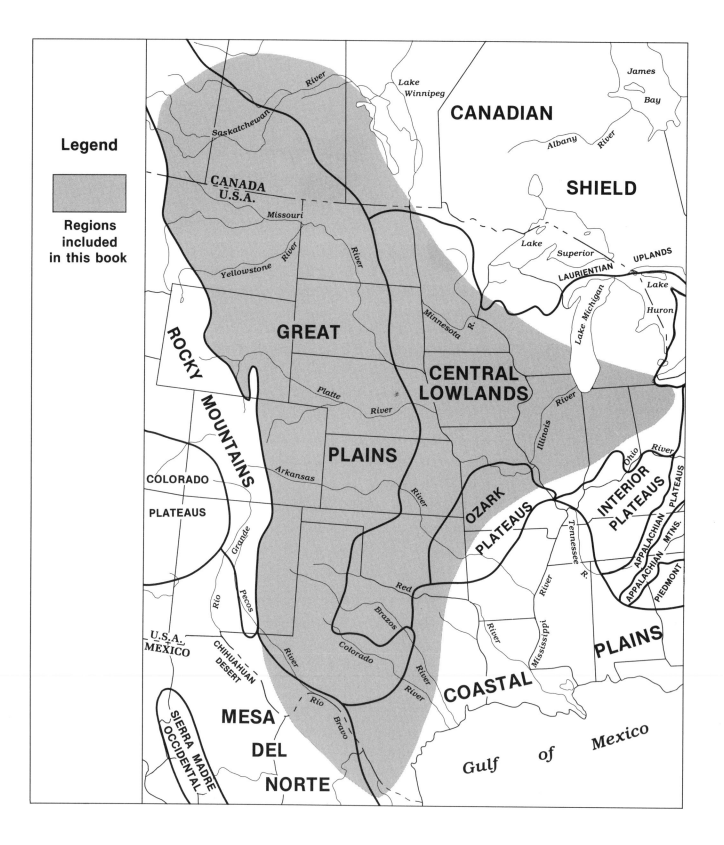

Legend

Regions included in this book

CANADIAN

SHIELD

James

Bay

Albany   River

Lake
Winnipeg

River

Saskatchewan

CANADA
U.S.A.

Missouri

Lake
Superior

UPLANDS

LAURIENTIAN

Lake
Michigan

Lake
Huron

Yellowstone   River

River

Minnesota

R.

GREAT

ROCKY

CENTRAL
LOWLANDS

River

COLORADO

MOUNTAINS

Platte

River

Illinois

PLATEAUS

PLAINS

INTERIOR
PLATEAUS

Ohio   River

Arkansas

River

OZARK

PLATEAUS

APPALACHIAN   PLATEAUS

Grande

Red

Tennessee   R.

APPALACHIAN   MTNS.

Rio

Pecos

Brazos

River

PIEDMONT

U.S.A.

MEXICO

CHIHUAHUAN
DESERT

River

Colorado

Mississippi

River

PLAINS

SIERRA MADRE
OCCIDENTAL

Rio

River

COASTAL

MESA

Bravo

DEL

NORTE

Gulf   of   Mexico

PART I

An Introduction for Wildflower Gardeners

This book is about growing wildflowers in the heartland of North America, a region extending from the eastern foothills of the Rocky Mountains to the Ohio River basin, and from the interior plains of Alberta to northern Mexico. This edition of *The Wildflower Gardener's Guide* focuses on the Great Plains and the Central Lowlands regions that support grasslands and prairies. It includes a variety of habitats, ranging from wet tallgrass sloughs to dry shortgrass prairies at the edges of deserts. Of the hundreds of wildflowers that grow in these habitats, 34 of the most easily cultivated and beautiful species have been selected for inclusion in this book. These wildflowers have been chosen to cover the range of flowering season and garden conditions typical of mid-continent North America.

Wildflowers of North American Prairies and Plains

The low, undulating topography and vast plains stretching from horizon to horizon give the Central Lowlands and Great Plains a majesty all their own. This environmental platform supports a vast array of plants and animals in an apparent simplicity that conceals an underlying complexity. Far from monotonous lawns of grass, the North American grasslands are rich mixtures of different grass, sedge, and wildflower species whose lives are delicately intertwined with one another and with the environment. Dramatic seasonal rhythms of weather are superimposed on longer-term cycles of climate, creating an ecological symphony of many movements. I urge you to incorporate the spectacular diversity of native species into your personal landscape — be it containers on a porch, flower beds in a modest yard, or a prairie restoration on a considerable ranch.

Although the topography and vegetation of the prairies and plains may appear at first glance to be uniform as far as the eye can see, the environment is highly variable from season to season, and from year to year. Summer temperatures in the Great Plains frequently exceed 95°F while winter temperatures are often 10°F or colder. Average annual precipitation varies from 12 inches in the Great Plains to 40 inches in prairies east of the Mississippi River. During droughts, however, it may be less than half that amount, and more than twice as much in wet years.

Some of the extremes, and even some of the normal seasonal changes of the continental climate of the heartland region — cold winters, prolonged dry spells, hot summer winds — can be hard on conventional gardens. Wildflowers provide solutions to many gardening problems since, unlike most domesticated horticultural plants, they have the ability to make it on their own without human assistance.

WILDFLOWER HABITATS

The native wildflowers of the Central Lowlands and Great Plains are the products of their varied habitats, geologic history, and human activities. Periodic disturbances ranging from drought to fires to grazing by mammals have been important natural elements maintaining these grassland landscapes.

The flatness of the landscape, perhaps the most striking feature of the Central Lowlands and Great Plains, has its origins in the distant past. At times over the past 500 million years, broad, shallow seas have covered the heartland of North America. The most recent such episode occurred about 135 million years ago when water inundated the region from the present foothills of the Rockies to the Mississippi River, and from the Gulf of Mexico to Northern Canada. During the millions of years that the continent was under water, sediments accumulated on the bottom of the shallow sea, smoothing its surface and eventually covering it with limestone, sandstone, and shale bedrock. Then, 65 million years ago, as dinosaurs were be-coming extinct and grasses were starting to evolve, the sea slowly receded. The newly exposed land surface was subjected to further smoothing through erosion and depositing of sediments carried by wind, rain, and flooding rivers.

About 6 million years ago the climate is believed to have become warmer and drier than it had been previously, allowing grasses to cover the broad central plains. The Cascades, Sierra Nevada, and Rocky Mountains then, as now, squeezed much of the moisture out of air masses moving eastward from the Pacific Ocean.

Grasses are well adapted to dry, even droughty, conditions, since they tend to have extensive root systems, leaves that curl tightly to conserve water in response to drought, and the ability to become temporarily dormant when the soil moisture is too low to sustain their growth. In some species of grass more than 80 percent of the plant is below ground, in its roots, and only 20 percent is above ground in green, leafy shoots. In general, grasses have evolved to grow actively when moisture is available and to rest when it isn't.

Between 18,000 and 15,000 years ago, the massive ice sheets of the Pleistocene glaciers covered the Canadian Shield, Laurentian Uplands, and northern portions of the Central Lowlands, pushing the tundra and coniferous forests far to the south. The prairies of this time, if they existed at all, were small patches of grasslands in what is now the southern Great Plains and northern Mexico. As the ice sheet retreated, more than 10,000 years ago, meltwater filled the Great Lake basins, scooped out by the southern advance of the glaciers. Glacial ice was also responsible for forming the "prairie pothole" lakes and ponds in the glaciated portions of the Dakotas, Manitoba, and Alberta.

During the late glacial period, Native Americans may have moved onto the plains, the descendants of those who migrated across the Bering Strait from Asia. These new residents encountered now-extinct large mammals such as giant beaver, ground sloth, mastodon, wooly mammoth, camels, yaks, and a primitive version of the horse, inhabiting a central North America that was cooler and more wooded than it is at present. Hunting and burning by the early Native Americans may have contributed to the extinction of many of those species.

It is probable that both the warming of the climate 5,000 years ago and the use of fire by Native Americans allowed the grasslands emerging along the eastern margins of the Rocky Mountains to expand eastward and cross the Mississippi River. Fires, set by lightning strikes or Native Americans and fanned by the persistent westerly winds blowing unobstructed from the Rockies, swept across the landscape, extinguished only where they encountered the infrequent rivers.

Grasses are well adapted to survive fires, with their vast root systems and subterranean buds. The soil covers and protects their growing zone, called the intercalary meristem, at the base of the leaf. In contrast, woody plants, their buds exposed at the ends of their branches, are for the most part damaged or killed by fires. Fire actually benefits many species of grasses and prairie wildflowers. It stimulates them to grow vigorously by releasing nutrients previously locked in undecomposed plant remains. It also cleanses the soil of naturally occurring inhibitors that limit plant growth, it removes thatch, and it darkens the soil so that it warms up more quickly in the spring. There is ample evidence that without fires, the eastern prairies would have been overgrown by trees and shrubs.

During the period of Native American dominance in the plains and lowlands, buffalo (Bison bison), pronghorn (Antilocapra americana), and small mammals such as prairie dogs (Cynomys ludovicianus) and jack rabbits (Lepus californicus and L. townsendii) may have played important roles in maintaining prairies and grasslands. Many species of grasses and prairie wildflowers grow more vigorously when grazed moderately, because their flowering is delayed. Intercalary meristems enable grasses to grow from below soil surface. In addition, it has recently been discovered that enzymes in the saliva of some mammals chemically stimulate the growth of these plants. Many grazers actually find grasses unpalatable: their leaves and shoots are rich in substances such as lignin that disrupt digestion, and their surfaces have high concentrations of silica. Grasses also benefit when mammals browse on competing woody plants such as basswood, elm, cottonwood, and sumac. Trees and shrubs were often destroyed by buffalo rubbing against them and making "wallows" as they seasonally migrated across the plains.

The life of the Plains Native Americans was intimately linked to the buffalo, which supplied them with food, clothing, tools, building materials, and even fuel. Today it is hard to imagine, but it is estimated that in the late 1700s 60 million buffalo roamed the central grasslands, with single herds of up to 12 million animals. The impact on the prairies of these large (1,000-2,000-pound) grazing animals, which migrated up to 300 miles each year in early summer and again in autumn, must have been considerable. Buffalo prefer to eat woody shrubs and grass in preference to forbs, and undoubtedly were an important factor in encouraging the growth of wildflower species like leadplant in the tallgrass prairie.

By 1889, the policy of wholesale slaughter of the buffalo in order to subjugate the Native Americans of the Plains had led to only 150 animals existing in a wild state. Five years later the last bison was shot in the wild, and the total population in captivity was only 250 animals. The 18th- and 19th-century influx of European pioneers to the Central Lowland prairies and Great Plains irrevocably changed the landscape. Domestic livestock displaced the bison and most of the native grazing mammals. Exotic grasses were planted in pasturelands, and overgrazing allowed for the spread of weedy European and Asian species. The prairies were put to the plow: native grasslands were converted to other grass crops such as corn, wheat, and barley in what was to become the "bread basket of the world." Wet sloughs were drained so that their rich soils could be cultivated. The flat unbroken topography was dissected by railroads, highways, fenced pastures, and irrigated fields. Any fires that started in the developing checkerboard landscape were quickly put out. The destruction of the Native American way of life, attuned as it was to native prairie ecosystems, gathered an irreversible momentum, right through the urbanization and suburbanization of the 20th century. The insult to the native prairie and plain landscape perhaps reached a peak in the Dust Bowl era of 1933 to 1939 when overgrazing and cultivation of marginal lands during a period of extreme drought led to massive wind erosion and degradation of vast portions of the Great Plains.

No longer are millions of bison free to roam across the prairies, no longer do prairie dog towns teem with populations in the millions, no longer can fires sweep across the landscape from horizon to horizon. Nevertheless, amid the current patchwork of cities, suburbs, countryside, ranches, corn and wheat fields, railroads, and highways, are the remnants of the plant communities that have nurtured native wildflowers for millions of years. The Great Plains and Central Lowlands may comprise the region of North

America most extensively altered by human activities; yet its inhabitants are also the most intensely active in restoring native vegetation to its natural state.

Tallgrass Prairie. As pioneers of European origin left the oak and hickory forests of the East and entered the prairies of the Mississippi River valley, they marveled at broad expanses of grasses tall enough to hide a person on horseback. These prairies, dominated by tall grasses and diverse wildflowers, stretch in a broad, irregular wedge from Minnesota to eastern Texas to Indiana and parts of Ohio. Some refer to the extension of the grasslands into the deciduous forests east of the Mississippi River as the "Prairie Peninsula."

The tallgrass prairie region, like other portions of the Central Lowlands and Great Plains, has a continental climate of cold winters and hot summers. In general, spring has the greatest precipitation, while the late summer through winter are the driest time of the year. There are substantial periods of ample rainfall, when precipitation exceeds the amount of water that can evaporate from the surfaces of plants and the soil. Every 15 to 25 years, however, there is a significant drought, a prolonged period in which evaporation greatly exceeds precipitation.

The soils of the tallgrass prairie region are some of the most fertile on earth. The close balance between rainfall and evaporation, along with the deep (often 8 feet or more) penetration by the extensive root systems of tallgrass prairie plants, tends to retain nutrients in the soil, rather than letting them wash away. The typical black color of these soils results from the decomposition of roots and the vigorous mixing of the soil by earthworms, rodents, insects, and other animals that coat the soil particles with humus and organic matter. One type of soil found extensively in the tallgrass prairie region is loess, a deep, rich, silty soil that was carried by the wind from the Great Plains thousands of years ago and deposited in the Central Lowlands.

The tallgrass prairie, like other North American grasslands, is a diverse mixture of grasses, sedges, and broad-leaved wildflowers, sometimes called "forbs" by agronomists and ranchers. The wet, marshy areas in the tallgrass prairies, where standing water can be found at least in the spring, are often called "sloughs." Prairie cordgrass (*Spartina pectinata*), also known as sloughgrass, is one of the tallest grasses of the prairies. Native Americans used it for thatching, and early "sodbusters" even used it as fuel. Canada wild rye (*Elymus canadensis*) is a tall grass that often encircles prairie cordgrass-filled sloughs and lines river banks, but is found throughout the prairie regions on dry, well-drained soils as well.

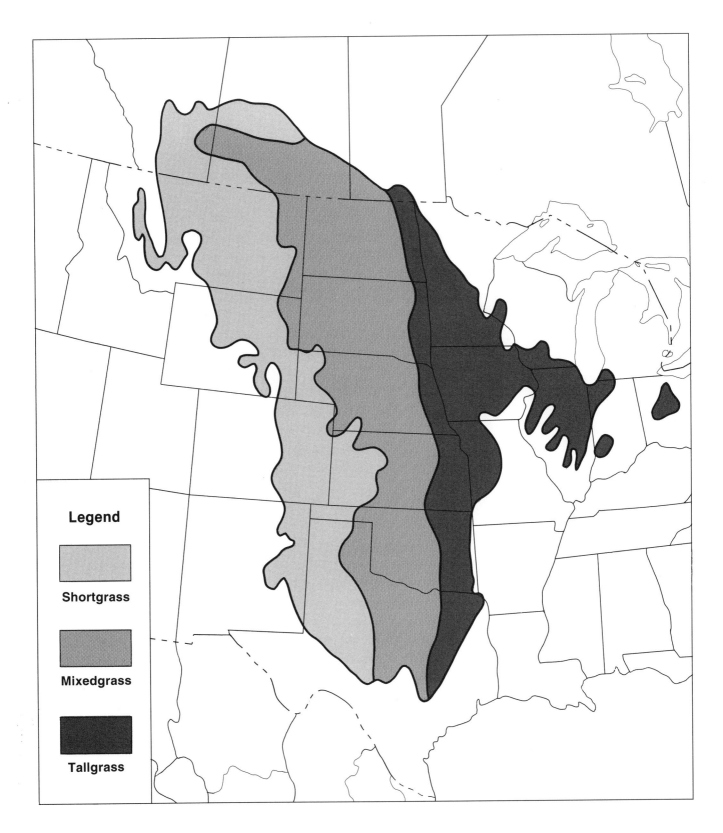

Legend

Shortgrass

Mixedgrass

Tallgrass

Lowland areas in the tallgrass prairie region that are not as wet as sloughs are often dominated by tall species of grass such as the sod-forming big bluestem (*Andropogon gerardi*), the bunch-forming Indian grass (*Sorghastrum nutans*), and switchgrass (*Panicum virgatum*), which grows either as a bunch grass or a sod grass depending upon conditions. These are "warm-season grasses" that start to grow in midspring and grow vigorously during the warm months until they flower in the late summer or early fall. Other species, such as the warm-season bunch grasses little bluestem (*Andropogon scoparius* or, sometimes, *Schizackyrium scoparium*) and prairie dropseed (*Sporobolus heterolepsis*) as well as the sedge *Carex pensylvanica* are more abundant in the drier areas in the tallgrass prairie regions, especially on uplands. Porcupine needlegrass (*Stipa spartea*), a "cool-season grass" that starts its growth in late winter or early spring and flowers by late spring or early summer, is found in the drier portions of northern tallgrass prairies. It gets its common name from the needle-like projections, known as "awns," on its fruits.

Along the northeastern and southeastern borders of the tallgrass prairies are forests dominated by various trees like bur oak (*Quercus macrocarpa*), post oak (*Q. stellata*), shagbark hickory (*Carya ovata*), and box-elder (*Acer negundo*), and shrubs like New Jersey tea (*Ceanothus americanus*) and smooth sumac (*Rhus glabra*). The climate of the tallgrass prairie region is moist enough that trees and shrubs could encroach into the grasslands were it not for the periodic fires, especially during droughts, that keep the forests in check.

Shortgrass Prairie. The natural vegetation of the Great Plains, stretching in a band east of the Rockies from central Texas to southeastern Alberta, is a prairie dominated by grasses of shorter stature (2-18 inches high) than those of the more humid tallgrass prairie. Not only are the summers hotter and the winters colder in the Great Plains than in the tallgrass prairies, but the annual rainfall is more scanty and less predictable as well. Grasses and wildflowers growing there are often subjected to seasonal moisture stress when evaporation from the soil and plant surfaces exceeds precipitation. In contrast to the deep-rooted plants of tallgrass prairies, plants of the shortgrass prairies have shallower, spreading roots that can quickly absorb the rainfall even if it doesn't penetrate very deeply into the soil.

Soils of the shortgrass prairies tend to be light brown, having much less organic matter than those of the prairie peninsula. The dry soils of the Great Plains also tend to be saltier and more alkaline than those to the east, because there is not enough precipitation to wash natural salts completely out of the soil. Sometimes an impervious "hardpan" of limestone-like calcium carbonate forms a foot or so deep in these soils, marking the depth to which rainwater has penetrated and carried salts.

Buffalo grass (*Buchloë dactyloides*), blue grama (*Bouteloua gracilis*), hairy grama (*Bouteloua hirsuta*), and sideoats grama (*Bouteloua curtipendula*), all warm-season plants, are important species in shortgrass prairies. They are also all bunch grasses that with sufficient moisture can grow so thickly they appear to form a sod. Indian ricegrass (*Oryzopsis hymenoides*) is a cool-season bunch grass that grows in the Great Plains and the foothills of the Rockies. While these species and their associated wildflowers are not as adapted to fires as tallgrass prairie plants are, they are quite tolerant of grazing by buffalo, pronghorn, prairie dogs, jackrabbits, and other mammals. Overgrazing by domestic livestock, cultivation of marginal lands, and too frequent burning of these grasslands can lead to encroachment by the bordering deserts and the deterioration of the shortgrass prairie landscape, such as happened during the Dust Bowl era of the 1930s.

Mixed-grass Prairie. Between the shortgrass prairies of the Great Plains and the tallgrass prairies of the Central Lowlands is a transitional or mixed-grass grassland where the species from the East blend with those from the West. The grama grasses of the shortgrass prairies mingle with little bluestem and other grasses of the eastern prairies. In addition, cool-season grasses such as the sod-forming western wheatgrass (*Agropyron smithii*) and bunch grasses like needle-and-thread (*Stipa comata*) and Junegrass (*Koeleria cristata*) are important in the mixed-grass prairie.

The climate and soils of the mixed-grass prairie belt, extending from Saskatchewan and the Dakotas south to central Texas, are also intermediate between tallgrass and shortgrass prairies. Although precipitation in the region amounts to about 24 inches per year, potential evaporation is greater, and where evaporation starts to exceed annual precipitation, there is a transition from tallgrass to mixed-grass prairie. Where calcium carbonate hardpans are found in the soil, they tend to be deeper (at depths of 1-4 feet) than in the shortgrass prairie because of the greater rainfall in this region. Mixed prairie soils have more organic matter than those of the western Great Plains, but are not as dark as those of the tallgrass prairies.

The composition of mixed-grass prairies often shifts with changes in the environment. As grazing increases, especially by domestic livestock, there is usually a shift from cool-season grasses like porcupine needlegrass to warm-season plants like buffalo grass. Species shifts also accompany the drought cycles of the prairies. During the drought of the Dust Bowl era, the boundary between mixed-grass and tallgrass prairies shifted east by more than 100 miles, and shifted back west when the drought was broken. During wet years in the mixed-grass prairie, buffalo grass tends to spread at the expense of blue grama grass, while in periods of drought blue grama does relatively better than buffalo grass, even though both species decline. Wet years often also cause an expansion of cottonwood, willow, elm, and oak outward from the ribbons of river bottomland forests into the prairie, only to be followed by their retreat during the next drought.

THE JOYS OF WILDFLOWERS

The beauty of prairie wildflowers has captivated botanists and gardeners from around the world for centuries, and Native Americans for thousands of years. Early European explorers, however, were somewhat mystified by the vast, treeless plains they discovered in the center of the continent.

Less than half a century after Columbus set eyes on North America, Francisco Coronado crossed the Rio Grande on April 23, 1541, to explore what later would be called the Great Plains, reaching as far north as present-day Kansas. His expedition did not find the gold and slaves it sought, but did provide Spain with the first descriptions of broad plains, Plains "Indians," and buffalo. At about the same time, Hernando de Soto became the first European to see the Mississippi River. His party wandered as far west as present day Oklahoma, recording massive floods in March, 1543. In their futile search for riches the early Spanish introduced the modern horse to the New World, an event that would profoundly affect the mobility and culture of the Native Americans of the Plains.

During the 17th century, French explorers and missionaries entered the Central Lowlands from "New France," the colony that later would become Canada. In 1673, Father Jacques Marquette accompanied Louis Joliet in the exploration of the Illinois and Mississippi rivers as far south as the mouth of the Arkansas River. Seven years later, René-Robert La Salle and Father Louis Hennepin started to explore the mid-Mississippi, during which time Hennepin was captured by the Sioux. He traveled northward with them through what is now southern Minnesota, but later escaped to give accounts of the tallgrass prairie and the fires set by his captors. In 1682 La Salle became the first European to travel the length of the Mississippi River, claiming the entire region south to New Orleans for the King of France.

It wasn't until more than a century later that the region would receive the attention of explorers interested specifically in plants. In 1793 Andre Michaux, a French botanist, was sent from Philadelphia with Meriwether Lewis to explore from the Missouri River to the Pacific Coast on behalf of the American Philosophical Society. The expedition was recalled, however, and it wasn't until 1795 that Michaux finally had the opportunity to collect plants, at his own expense, in the prairies of Indiana, Illinois, and Missouri.

A decade later Meriwether Lewis would also return to the central prairies and the Great Plains, en route to the Pacific Ocean with the Lewis & Clark Expedition of 1804 to 1806. Under orders from President Thomas Jefferson, Captains Meriwether Lewis and William Clark were to explore the newly acquired Louisiana Purchase, observing "...the face of the country, its growth and vegetable productions; especially those not of the U.S. [only 17 states at the time]."

Although he was not a botanist, the list of plants Meriwether Lewis discovered and collected on his journey to the Pacific is truly impressive: in total, 178 plants not previously described were cataloged. There would have been more prairie plants in his collection if most of the plants collected from east of the Rockies had not been washed away by flood waters during the winter of 1805-6. Dried plant specimens from the expedition were taken back to the East Coast where botanists named the newly discovered species, including snow-on-the-mountain (*Euphorbia marginata*), blanket-flower (*Gaillardia aristata*), and prairie smoke (*Geum triflorum*). Horticulturalists like Bernard McMahon of Philadelphia grew plants from seeds collected by the expedition and introduced many of these new plants into the garden trade.

While the tallgrass and mixed-grass prairie regions were settled by Europeans in the early 1800s, many people misperceived the Great Plains region as "The Great American Desert" until the mid-19th century. By the end of the 1800s, the Great Plains and Central Lowlands would nurture many of the North American scientists conducting research in the emerging discipline of "ecology." It was here also that the prairie restoration/ preservation movement gained momentum after World War II, spurring a continent-wide interest in reestablishing native plants on a large scale.

INDIVIDUAL WILDFLOWERS

Modern-day gardeners can share the botanists' fascination by introducing wildflowers into their own gardens — and even the most common of native species can bring great pleasure as one learns their secrets.

Butterfly weed. Butterfly weed (*Asclepias tuberosa*) is a widespread native perennial that grows from Arizona and Utah to Massachusetts and Florida. In the center of its range, the Midwestern tallgrass prairie, butterfly weed has bright red-orange flowers. The colors of the flowers change toward the edges of its range, however, becoming yellow-orange from Minnesota to the Great Plains and yellow in the Southwest. Along the eastern seaboard the flowers are a medium orange. The shapes of the leaves also vary geographically, those in the East having tapering bases, those in the Midwest having heart-shaped bases, and those in Florida and the Gulf Coast having flat bases.

While the shapes of leaves and colors of flowers may be variable, the unusual shape of the butterfly weed flower is consistent across its range. Clusters of up to 50 flowers are borne at the top of the plant, so that their color and fragrant nectar catch the attention of passing bees, wasps, and, as its common name implies, butterflies.

The flowers have evolved a peculiar form especially suited to pollination by these hairy-legged insects, especially heavy bees. The pollen of butterfly weed, unlike most other wildflowers, is produced in 2 sticky masses known as *pollinia*. These *pollinia* are attached to each other by a straplike tissue with a grooved gland called a *corpusculum*. Five pairs of these pollen masses are packed in open sacs near the center of the flower. The 5 downward-sloping petals of the butterfly weed flower are difficult for insects to land on, but the 5 hoods that cluster around the polished female nectar-producing structures in the center of the flower make a perfect landing platform — or almost perfect. Frequently, when an insect alights and probes for nectar around the center of the flower, its feet slip and get stuck on a corpusculum. Struggling to free itself, it usually yanks the pollinia out of the flower. These cling to its legs like drooping golden anchors as it flies on to the next flower. Upon landing the insect will frequently stick its leg into special pouches, part of the female floral structure, thereby freeing its leg of the unwanted pollinia and accomplishing pollination at the same time.

Butterfly weed cannot pollinate itself, so without its insect visitors it would not produce any fruit. At best only 1 or 2 of the flowers in a cluster produce fruit, but each fruit contains many tufted seeds that catch the autumn winds to be carried great distances.

Other Species. The wildflower garden may have other delights awaiting discovery. Blanketflower (*Gaillardia aristata*) often covers the northern Great Plains with its red and yellow flowers. Look carefully at its flower heads and you may discover that the flower moth *Schinia masoni* has taken sanctuary there. It hides from bird predators during the day with its head and yellow body pointing toward the yellow tips of the ray flowers and its crimson wings overlapping the red bases of the florets. In the evening the flower moths become more active, searching for nectar from blanketflower blos-

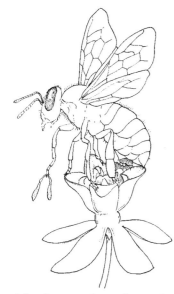

A bee leaving a butterfly weed flower with pollinia attached to its foreleg.

soms. The caterpillars of flower moths also depend on blanketflower for food, eating some of the developing seeds in the flower heads.

Moths are also an important pollinator of the Missouri evening primrose (*Oenothera missouriensis*), whose flowers open as the sun is setting. By the heat of the next day the large yellow flowers wither and turn orange, becoming less attractive to the moths, which are active from dusk to dawn. The fruits of some wildflowers, such as birdsfoot violet (*Viola pedata*) and prairie phlox (*Phlox pilosa*), open explosively, shooting their seeds several feet in the process. Other plants, like pasqueflower (*Anemone patens*) and prairie smoke (*Geum triflorum*), have hairy, wispy fruits that are blown away by the wind. Still others, like showy tick trefoil (*Desmodium canadense*), have fruits with minute bristles that cling to animals as they pass by.

This book presents but a few of the hundreds of wildflowers that are worthy of introduction into gardens in the heartland of North America. Although some of us greatly enjoy studying those intricacies of wildflower life cycles that can be discovered only through close observation, others may be perfectly content simply appreciating the subtle colors and graceful forms of these elements of our natural heritage.

Getting a Start

This book presents 34 wildflowers native to North American prairies and meadows. You may already be familiar with some of these species, such as black-eyed Susan, lance-leaved coreopsis, and bluebonnet. Others, such as birdsfoot violet, compass plant, and meadow beauty, may be new to you. The selected species are well adapted to the range of conditions likely to exist in gardens of the region and can be propagated without much difficulty. Although any wildflower becomes scarce near the edges of its natural range, none of the species included in this book is designated "rare" or "endangered." They are generally available from reputable wildflower suppliers who sell nursery-propagated stock, or from seed companies.

It is delightful to watch the parade of wildflowers through the growing season, and the species chosen for this edition will provide a succession of flowering from late winter through autumn. These wildflowers can be grown in a wide variety of conditions, from conventional gardens to grassland restorations, from meadows to shade; some can even be grown in containers on your porch or patio. Hopefully, the wildflowers in this book will be only a starting point for your gardening with native plants.

Many other species are presented in other regional editions of *The Wildflower Gardener's Guide*, *A Garden of Wildflowers*, and other books on native-plant gardening suitable for central North American gardens.

Some wildflowers that are not included in this book are difficult to bring into the garden because of their demanding soil or cultural requirements. For example, Indian paintbrushes have green leaves yet are parasitic on the roots of other plants; most species are nearly impossible to cultivate in a garden. They are best left growing where they are in the wild and should be moved into your garden only if they are in imminent danger of destruction by development.

WILDFLOWER CONSERVATION

One safeguard of our native wild plants is the Federal Endangered Species Act of 1973, administered by the U.S. Fish and Wildlife Service. This act gives protection to those native species that are recognized as endangered in the United States. This law applies only to federal lands, however, and to the interstate traffic of rare plants. The protection of endangered wildflowers on other public and private lands is left up to the states, as is the protection of species that might become locally rare or endangered through collection by native-plant suppliers and wildflower fanciers. State laws protecting wildflowers are far from uniform, and even where there is protective legislation, the enforcement of these laws is sometimes weak.

Wildflower gardeners should become aware of their state's laws concerning the protection of native plants. If your state lacks such protective legislation, or if the enforcement of the laws is weak, become an advocate for passage of strong and effective measures. The World Wildlife Fund and the Environmental Defense Fund, whose addresses can be found in Appendix C, can provide information concerning model native-plant protection legislation.

The wildflower gardener is faced with moral and ethical considerations that do not confront the gardener of cultivars. Essential to the enjoyment and appreciation of wild, native plants is a respect for living organisms in their native habitats. The wildflower gardener's code of conduct should protect naturally occurring populations of native plants, not only so that others can enjoy them, but also to preserve the ecological roles these plants play. Individual actions do make a difference, both positively and negatively. Wildflower gardeners have the chance to counteract the tragedy of habitat destruction and reduction in native-plant populations occurring around the world.

PLANTING STOCK

One of the first questions one might ask is where to obtain seeds or plants to start a garden of wildflowers. Where not to obtain plants is easier to answer. *Plants growing in their native habitats should never be dug up for the garden.* Apart from the laws that protect wildflowers in many states, it is unethical to uproot native plants. Furthermore, many deeply rooted perennials are nearly impossible to transplant even with a backhoe.

The propagation instructions given for the 34 species of wildflowers in this book are intended for gardeners who desire to make divisions of their own plants only, not of those growing in the wild. The only circumstance

WILDFLOWER CONSERVATION GUIDELINES*

1. Let your acts reflect your respect for wild native plants as integral parts of biological communities and natural landscapes. Remember that if you pick a wildflower, your action affects the natural world. The cumulative effects of the actions of many people can be particularly harmful.

2. Do not collect native plants or plant parts from the wild except as part of rescue operations sponsored by responsible organizations. Even then, any parts, including seeds, of wildflowers on state or federal threatened, rare, or endangered lists cannot be collected without a permit.

3. Encourage the use of regional and local native plants in home and public landscapes. Before obtaining wildflower plants or seeds for your home landscape, however, learn enough about their cultural requirements to be sure you can provide a suitable habitat.

4. If you collect seeds from the wild, collect a few seeds or fruits from each of many plants and only from common species that are locally abundant. Purchase wildflower seeds only from companies that collect responsibly.

5. Purchase live wildflower plants only from suppliers or organizations that propagate their own plants or that purchase their material from those who propagate them. Ask sellers about the origin of the plants you are considering buying. Beware of plants labeled "nursery grown"; they may have been collected from the wild and kept in a nursery for only a short period of time. If there is any doubt about a plant's origin, do not purchase it.

6. Be cautious and knowledgeable in the use of exotic wildflowers. While many non-native species can be attractively used in gardens and landscapes, some are overly aggressive and these weeds may displace native species. Become aware of your state's noxious weed laws by contacting your state Department of Agriculture or Agricultural Extension Service.

7. When photographing wildflowers, or inspecting them closely, be careful not to trample plants nearby. Respect state and local trespassing laws by obtaining permission to be on private land.

8. If you pick wildflowers, dried seed stalks, or greens for home decoration, use only common species that are abundant at the site. Leave enough flowers or seeds to allow the plant population to re-seed itself. Avoid picking herbaceous perennials such as wild orchids, lilies, or gentians which, like daffodils and tulips, need to retain their vegetative parts to store energy for next year's development. Avoid cutting slow-growing plants such as cacti.

9. Become familiar with your state's wildflower protection laws. If your state does not have laws protecting wildflowers, or if the existing laws are weak, support the passage and enforcement of strong and effective legislation for the preservation of native plants. Report unlawful collection of plants to proper authorities and, when necessary, remind others that collecting plants or disturbing a natural area is illegal in parks and other public places.

10. If you learn that an area with wildflowers is scheduled for development, notify a native plant society in your region. Discuss with the developer the possibilities of compatible development alternatives or, if alternatives cannot be negotiated, of conducting a wildflower rescue operation.

11. It is important to protect information about the locations of rare species. If you discover a new site of a plant species that you know is rare, report it to responsible conservation officials, such as your state's Natural Heritage Program, a native plant society, a Nature Conservancy chapter, or the U.S. Fish and Wildlife Service, as soon as possible and before discussing it with others.

* Adapted from the Virginia Native Plant Society's "Wildflower Conservation Guidelines," with modifications suggested by the California Native Plant Society.

in which it is acceptable to dig up wildflowers is when they are imminently threatened by highway development or construction, and preservation on the site cannot be arranged. In those cases, prior approval must be obtained from the proper authorities, and if possible, plants should be dug while dormant.

Nursery-grown material usually yields the best wildflower gardening results. Before ordering plants by mail or from a local retail outlet, determine whether the plants have been propagated in a nursery, not merely "grown" there for a while. Do not buy plants that have been collected in the wild, since this practice may deplete natural populations of plants deserving protection. When ordering wildflowers you may wish to purchase seeds or live plants from a producer who is relatively close by, since there is a greater likelihood that the stock is better adapted to your local environmental conditions.

Seeds. Much can be gained by propagating wildflowers by seed, even apart from seeds' year-round availability, durability in shipping, and relatively low cost. Raising wildflowers from seed gives the gardener a chance to become familiar with the complete life cycle of plants. Some of the species in this book will self-seed once established, and therefore it is useful to know from firsthand experience what the seedlings of the species look like. Often the leaves of seedlings look different from those of mature plants, and without this knowledge they might be accidentally removed as weeds.

You can collect the seeds of most perennials growing in the wild without fear of significantly affecting their populations, if you take only a small proportion of the seeds produced. Since annuals reproduce only by seed, collect seeds from them only in locations where their populations are abundant. Before collecting any seeds get permission from the property owner.

Wildflower seeds are usually available throughout the year from mail-order suppliers. Since some wildflower species vary genetically from one part of their range to another, it is prudent to purchase seeds originating as close as possible to where they will be planted. By using seeds propagated close to home you are likely to have greater success and at the same time help to preserve the gene pool of these native plants. Some perennial prairie wildflowers have enhanced germination when their seeds are chilled or stratified for several months. Check with the supplier to determine whether the seeds you purchase have been pretreated or if they would benefit from additional cold treatment.

Wildflower Seed Mixtures: Caution! You should be very cautious and fully informed before purchasing commercial wildflower seed mixtures, which recently have been gaining popularity. Some suppliers painstakingly formulate mixtures that are representative of native wildflowers of specific regions or habitats. Others, however, formulate mixes for broad geographic regions and may include species that are not particularly adapted to your local conditions. Furthermore, it is often difficult to know just what species are contained in some of the mixtures and in what proportions. Some of the producers of the wildflower mixtures will vary the composition depending upon the temporary availability of seeds, so there is no guarantee that the product will be uniform from year to year. Often the mixes contain an abundance of annuals that provide a splash of color the first year but have difficulty in reseeding themselves. The lack of perennials in these mixes may mean disappointment in subsequent years. As long as you are investing in wildflowers, you might as well pay only for what you want, not just a pretty can or a packet mostly of roadside weeds.

A further difficulty with some of the mixes is the inclusion of weedy, non-native wildflower species which, while attractive, may become aggressive. An analysis of various wildflower seed mixes by the New England Wild Flower Society in 1985 found them to be comprised of 8 to 34 different species, of which zero to 100 percent were native. The following are some non-native species that are commonly found in wildflower mixes:

SPECIES	PLACE OF ORIGIN	SPECIES	PLACE OF ORIGIN
Oxeye daisy	Europe	Dame's rocket	France
Corn poppy	Europe	African daisy	South Africa
Sweet alyssum	Europe-W. Asia	Foxglove	Europe
White yarrow	Europe	Candytuft	S.E. Europe-W. Asia
Baby's breath	S. Europe	Four-o'clock	Peru
Purple loosestrife	N. Europe	Queen Anne's lace	Europe
St. John's-wort	Europe-Africa	Chicory	Europe
Bouncing bet	Europe-Asia	Cornflower	Europe

Live Plants. Since it often takes several years for perennial wildflowers to bloom when started from seed, the fastest way to establish them in the garden is to purchase live plants from reputable suppliers. Planning is essential. Perennial wildflowers are best shipped and planted when they are dormant. Many mail-order suppliers ship only during a limited season, so you should contact suppliers to determine the season of availability and whether there are any other constraints in shipping the specific live wildflowers you wish to plant.

SUPPLIERS The number of reputable commercial producers and distributors of wild-flower plants and seeds is steadily increasing. Some commercial sources are listed in Appendix A, although their inclusion is in no way an endorsement by the author or publisher. Most suppliers have catalogs or lists giving prices of seeds, live plants, and other items useful in wildflower gardening. Many of these catalogs are extremely useful sources of information about growing native plants. As is noted in Appendix A, some of the suppliers have a small charge for their catalogs and some refund that charge with the first order. It is a good idea to order catalogs several months in advance of your anticipated planting time. Some suppliers have shipping restrictions across international boundaries, and where these are known they are mentioned in Appendix A. Most suppliers prefer payment in the currency of their own country, and some require it.

If you are planning to plant large areas with mature bulbs and rootstocks, some of the suppliers listed in Appendix A sell large quantities of live plants (and seeds) to the public at wholesale prices. Although many suppliers give wholesale discounts to the public, some sell at wholesale rates only to registered retailers, so check with the supplier first.

MORE INFORMATION This book may be just a beginning for you. Further information is available from many sources, some of which are listed in the appendices to this book.

Botanical Gardens. Botanical gardens, nature centers, and arboreta are excellent sources of information about gardening with native plants. A state-by-state listing of such institutions is given in Appendix B. This listing includes the admission fee, if any, the season of operation, and the phone numbers. The resources of these gardens and centers usually extend beyond their collections of living native plants. Many offer workshops, symposia, tours, or lecture series on wildflower gardening. Some publish magazines, newsletters, and brochures that include information on native plants, and they often have shops that sell books on wildflowers as well as wildflower seeds and live plants.

Many botanical gardens offer memberships that entitle members to use library facilities, attend special events at reduced prices, go on field trips to various natural areas, consult with the horticultural staff, use a phone "gardening hotline," and enjoy other benefits. If you become interested in the institution's activities, they may have a program in which you could become a volunteer.

There are numerous other places not listed in Appendix B to observe wildflowers. Many local, regional, state, and national parks have preserved areas of native vegetation. National Forests and National Wildlife Refuges are also ideal places to see native wildflowers, as are lands owned by various chapters of the Audubon Society and the Nature Conservancy.

Botanical Organizations. Native plant societies and some horticultural organizations are excellent sources of information about native plants, as well as a means of becoming involved with wildflowers. The activities and resources of these societies are quite varied, ranging from projects to conserve rare and endangered plants to field trips, lecture series, and seed exchanges. Many of the native plant societies periodically publish newsletters or bulletins and have smaller local chapters that hold regular meetings. Some of the societies are affiliated with specific botanic gardens or arboreta, while others have a more regional or national focus. Appendix C lists botanical organizations that are concerned with wildflowers.

One organization concerned with native plants across the continent is the National Wildflower Research Center, located in Austin, Texas. The N.W.R.C., founded in 1982, is a clearinghouse for wildflower information, an institution conducting research on the propagation and cultivation of native plants, and an advocate for wildflower conservation and preservation. The public is encouraged both to contact the N.W.R.C. for information about native plants and to join them in their cause. The address of the National Wildflower Research Center is given in Appendix C.

On a state level, all states in the Great Plains and midwestern United States have Natural Heritage Programs, cooperative efforts between the Nature Conservancy and state departments of fish and game or natural resources to take inventory of rare plants, animals, and biological communities. The first Natural Heritage Program was started in South Carolina in 1974, to provide that state with biological inventory data augmenting the Federal Endangered Species Act. The offices of Natural Heritage Programs listed in Appendix C can provide you with current information on rare and endangered wildflowers and plant communities in your state.

The National Council of State Garden Clubs, Inc. is also active in wildflower preservation, and advocates using native plants for landscaping roadsides and public spaces. The organization sponsors "Operation Wildflower," a cooperative effort among state garden club federations, state highway agencies, and the Federal Highway Administration to beautify the nation's highways with native species, providing a low-cost, low-maintenance alternative to the exotic grasses and weeds that dominate our roadsides. Since its inception in 1972, Operation Wildflower has extended its horizons beyond the roadside to include projects in public parks, gardens, and wildflower preserves.

References. An annotated bibliography of books and published resources on wildflower gardening is contained in Appendix D.

Theme Gardens

Cultivating native prairie wildflowers can open new horizons in low-maintenance gardening. A sense of satisfaction accompanies the reestablishment of plants that were once more widespread in the region. Whether you use native plants to complement existing gardens or establish new plantings of species with different environmental requirements, you don't have to start out on a grand scale. Some of the most successful wildflower gardens are small flower beds at the corner of a house or on small patches of land otherwise unused. Even those areas that you can't mow anyway, like the corners of fences or between the roots of the trees in the front yard, can be enhanced by plantings of wildflowers.

Wildflowers let you adapt landscapes for specific purposes, such as "xeriscaping" with drought-tolerant plants to reduce water consumption or planting prairie wildflowers instead of lawns. Wildflowers can also be used in restoring natural habitats.

HORTICULTURAL GARDENS

Beds and Borders. The simplest approach is to use wildflowers in existing gardens to complement your ornamental plants. Conventional flower beds might include a progression of species like lance-leaved coreopsis, blanketflower, Mexican hat, gayfeather, and false dragonhead, whose long stems and long-lasting flowers make them ideal cut flowers.

Many prairie native plants are ideal for sunny borders. Missouri evening primrose, birdsfoot violet, and wine cup, with their low growth forms and interesting foliage, make excellent border plants. If your border is shady, try Canada anemone, but keep an eye on it, lest it crowd out other plants.

Butterfly and Hummingbird Gardens. If you want to attract butterflies to your garden, plant species such as New England aster, silky aster, purple coneflower, blanketflower, and Mexican hat, which have contrasting flower colors or sweet nectars to attract adult butterflies. Butterfly weed attracts

Wildflowers That Attract Bees

American bellflower
Black-eyed Susan
Blanketflower
Bluebonnet
Butterfly weed
Culver's root
Gayfeather
Lance-leaved coreopsis
Mexican hat
Purple prairie clover
Wild bergamot

multitudes of butterflies to its fragrant flowers. Another approach is to plant wildflowers that the developing caterpillars like to eat. For example, fritillary butterfly larvae feed on violet leaves, crescent butterfly caterpillars eat the leaves of various asters, and the larvae of many species of skippers consume the foliage of members of the bean family, such as showy tick trefoil and purple prairie clover. One obvious reason to refrain from using insecticides in wildflower gardens is the harm they cause to butterflies.

Hummingbirds are attracted to red or pink flowers that point outward or hang down. To lure hummingbirds to your garden, try planting wild columbine and prairie phlox. Bees are attracted to wildflowers such as American bellflower whose shape fits their bodies, or to flowers with sweet nectar and contrasting colors, like bluebonnets. Planted as companions to those that attract butterflies, these wildflowers will provide a long season of winged guests.

Prairie Wildflowers for Butterflies & Moths

WILDFLOWER	BUTTERFLY
Blanketflower	Flower moth (*Schinia masoni*)
Butterfly weed	Monarch (*Danaus plexippus*) Orange sulfur (*Colias eurytheme*)
Culver's root	Many for nectar.
Gayfeather	Many for nectar.
Leadplant	Marine blue (*Leptotes marina*)
Lance-leaved coreopsis	Many for nectar.
Mexican hat	Dakota skipper (*Hesperis dacotae*) Poweshiek skipperling (*Oarisma poweshiek*)
New England aster	Pearl crescentspot (*Phyciodes tharos*) Field crescentspot (*Phyciodes campestris*) Silvery crescentspot (*Charidryas nycteis*)
Prairie phlox	Many for nectar.
Purple coneflower	Ottoe skipper (*Hesperis ottoe*)
Purple prairie clover	Sulphur butterflies (*Colias species*)
Silky aster	Many for nectar.
Wild bergamot	Many for nectar.
Wild columbine	White-lined sphinx moth (*Hyles lineta*) Columbine duskywing (*Erynnis lucilius*)

Butterfly and hummingbird garden.

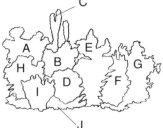

A. Wild bergamot
B. Purple coneflower
C. Gayfeather
D. Prairie phlox
E. Butterfly weed
F. Leadplant
G. Wild columbine
H. New England aster
I. Purple prairie clover
J. Silky aster

Wildflowers for Shady Gardens. Some prairie wildflowers grow in woodlands and forests as well as grasslands. These species are ideally suited to gardens where shade is present some or most of the day. Wild columbine is found growing in the shade of deciduous forests in eastern North America, while Canada anemone, showy tick trefoil, closed gentian, and birdsfoot violet grow in woodland gaps among the trees. Missouri evening primrose and American bellflower grow along the margins of woodlands on the Ozark Plateau. Culver's root is also quite tolerant of shade.

Rock Gardens. No rock garden is truly complete without representative native species. By their very nature, prairie wildflowers are adapted to rock garden conditions. When using wildflowers you can create rock gardens for sun or partial shade, and for moist or dry conditions. Take the environmental preferences of various wildflowers into consideration when planning your rock garden.

Plant wine cup, pasqueflower, prairie smoke, and prairie phlox in dry, sunny places such as the south-facing exposure near the top of the garden. Wild columbine and birdsfoot violet, on the other hand, tolerate partial shade and might be planted on east- or west-facing slopes. Meadow beauty should be planted only in low nooks where it can receive more moisture than the other rock garden plants. If you have a large space for a rock garden you might consider growing more aggressive wildflowers like Canada anemone.

Container Gardening. Growing wildflowers in containers is an easy way to enjoy native plants if you live in a city, if your gardening space is limited, or if more intensive care is needed because your local conditions are quite different from those usually required by a particular species. One advantage to container gardening is that you can move the plants seasonally, indoors or out, to match the needs of the species. When lance-leaved coreopsis or wood lily is planted densely in large containers it provides stunning accents for courtyards, balconies, or patios. Wooden or masonry boxes planted with the low-growing wine cup, meadow beauty, or birdsfoot violet are especially attractive along side paths and stairways.

A wide variety of containers can be used: conventional pots, wooden tubs, window boxes, hanging baskets, drainage tile, and chimney flue liners, to mention a few. Containers made of porous ceramic material, like clay pots, tend to dry out faster, so wildflowers planted in them need to be watered more frequently than those planted in impervious glass, glazed ceramic, or plastic containers.

Good drainage is essential for container gardening, since water-logged soils not only prevent the roots from getting needed oxygen, but also encourage diseases. Many plants adapted to dry soil conditions simply cannot tolerate wet soils. First, be sure the container has a drainage hole, and line the bottom of the pot with a layer of gravel. The soil you use should be light and porous. Equal measures of top soil, peat moss, and builder's sand, mixed thoroughly, make a good potting mixture for most plants. With the plant in place, the pot should be filled to about 1 inch from the top with this loamy soil mix.

The root growth of plants in containers tends not to be as extensive as that of plants growing in conventional gardens, so additional water is usually required. Water the container garden only after the surface of the soil has become dry to the touch, and then water sufficiently for water to drain out and carry the dissolved salts out the drainage hole. Otherwise, salts may build up in the soil and damage the plants. Regular watering will remove some of the necessary plant nutrients from the soil, so periodically add small amounts of slow-release fertilizers to replace them.

NATURAL GARDENS AND LANDSCAPES

A highly successful way to use native plants is to plant wildflowers in appropriate natural settings. This also allows you to brighten up areas of your property that are difficult to plant, such as poorly drained or dry, droughty spots. As a result your personal landscape will be adapted to its natural environment and require far less time, energy, and resources to maintain it.

Xeriscape garden.

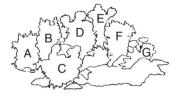

A. Mexican hat
B. Purple prairie clover
C. Wine cup
D. Butterfly weed
E. Lance-leaved coreopsis
F. Snow-on-the-mountain
G. Blanketflower

"Xeriscaping" — Gardening with Less Water. Xeriscaping is a new gardening and landscape approach gaining popularity in the Great Plains and the West as it becomes painfully obvious that water is an ever more scarce and expensive resource. The term "xeriscaping" is derived from the Greek word *xeros* meaning "dry," and is applied to techniques that reduce the water required to maintain gardens. The xeriscaping movement had its birth in the Denver area in the early 1980s. It gathered momentum later in the decade as an increasing number of cities enacted ordinances requiring water-conserving landscaping for new industrial, commercial, and residential developments.

Xeriscaping stresses the establishment of landscapes adapted to the dry environments around them, rather than trying to transplant and maintain water-consumptive landscapes from the humid East Coast or tropics. Included among the several techniques used to create water-thrifty gardens and landscapes are: reducing the areas devoted to lawns, planting water-conserving plants, using mulches where possible to conserve water, using soil amendments to increase the water-holding capacity of soils, grouping plants with similar water requirements close together, and, if absolutely needed, installing micro-irrigation systems that most efficiently meet the plants' water needs. These techniques can allow you to use 30 to 80 percent less water than in the traditional "humid" garden.

In designing a xeriscape take advantage of the water draining from roofs, driveways, and impervious surfaces for supplemental irrigation. Also consider planting species with greater water needs in swales and depressions that collect rainwater at the beginning of the dry season. Even water-conserving species may initially need additional irrigation, but once established they should require only natural rainfall.

Native plants play a natural role in prairie xeriscapes, since they, above all species, are adapted to the local environment. The wildflowers presented in the section on summer dry prairie species (starting on page 132) are obvious candidates for water-conserving landscapes; in addition, some spring species like wine cup and fall species like silky aster are also quite drought tolerant. Also effective in xeriscapes are trees such as ponderosa pine and shrubs such as sagebrush (*Artemesia tridentata*), golden currant (*Ribies odoratum, R. aureum*), mountain mahogany (*Cercocarpus montanus*), and Woods's rose (*Rosa woodsii*). Be sure to prune shrubs periodically so that they remain a manageable size, old wood is removed, and new vigorous growth is encouraged.

Further information about xeriscaping is available from the Agricultural Extension Service, city or regional water authorities, botanic gardens, or the Xeriscaping Council, Inc., the address of which appears in Appendix C.

Meadows and Prairies. Wildflower meadows are becoming increasingly popular alternatives to lawns, and prairie natives such as pasqueflower, wine cup, Canada anemone, prairie phlox, purple coneflower, black-eyed Susan, blanketflower, Mexican hat, New England aster, and closed gentian can fill open spaces with color from late winter to fall. Native wildflower meadows cost less than lawns to maintain, and consume less water, gasoline, fertilizers, and time. Furthermore, they are vastly more interesting to look at.

Planning the Prairie. Grasslands and prairies are a combination of wildflowers and grasses. When planning your wildflower meadow select the grasses with great care. The chart below lists native grasses suitable for prairie meadows. Some of these grasses are "cool-season" grasses that grow in the winter and spring in response to seasonal rains and then dry out and go into dormancy during the summer. The best grasses to interplant with the wildflowers are bunch grasses — species that grow in clumps. Their shoots will provide support and the ideal amount of competition to enable the wildflowers to grow straight and tall. While sod-forming grasses are ideal for lawns or filling in wet swales, avoid planting them in wildflower meadows and prairies where a mix of grasses and wildflowers is desired.

Native wildflower seeds should be combined with a mixture of native grasses appropriate to the region and habitat. If you have a field with both damp and dry conditions, plant a mixture of species and let nature sort

---

Wildflowers for Xeriscaping

Blanketflower
Butterfly weed
Lance-leaved coreopsis
Mexican hat
Missouri evening primrose
Purple prairie clover
Snow-on-the-mountain
Wine cup

Cut border garden.

A. Canada anemone
B. Showy tick trefoil
C. Black-eyed Susan
D. Blanketflower
E. False dragonhead
F. Mexican hat
G. Gayfeather
H. Lance-leaved coreopsis

them out later rather than trying to plant just dry-adapted species in dry areas and moisture-loving species in the moist areas.

Prairie grass and wildflower seeds can be purchased from many of the suppliers listed in Appendix A. If you are planning to plant a large area, you should inquire about wholesale prices for wildflower and native grass seed. And if you purchase formulated wildflower-grass seed mixtures, be sure they contain only those native species you really want in your meadow. Some wholesaler dealers can even make arrangements to plant large areas with mechanized equipment.

Whenever possible, purchase grass and wildflower seeds from a supplier who has produced them close to where they will be planted. This way your plants will be better adapted to your local conditions and representative of the genetic varieties native to your region.

Many grasses and wildflower have seeds that need conditioning or special handling before they are planted. Many species of wildflowers and warm-season grass, for example, require a cold treatment known as *stratification* in order to germinate properly (see page 60). Leguminous species may need the addition of soil inoculants containing "rhizobia" bacteria if they are not already present in your soil (see page 63).

Grasses should make up 60 to 90 percent and wildflowers 10 to 40 percent of the mix. The wildflower and grass seed mixture should be sown at a rate of 5 to 20 pounds of live seeds per acre, depending on the species composition. If species with small seeds make up the bulk of the seeds, the seeding rate should be lower than with species with large, heavy seeds. The supplier from whom you purchase wildflower and grass seed in bulk can make specific seeding rate recommendations, but typically 6 to 7 pounds of wildflower seeds are mixed with enough grass seeds to sow an acre, yielding 10 to 20 seeds per square foot.

Since it takes several years for meadows and prairies to become established, plan to include some species such as purple coneflower, black-eyed Susan, showy tick trefoil, rattlesnake master, or bluebonnet in the seed mixture. They germinate quickly and produce flowers the first growing season.

Preparing the Site. The easiest time to create a wildflower meadow is when the land is bare and you do not have to deal with established, competing grasses, weeds, herbaceous plants, or woody seedlings. If the site is small, you can cultivate and rake out the soil surface by hand, otherwise mechanized equipment may be needed.

More commonly, you are confronted with an existing lawn or field filled with exotic grasses and weeds that you want to convert to a native wildflower meadow. *Resist the impulse to use herbicides or fumigants to kill the existing vegetation.* Herbicides are likely to create more problems for the wildflower enthusiast than they solve. Apart from the damage they cause to the environment, they are not likely to save you time in establishing a wildflower meadow. Hand weeding may take longer than spraying herbicide, but it is much safer. Cultivation, mowing, and the appropriate use of fire generally give better results and are less damaging to the environment.

One way to turn an existing small field into a wildflower meadow is to start on a modest scale by clearing small patches or strips in the fall, sowing native annual wildflowers and grasses, and transplanting additional live perennials the next spring. Just scattering seeds among established grasses *never* works. An even more successful approach is to start perennial grass and wildflower plugs (see page 62) a year ahead and then to prepare the site a spring in advance, before the unwanted existing field plants produce seeds.

Make patches by turning over sections of the field with a sharp spade or a rototiller. Remove as many of the roots of non- native grasses as possible by hand, and cultivate the soil shallowly so as not to bring many weed seeds to the surface. The patches should be 3 to 8 feet in diameter and dug in a random pattern, to create a more natural effect. If you prefer a border effect, clear strips in the field with a rototiller. Remove as many of the existing grass roots as possible, and water the soil to encourage the germination of any weed seeds that you have inadvertently stirred up in the process. Then cover the patch with heavy-gauge black plastic sheet "mulch," pieces of discarded carpet, or even thick sections of newspaper. If you do not care for the sight of such coverings, you can spread a layer of bark mulch or soil on top of them. The covering will eventually shade out and kill off the remaining clumps of grass and the newly germinated weed seedlings.

Native Prairie Grasses

Common name	Latin name	Height	Comments
Western wheatgrass Period: Cool-season grass. Region: Tall, mixed, short. Habitat: Moist, alkaline soil.	*Agropyron smithii*	12-24"	Tolerates both heat and cold; can be mown for a tolerable lawn.
Big bluestem Period: Warm-season grass. Region: Tallgrass, mixed. Habitat: Medium moist.	*Andropogon gerardi*	36-96"	Attractive, tall grass; seedheads arranged in 3s. Plant seed in fall.
Little bluestem Period: Warm-season grass. Region: Tallgrass, mixed. Habitat: Well-drained soils.	*Andropogon scoparius or Schizachyrium scoparium*	20-60"	Very attractive purple and orange stems when in fruit; fluffy fruits; good on dry soils. Plant seed in fall.
Sideoats grama Period: Warm-season grass, grows in cool too. Region: Tall, mixed, short. Habitat: Well-drained soils.	*Bouteloua curtipendula*	24"	Good drought resistance and erosion control; excellent for desert meadows; can be mown as a lawn; plant seeds in fall.
Blue grama Period: Warm-season grass. Region: Mixed and shortgrass. Habitat: Dry, alkaline soils.	*Bouteloua gracilis*	15"	Very attractive seed heads; *very low water use*; can be mown to 1½ inch. Sow in fall.

Short grasses: ½"= 6"

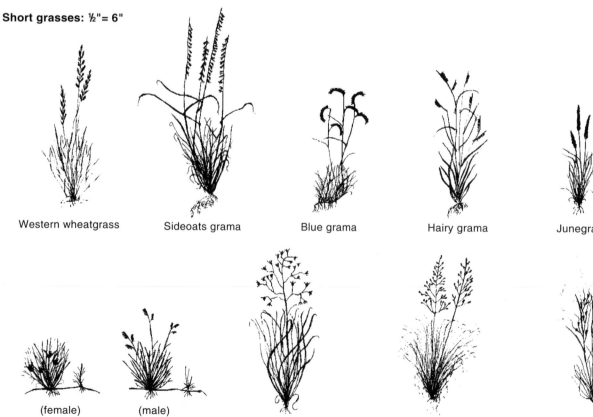

Western wheatgrass   Sideoats grama   Blue grama   Hairy grama   Junegrass

(female)   (male)

Buffalo grass   Indian ricegrass   Prairie dropseed   Needle-and-thread

Native Prairie Grasses
(continued)

COMMON NAME	LATIN NAME	HEIGHT	COMMENTS
Hairy grama PERIOD: Warm-season grass. REGION: Mixed and shortgrass. HABITAT: Dry sandy and rocky soils.	*Bouteloua hirsuta*	8-24"	Densely tufted clumps, slender, hairy leaves; flattened, brushy seed heads.
Buffalo grass PERIOD: Warm-season grass. REGION: Mixed and shortgrass. HABITAT: Dry loams and clay.	*Buchoë dactyloides*	2-5"	Low growing, can use as lawn; very drought resistant; spreads by runners; gray-green foliage. Has separate male and female plants.
Canada wild rye PERIOD: Cool-season grass. REGION: Nearly coast to coast. HABITAT: Moist or dry soils.	*Elymus canadensis*	24-60"	Grows throughout prairie region; dense seed heads bend when mature.
June grass PERIOD: Cool-season grass. REGION: Tallgrass and mixed. HABITAT: Dry, sandy soils.	*Koeleria cristata*	6-24"	Grows well on dry soil; flattened gray-green spikelets. Plant seed in spring.
Indian ricegrass PERIOD: Cool-season grass. REGION: Shortgrass and foothills. HABITAT: Sandy and rocky soil.	*Oryzopsis hymenoides*	20"	Excellent for meadows or rock gardens; has attractive flowers that can be dried for arrangements; seeds are edible; drought resistant.
Switchgrass PERIOD: Warm-season grass. REGION: Tallgrass. HABITAT: Moist soils.	*Panicum virgatum*	36-60"	Robust plant with leaves that turn pale yellow. Plant seeds in fall.

Tall grasses: ½"=1'

Big bluestem

Little bluestem

Canada wild rye

Switchgrass

Native Prairie Grasses

(continued)

COMMON NAME	LATIN NAME	HEIGHT	COMMENTS
Indian grass PERIOD: Warm-season grass. REGION: Tallgrass. HABITAT: Moist to dry soils.	*Sorghastrum nutans*	36-60"	Large plumes of glossy seeds; can be aggressive; plant seeds in fall.
Sloughgrass PERIOD: Warm-season grass. REGION: Tallgrass. HABITAT: Wet soils.	*Spartina pectinata*	24-90"	Forms sods from rhizomes; use in wetlands only, aggressive.
Prairie dropseed PERIOD: Warm-season grass. REGION: Tallgrass. HABITAT: Medium moist to dry soils.	*Sporobolus heterolepis*	12-24"	Beautiful tufted clumps of light green leaves; sweet-smelling seeds. Plant seeds in fall.
Needle-and-thread PERIOD: Cool-season grass. REGION: Mixed. HABITAT: Dry plains and hills.	*Stipa comata*	8-24"	Attractive sharp-pointed seeds; twisted golden tops when dry.
Porcupine needlegrass PERIOD: Cool-season grass. REGION: Tallgrass, mixed. HABITAT: Dry soils.	*Stipa spartea*	24-40"	Straw-colored leaves in summer; long, sharp-pointed fruits.

Tall grasses: ½"=1'

Indian grass

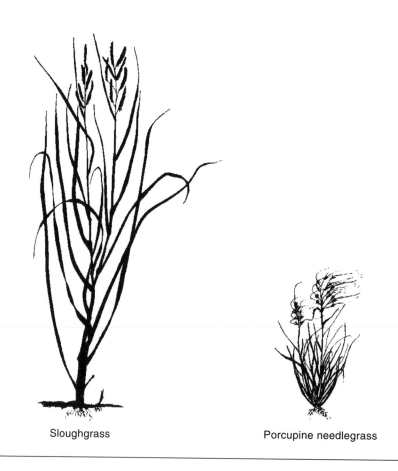

Sloughgrass

Porcupine needlegrass

Remove the coverings in mid-autumn just before planting the field. If black plastic mulch or carpet sections have been used, you may be able to use them again. Just place them where you intend to create the next year's patches.

Plant the grass plugs in the patch, spacing them 12 to 15 inches apart. Transplant perennial native plants in between the clumps of grasses, and sow the seeds of annual wildflowers. The meadow will benefit from a light mulching with seed-free straw to conserve moisture and reduce erosion.

If your meadow already has bunch grasses, and you do not care to introduce new grass species, wildflower plugs and sods can be planted directly into the field in late autumn. Clear a small patch about a foot in diameter with a cultivator and pick out the grass roots. Set the live plants so the bases of their shoots are at the ground level. Press them down firmly so the roots are in good contact with the soil beneath, and water them.

Larger areas usually require the use of heavy, mechanized equipment. If the field can be prepared a year in advance the results will be better than if it is prepared only just before planting.

In the tallgrass prairie region plow the field the fall before you wish to plant, then harrow it shallowly to break up surface grass rhizomes. The next spring, as soon as the soil can be worked, cultivate shallowly to disrupt weed seedlings and further break up grass rhizomes. Repeat cultivations every several weeks until you plant seed in late spring.

In the shortgrass prairie region, plow the field in early summer and plant a cover crop of grain sorghum. In the early fall cut the grain sorghum 8 inches high and drill seeds into the stubble.

Planting the Prairie. Meadows and prairies can be seeded either in autumn or in the spring, and there are advantages and disadvantages to either season. Choose a time when there will be sufficient moisture for the next 3 warm months to give the grass and wildflower seedlings an opportunity to become established.

Fall is generally the best time to plant prairies in Texas and the Great Plains. Many species release their seeds in fall, and the coming winter naturally provides the chilling treatment many seeds need to germinate the next spring. The only problem with fall planting is that if germination occurs early, frosts in the soil may damage the tender seedlings, or animals may eat them over the winter.

Early spring planting gives good germination if seeds have artificially been given the necessary chilling treatment. It is a good time to plant sandy soils, but clay soils are usually too wet to be worked at this time of the year. A

Shade garden.

A. Birdsfoot violet
B. American bellflower
C. Culver's root
D. Showey tick trefoil
E. Wood lily
F. Wild columbine
G. Birdsfoot violet
H. Missouri evening primrose

disadvantage of planting in the early spring is that weed control is more difficult than when planting is done later.

Late spring is generally the best time to plant in the tallgrass prairie region. The field to be planted can be cultivated for several months to kill exotic grass rhizomes and emerging weeds before planting in June. The seedlings of warm-season grasses develop rapidly at this time, sending their roots down to considerable depths even if their shoots remain small. The drawback of late spring planting is the risk of seedlings dying during periodic summer droughts.

Do not use fertilizers when planting a meadow or prairie since exotic weeds tend to respond more vigorously than the native wildflowers do to the application of additional nutrients. Furthermore, improper fertilizer application can severely retard the growth of leguminous plants like bluebonnets, showy tick trefoil, and purple prairie clover.

Sow the seeds on a windless day, broadcasting them by hand or using a whirlwind seeder if the area is small. Rake the seeds into the soil, then tamp down or roll the surface so the seeds can have good contact with the soil. On large areas hand seeding can be done from the back of a pickup truck, but drilling the seeds or applying them with a hydroseeder may be more practical.

Keep the soil moist, but not wet, until the seeds have germinated and seedlings start to become established. A light covering of seed-free straw will help to conserve moisture and reduce erosion until the meadow is established. Do not, however, use baled field hay, which is likely to contain the seeds of exotic grasses, species you want to keep from invading your meadow.

Prairie and Meadow Maintenance. Prairies and wildflower meadows require some attention in the beginning until they become fully established. Early on, weeds may be a problem, but don't become discouraged; it takes time for native perennial grasses and wildflowers to become reestablished. The fast-growing weeds can be mowed down during the first summer, but set the mower height above the slower-growing native wildflowers. The second year the prairie or meadow may be sufficiently developed to be burned to kill many of the exotic weeds as well as invading shrub and tree seedlings. Creating a meadow or prairie may be a slow process, but even in nature a beautiful wildflower grassland, resplendent with a high diversity of desirable plants, isn't produced in a single year.

Once the wildflower meadow is established it is relatively easy to maintain. Mow the meadow once a year with a rotary mower after the seeds have set, or burn it periodically. Do not burn a meadow until after the second season, but then you can burn it every two to three years. Do the burning on windless days in the early spring, when the dormant grass is dry but the soil is still wet. If the meadow grass is too thin to support the fire, dry straw can be scattered about and ignited. Be certain to observe local, state, and federal regulations concerning outdoor burning, in addition to the usual safety practices. Check with your local fire department for assistance in planning any controlled burns and to obtain an outdoor burning permit.

In some suburbs there are ordinances dictating aesthetic standards for landscaping. If you live in such a community you might want to check with your city hall before converting your front yard into a prairie. If there are prohibitions, you can always try to get the law changed to encourage the landscaping use of native plants. Native plants are rarely the "weeds" that these ordinances are trying to prohibit, and it is unlikely that your blanketflowers or silky asters are going to march through your neighbor's water-consuming Kentucky bluegrass.

Plant Descriptions

The technical terminology used in the descriptions of the flowers, leaves, shoots, and roots for the species in this book has been kept to a minimum. The knowledge of some botanical terms is essential, however, and relatively painless to acquire.

FLOWERS   Illustrated below are two typical flowers with all the parts that are usually present. *Complete flowers* have all the parts illustrated, but some of the wildflowers in the book lack one or more of the parts or they may be fused together in different arrangements. The trillium (below left) is a *simple flower*. The blanketflower (below right) is a *composite flower*.

In simple flowers, the flower parts are attached to a fleshy pad (the *receptacle*) atop the flower stem or *peduncle*. The outermost parts of the flower are the *sepals*, which are usually small, green, leaflike structures that cover and protect the flower while it is in the bud. Collectively, all of the sepals are called the *calyx*, Latin for "cup." In some species the sepals are fused together to form a tubular calyx, and

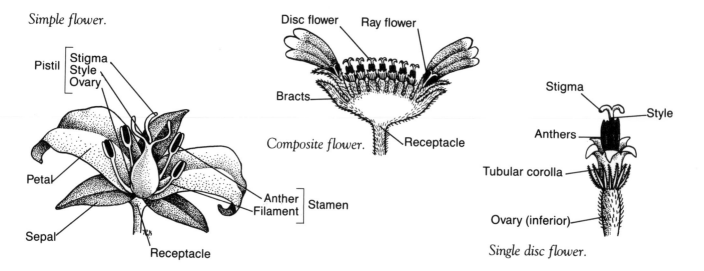

Simple flower.

Composite flower.

Single disc flower.

in other species they resemble petals. Immediately inside the sepals are the petals, which may take on a variety of forms, some species having petals fused together into a tube, and others having petals that are free and unattached. On some flowers the petal arrangement is radially symmetrical, but on others, the petals take irregular forms. Collectively the petals are called the *corolla*, which means "small crown" in Latin.

In the center of the flower are the sexual parts, the male *stamens* and the female *pistil*. There may be one or several pistils, depending upon the species, but most flowering plants have more than one stamen. The stamen consists of a slender stalk, the *filament*, to which the pollen-bearing sacks, the *anthers*, are attached. The pistil has three major parts whose shapes may vary widely among species. The upper surface of the pistil, which receives pollen grains, is the *stigma*. The stigma is attached to the *ovary* at the base of the pistil by a usually slender tissue known as the *style*. Inside the ovary is a chamber containing the *ovules*, the female sex cells. After the pollen grains are deposited on the stigma, they germinate, sending microscopic tubes down through the style, through portions of the ovary, and finally into the ovules. Following fertilization, the ovules mature into *seeds*, and the ovary matures into the *fruit* of the plant.

The flowers of plants in the aster family, such as blanketflower and black-eyed Susan, have a more complex structure. These species usually have two types of small flowers clustered together in a composite *flower head*. The small flowers or *florets* share a broad receptacle which is usually enclosed from below by many leafy bracts. The *ray flowers* usually form a ring around the outside of the head. Each ray flower has a relatively long, straplike petal which upon close inspection can be seen to be several small petals fused together. Often ray flowers are sterile and lack stamens and pistils entirely. In the center of the flower head are the even smaller *disc flowers*, with minute, tubular corollas. The stamens and the pistils in these flowers are surrounded by the petals, but are usually so small that magnification is required to see them clearly.

COLOR AND HEIGHT

Color of the flower and height of the plant are the gardener's first two concerns in deciding what species to plant. To aid in planning, the 34 species of plants described in this book are listed on page 38 by flower color and on page 39 by height. Use the information in these charts as a rough guide only. Keep in mind that some species, such as butterfly weed and Mexican hat, can appear in a range of colors. Also, the height of the plant depends on the environmental conditions in which it is grown. Further information concerning flower color and plant height is given in the descriptions of individual species.

FLOWER COLOR

Species	Page	Brown	White	Pink	Red	Orange	Yellow	Green	Blue	Purple	Lavender
Black-eyed Susan	124	■					■				
American bellflower	112		■						■		
Bluebonnet	94		■						■		
Canada anemone	106		■								
Culver's root	116		■								
Pasqueflower	92		■						■		■
Rattlesnake master	122		■					■			
Snow-on-the-mountain	140		■					■			
Nodding wild onion	126		■	■							■
False dragonhead	156			■							■
Pasture rose	110			■							
Prairie phlox	102			■							■
Wine cup	96			■						■	
Queen-of-the-prairie	120			■							
Showy tick trefoil	158			■					■		■
Prairie smoke	98			■							
Wild columbine	104			■			■				
Meadow beauty	154			■							■
Blanketflower	150				■		■				
Mexican hat	138				■		■				
Purple coneflower	130			■							■
Wood lily	114				■	■					
Butterfly weed	144					■					
Missouri evening primrose	136						■				
Silky aster	164						■		■		■
Compass plant	118						■				
Lance-leaved coreopsis	134						■				
Closed gentian	160								■		
Leadplant	142									■	
New England aster	162						■			■	
Birdsfoot violet	100									■	■
Purple prairie clover	146									■	■
Gayfeather	128										■
Wild bergamot	148										■

PLANT HEIGHT

Species	Page
Birdsfoot violet	100
Pasqueflower	92
Meadow beauty	154
Bluebonnet	94
Prairie smoke	98
Wild columbine	104
Wine cup	96
Missouri evening primrose	136
Lance-leaved coreopsis	134
Prairie phlox	102
Wood lily	114
Canada anemone	106
Closed gentian	160
Nodding wild onion	126
Silky aster	164
Black-eyed Susan	124
Butterfly weed	144
Pasture rose	110
Purple prairie clover	146
Snow-on-the-mountain	140
Gayfeather	128
Rattlesnake master	122
Mexican hat	138
Leadplant	142
Blanketflower	150
False dragonhead	156
Queen-of-the-prairie	120
Wild bergamot	148
New England aster	162
Purple coneflower	130
American bellflower	112
Culver's root	116
Showy tick trefoil	158
Compass plant	118

Height scale: 0' 1/2' 1' 2' 3' 4' 5' 10' 15'

FRUITS AND
SEEDS

Fruits are as intriguing and varied as the flowers that produce them. The main function of fruits, which are formed from ripened ovaries, is to aid in the dissemination of the seeds they contain. The structure of various fruits often gives clues about how the seeds are disseminated. Many species that inhabit open spaces, like pasqueflower, butterfly weed, and asters, depend upon the wind to carry their seeds away from the parent plants and often have light seeds with tufts of hairs to keep them buoyed by air currents.

Other wildflowers use different devices to disseminate their seeds. As the long stems of wild columbine wave in the wind, for example, the seeds are flung out of openings in the tops of the capsule fruits. The fleshy fruits of pasture rose are eaten by various birds and mammals, and the seeds are then dropped after travelling through their digestive systems. Birdsfoot violet seeds have a small, oily bodies known as "elaiosomes" attached to their surfaces. Ants find the elaiosomes irresistible, and carry the seeds off, chew off the elaiosome, and discard the seeds some distance from the parent plants. The seeds chewed upon by ants usually germinate better than those which the ants have missed.

ROOT SYSTEMS

The forms of the underground portions of the 34 wildflowers described in this book vary greatly and may influence the types of habitats in which they can be grown. The root system also affects how easily a plant can be propagated. Six of the eight most common "root types" illustrated on page 41 are actually the underground stems, or "rootstocks," of perennials. The remaining two are true roots and lack leaf buds.

True Roots. True roots (illustrated on page 41) may be either diffuse and fibrous, as with many garden plants and wildflowers like silky aster and prairie phlox, or they may be a strongly vertical, carrotlike tap root as with compass plant. The root systems of some wildflowers are intermediate between the two basic types.

Runners and Stolons. Underground stems take a variety of forms. The simplest rootstock has thin horizontal branches, which give rise to new plants. These branches are usually called runners if they are above ground, as with strawberries, and stolons if they are below ground, as with mint and false dragonhead.

Tubers. If the tip of a stolon produces a swollen, fleshy storage organ, it is called a tuber. The leaf buds of tubers are frequently called "eyes." The potato is probably the most familiar example of a tuber, but wildflowers such as butterfly weed and meadow beauty also have tuberous roots.

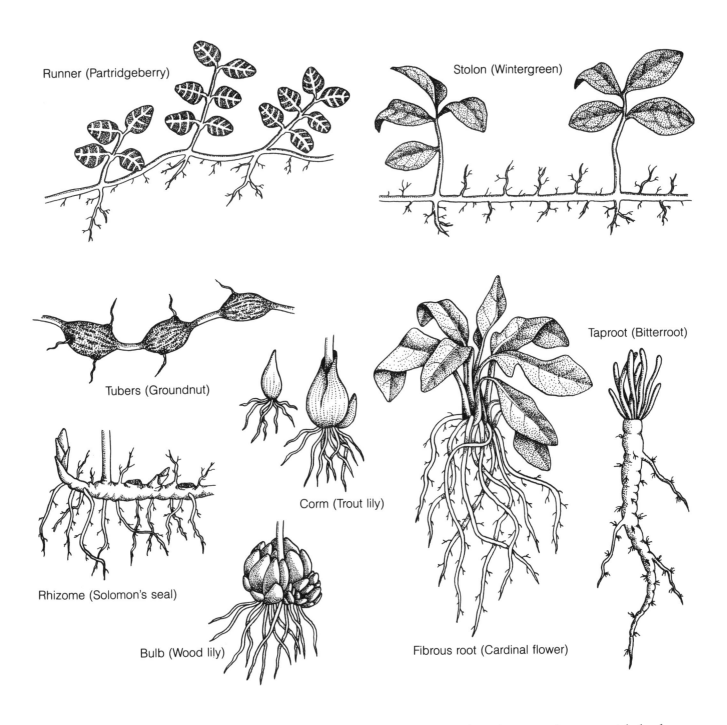

Runner (Partridgeberry)

Stolon (Wintergreen)

Tubers (Groundnut)

Taproot (Bitterroot)

Corm (Trout lily)

Rhizome (Solomon's seal)

Bulb (Wood lily)

Fibrous root (Cardinal flower)

Rhizomes. Thick, fleshy, horizontal underground stems with buds on their top surfaces and roots on their bottom surfaces are called rhizomes. Rhizomes, like those of prairie smoke and Canada anemone, store large amounts of starch, which is used to nourish the shoots and flowers of perennials as they emerge from dormancy.

Corms and Bulbs. Rootstocks may also be round and bulbous. A true bulb is a bud atop a very short stem, surrounded by fleshy leaf scales, as with nodding wild onion and wood lily. Corms look like bulbs but are rootstocks formed from the swollen, solid base of the stem, as with gladiolus and gayfeather.

Flowering Season

A great number of factors, some genetic and some environmental, affect the onset and length of the flowering season of wildflowers. Complex interactions among climatic factors such as amount of sunlight, length of day, moisture, and temperature of air and soil influence exactly when plants start flowering.

Annual species usually have longer flowering seasons than perennials do and, of course, flower in a single growing season. Annuals may become persistent, even to the point of being considered weeds, through self-seeding. Perennials, on the other hand, may require several or many years to reach maturity and flower, but once established they generally require little maintenance, and reliably reappear year after year.

CLIMATE   The overall climatic patterns of temperature and precipitation have a considerable effect on the blooming of wildflowers. In general, mid-continental areas lack the moderating effects of oceans and therefore have more or less constant temperatures, less reliable precipitation, and shorter growing seasons than do coastal regions. However, in the immediate vicinity of the Great Lakes the growing season may be prolonged.

Precipitation and temperature are critical, influencing the timing of germination, the renewal of perennial growth, and the abundance of wildflowers. In years when the winter rains are erratic or far below average, especially if it is also unusually cold, springtime flowering may be delayed. On the other hand, if the rainy season precipitation is well distributed and temperatures are slightly above average, flowering may be accelerated.

Even though exact flowering times frequently vary, the flowering order of wildflower species within the same geographic area tends to be consistent from year to year. The general seasonal progression of flowering of the wildflowers in this book is shown on page 44. The seasons of flowering are given, rather than calendar months, because the onset of the growing season varies from locale to locale and from year to year. The seasons refer to the flowering of a given species near the center of its native range, and the gardener may find that the flowering sequence may be slightly different for plants obtained from different areas.

LOCAL CONDITIONS

The exact time of flowering in your garden may also be influenced by local conditions such as slope, elevation, soil type, and mulches. If your garden slopes to the south, it will be warmer and spring will arrive sooner than if it slopes to the north. The warmest slopes are those on which the sun's rays strike most perpendicularly, but even a 5-degree south-facing slope may have a microclimate equivalent to that of a flat surface 300 miles farther south. A similar slope facing north would be correspondingly cooler. A garden located at the base of a mountain or a hill, on the other hand, may be chilled by the downslope settling of cold air, especially in the spring and fall. Flowering dates may vary by as much as several weeks, therefore, depending on the local topography.

The elevation of a garden will also influence how rapidly spring arrives. At a given latitude air temperatures generally decrease 3 degrees F per 1,000 feet of rise. For each 100-foot increase in elevation, the air temperature is only three-tenths of a degree cooler, but flowering is delayed by about one day.

Proximity to the Great Lakes, especially during the spring, may influence how rapidly plants grow and flower. It is not uncommon for sites on the downwind sides of lakes to be 10 degrees F cooler than areas several miles inland. Yet although onshore winds tend to lower air temperatures during the spring and summer, they raise them in the fall and winter, placing these areas in warmer hardiness zones than adjacent inland sites.

Soil conditions may advance or retard the progression of flowering. Sandy soils generally warm up more rapidly in the spring than do peaty or clayey soils. Dark-colored soils, or those blackened by recent fires, will warm more rapidly than light-colored soils will. Heavy mulches, while reducing frost and keeping soils warmer in the winter, provide an insulation layer that may both slow warming in the spring and maintain cooler soils in the summer.

GENETIC FACTORS

Some plants, but not all, are genetically programmed to flower in response to specific day lengths or hours of darkness. This characteristic is found in a wide variety of wildflowers, including annuals, biennials, and perennials. Some plants, such as black-eyed Susan and Mexican hat, flower most abundantly when days lengthen and nights become short. They are known as "long-day" plants, although they are actually responding to the short nights associated with late spring and early summer. The northern regions of North America,

FLOWERING PROGRESSION

Species	Page	Late Winter	Early Spring	Midspring	Late Spring	Early Summer	Summer	Late Summer	Early Fall	Fall
Pasqueflower	92	■	■							
Bluebonnet	94	■	■	■						
Wine cup	96		■	■	■	■	■			
Prairie smoke	98		■	■	■					
Birdsfoot violet	100			■	■					
Prairie phlox	102			■	■	■				
Wild columbine	104			■	■					
Canada anemone	106				■					
Pasture rose	110				■					
Wood lily	114					■	■			
Lance-leaved coreopsis	134				■	■	■			
Missouri evening primrose	136				■	■	■			
Mexican hat	138				■	■	■	■	■	
Snow-on-the-mountain	140				■	■	■	■	■	■
American bellflower	112					■	■			
Culver's root	116					■	■			
Leadplant	142					■	■			
Butterfly weed	144					■	■			
Compass plant	118					■	■			
Queen-of-the-prairie	120					■	■			
Rattlesnake master	122					■	■			
Black-eyed Susan	124					■	■	■	■	
Nodding wild onion	126					■	■			
Gayfeather	128					■	■	■		
Purple prairie clover	146					■	■	■		
Purple coneflower	130						■	■	■	
Wild bergamot	148					■	■			
Blanketflower	150						■	■	■	
Meadow beauty	154						■	■		
False dragonhead	156						■	■	■	
Showy tick trefoil	158						■	■	■	
Closed gentian	160							■	■	■
New England aster	162							■	■	■
Silky aster	164								■	■

with relatively longer spring and summer day lengths, have a greater proportion of long-day plants than do southern regions. In fact, day length determines the southern limits of some long-day species.

Other species, such as the New England and silky asters, are "short-day" plants and flower when days are short and nights are long. These species are stimulated to flower by the long nights of late summer and fall.

Regional differences in climatic patterns and day lengths have led to the evolution of genetically distinct varieties in some wildflower species. Known as "ecotypes," these varieties are well adapted to local conditions. When individuals of different ecotypes are planted together in the same garden, they frequently will flower at different times.

EXTENDING THE FLOWERING SEASON

There are several ways in which the flowering season can be prolonged. The easiest way to extend the flower season of annual wildflowers is to make successive plantings at three-to-four-week intervals from spring to early summer. Some of the late sowings may not bear flowers, but there will still be blooms after the flowers of the first sowing have long withered. Black-eyed Susans grown from seeds will tend to flower later the first year than in subsequent years. By planting new seeds in the late spring each year, you can have black-eyed Susans flowering in autumn well after the flowers have withered on plants established in previous years. Some wildflowers will bloom longer if additional water is provided during the dry season, while others will simply rot. Consult the cultural requirements for individual wildflowers presented in Part III.

With species like butterfly weed, trim some of the plants just before they set flower buds. That will delay their flowering by several weeks, and the clipped plants will come into bloom as the flowers on the untrimmed plants are fading. Many species, both annuals and perennials, will bloom longer if fading flowers are removed ("deadheaded") before the fruits and seeds start to mature. The only drawback of this technique is that you sacrifice production of seed that could be used for further propagation.

If you have a number of different garden sites with varying slopes and exposures, the differences in microclimates may be sufficient to accelerate flowering in some plants and delay it in others. Another way to extend the flowering season of a given species in the garden is to purchase seeds or plants from suppliers in various geographic regions, so that different ecotypes are represented in the garden. The differences in their flowering times may be sufficient to prolong the season even of those species with short-lived flowers. This approach is not recommended for restoring prairies or planting large meadows, since it may alter the local gene pool.

Wildflower Culture

LIGHT CONDITIONS While the vast majority of domesticated horticultural species planted in the garden require full sunlight for optimum growth, native plants have evolved to survive in a wide variety of light conditions, from full sun to shade. Therein lies an opportunity in gardening with wildflowers. The light preferences of the 34 species of native plants included in this book are given on page 47. While some species are successfully grown only in a rather restricted range of light conditions, others can be cultivated in either sun or shade. The form of the plant often changes when grown under different light conditions. Typically when a plant is grown in the shade its leaves are thinner and larger and its stems are more spindly or "leggy" than when it is grown in the open. Some prairie species, however, such as wild columbine, are adapted to shade and can grow vigorously under the cover of deciduous forest trees.

TEMPERATURE Most gardeners are familiar with hardiness zones, which indicate the relative mildness or severity of winter temperatures. (See page 70, U.S.D.A. Hardiness Zone Map.) The higher the hardiness zone number, the milder the winter climate. There is a great deal of similarity between hardiness zones and the length of the frost-free season (see map on page 69). Hardiness zones are based only on the average annual minimum winter temperature, however, and the frost-free season is the average length of time between the last killing frost in the spring and the first frost in the autumn. As you move from southern to northern interior regions of central North America, you will generally encounter shorter frost-free seasons and lower hardiness zone numbers, but this pattern is by no means uniform. The east sides of the Great Lakes have significantly milder winters and longer growing seasons than do the upwind, western lakeshores and mid-continental regions at the same latitude.

LIGHT CONDITIONS

Species	Page	Open Full Sun	Filtered Sun Partial Shade	Light Shade	Heavy Shade
Blanketflower	150	▓			
Bluebonnet	94	▓			
Butterfly weed	144	▓			
Compass plant	118	▓			
Lance-leaved coreopsis	134	▓			
Leadplant	142	▓			
Mexican hat	138	▓			
Missouri evening primrose	136	▓			
Nodding wild onion	126	▓			
Purple prairie clover	146	▓			
Rattlesnake master	122	▓			
Snow-on-the-mountain	140	▓			
Wine cup	96	▓			
Pasqueflower	92	▓▓			
Purple coneflower	130	▓▓			
Birdsfoot violet	100	▓▓▓			
Black-eyed Susan	124	▓▓▓			
Gayfeather	128	▓▓▓			
Meadow beauty	154	▓▓▓			
New England aster	162	▓▓▓			
Prairie phlox	102	▓▓▓			
Silky aster	164	▓▓▓			
Wild bergamot	148	▓▓▓			
Pasture rose	110	▓▓▓▓			
Showy tick trefoil	158	▓▓▓▓			
American bellflower	112	▓▓▓▓▓			
Canada anemone	106	▓▓▓▓▓			
Closed gentian	160	▓▓▓▓▓			
False dragonhead	156	▓▓▓▓▓			
Prairie smoke	98	▓▓▓▓▓			
Queen-of-the-prairie	120	▓▓▓▓▓			
Wood lily	114	▓▓▓▓▓			
Culver's root	116	▓▓▓▓▓▓			
Wild columbine	104	▓▓▓▓▓▓▓			

Most perennials have a limited range of hardiness zones in which they can survive. The approximate range of hardiness zones for the species of wildflowers in this book is given on page 49 and is shown on the individual range maps. The hardiness ranges indicated are approximate. You can usually cultivate perennials in colder areas if you insulate them with a heavy overwinter mulch to prevent frost penetration in the soil. Be careful to remove the mulch in the spring and to choose a mulching material that will not alter the desired acidity/alkalinity conditions for pH-sensitive species, as is explained in the section to follow concerning soils.

Many wildflowers and grasses need chilling of their seeds as well. These seeds require or are enhanced by weeks or even months of exposure to temperatures of 40°F or below, to break their dormancy and germinate properly, as is discussed in the following section on propagation.

MOISTURE CONDITIONS

Just as prairie wildflowers have adapted to different temperature and light conditions, they have evolved to survive under different moisture conditions, ranging from the dry Great Plains to the moist Prairie Peninsula. Precipitation in mid-continent North America is generally most abundant during the late spring, but can be scanty during the summer growing season when evaporation is greatest.

The geographic distribution of precipitation is far from uniform. Moisture-laden air masses, traveling inland from the Pacific Ocean, are forced to rise over the summits of the Cascades, Sierra Nevada, and Rocky Mountains, cooling and releasing snow or rain. The passage up the western slopes depletes the moisture from the air masses, which become warmer and even drier during their descent down the eastern slopes. As a result the western Great Plains are in a "rain-shadow" of the western mountains. Moisture is replenished in the air by air masses moving northward out of the Gulf of Mexico, especially during late spring and summer, meeting air masses travelling from west to east across the middle of the continent. Precipitation generally increases west to east, therefore, from the Rocky Mountains, across the Great Plains, to the eastern deciduous forest regions. The greater precipitation in the southern portion of the tallgrass prairie region is an influence of the Gulf of Mexico (see the map on page 68).

On a local scale, the gardener should choose wildflowers adapted to the soil-moisture conditions that are present, as shown in the chart on page 51. Some species, such as closed gentian and meadow beauty, thrive in damp soils, yet can also be easily cultivated in well-drained soils of moderate moisture — conditions typical of most flower gardens. Many species need

HARDINESS ZONES

Species	Page	Hardiness Zones
Pasqueflower	92	1–6
Prairie smoke	98	2–5
Canada anemone	106	2–6
Blanketflower	150	2–8
False dragonhead	156	2–9
Closed gentian	160	3–5
Showy tick trefoil	158	3
Leadplant	142	3–7
New England aster	162	3–7
Black-eyed Susan	124	3–8
Purple coneflower	130	3–8
Prairie phlox	102	3–8
Purple prairie clover	146	3–8
Birdsfoot violet	100	3–8
Culver's root	116	3–8
Compass plant	118	3–8
Queen-of-the-prairie	120	3–8
Wild columbine	104	3–8
Silky aster	164	3–8
Gayfeather	128	3–9
American bellflower	112	3–9
Wild bergamot	148	3–9
Butterfly weed	144	3–10
Wood lily	114	4–6
Wine cup	96	4–8
Nodding wild onion	126	4–8
Missouri evening primrose	136	4–8
Pasture rose	110	4–9
Lance-leaved coreopsis	134	4–9
Rattlesnake master	122	4–9
Meadow beauty	154	5–9
Mexican hat	138	5–9
Bluebonnet HA	94	
Snow-on-the-mountain HA	140	

HA (Hardy Annual): Planted in fall or spring, grows early spring to early fall.

moisture while they are becoming established in the garden, but then grow better if the soils are not overly wet. Wildflower gardeners should be judicious with the hose; wild bergamot, Mexican hat, blanketflower, and other species suffer from root rot or leaf mildews if they are kept too wet, and seedlings of most wildflowers are especially sensitive to fungal attack when soils are cold and wet.

Cultivating wildflowers is easiest when you match a species' optimal requirements with those naturally occurring in the garden, so consider your soil before selecting wildflowers. If your soil is sandy, it will probably drain quickly, and you should consider planting species that do well in drier conditions. Clayey and peaty soils are often poorly drained, making them hospitable to species preferring plenty of soil moisture during the rainy season, but they can become excessively dry during the remainder of the year.

If your soil conditions do not quite suit a particular species, however, you may be able to add the proper soil amendments before planting. A little extra time and energy invested in site preparation will pay large dividends in the future, so do not rush your wildflowers into soils to which they are ill adapted. Avoid merely piling soil amendments on top of the soil where they will have marginal effect; instead, work them thoroughly into the soil. Organic matter well mixed into the soil will aerate it and increase its water-holding capacity.

If your soil is too dry, the garden not too large, and your hose long enough, it is obviously easy to increase the soil moisture by watering. However, adding clay, compost, humus, or even coarse organic matter such as leaves may be a more effective way of assuring the long-term retention of moisture. Mulches are an integral part of xeriscaping in dry regions because they reduce evaporation from the soil surface. They are excellent to use around the bases of perennials, but may prevent small seeded annual wildflowers from self-seeding.

If the soil is too wet during the spring and early summer because of an overabundance of clay, you can improve the drainage by adding sand or gravel mixed with copious amounts of compost or other organic matter. The organic matter creates additional air spaces in clayey soil and helps to prevent the clay from merely coating the grains of sand. Alternatively, gypsum (calcium sulfate) can be added to clayey soil to improve drainage. Since gypsum is an acidifying agent, it should be used where you will be planting wildflowers that thrive in acid soil, with a pH of 5.5 and below. Gypsum has the additional benefit of helping conserve nitrogen compounds in the soil. It is available at many garden or building-supply centers.

SOIL MOISTURE CONDITIONS

Species	Page	Wet	Damp	Moist	Moderately or Seasonally Dry	Arid
Meadow beauty	154	▓	▓			
False dragonhead	156		▓			
Queen-of-the-prairie	120		▓	▓		
Culver's root	116			▓		
New England aster	162			▓		
Nodding wild onion	126			▓		
Prairie smoke	98			▓		
Canada anemone	106			▓	▓	
Showy tick trefoil	158			▓	▓	
Wild columbine	104			▓	▓	
Snow-on-the-mountain	140			▓	▓	
Purple coneflower	130			▓	▓	
Gayfeather	128			▓	▓	
Closed gentian	160			▓	▓	
Black-eyed Susan	124			▓	▓	
Compass plant	118			▓	▓	
Pasture rose	110			▓		
American bellflower	112			▓		
Wood lily	114			▓	▓	
Wild bergamot	148			▓	▓	
Rattlesnake master	122			▓	▓	
Prairie phlox	102			▓		
Birdsfoot violet	100			▓		
Lance-leaved coreopsis	134			▓	▓	
Blanketflower	150			▓	▓	
Mexican hat	138			▓	▓	
Silky aster	164				▓	
Leadplant	142				▓	
Pasqueflower	92				▓	
Butterfly weed	144				▓	
Bluebonnet	94				▓	
Wine cup	96				▓	
Purple prairie clover	146				▓	
Missouri evening primrose	136				▓	

pH, SALINITY, AND OTHER SOIL CONDITIONS

The specific soil requirements of 34 native plants are given on the individual species description pages. Some species thrive where nutrient levels are high and humus is abundant in the soil. Other species do best where there is little organic matter and the soil fertility is low. In general it is not necessary to apply fertilizers to plantings of native prairie wildflowers and grasses. For many species it can do more harm than good, and frequently just encourages exotic weed growth.

One of the most important conditions in the cultivation of many wildflowers is the pH of the soil. The pH is simply a measure of the relative acidity or alkalinity on a scale from 0 (most acidic) to 14 (most alkaline), with a value of 7 indicating neutral conditions. The pH units are based on multiples of ten, so that a soil with a pH of 4.0 is 10 times more acidic than a soil with a pH of 5.0, and 100 times more acidic than a soil with a pH of 6.0. Likewise, a pH of 9 is 10 times more alkaline than a pH of 8, and so forth.

The pH of the soil is important because it influences the availability of nutrients essential for plant growth. Nutrients such as phosphorus, calcium, potassium, and magnesium are most available to plants when the soil pH is between 6.0 and 7.5. Under highly acidic (low pH) conditions these nutrients become insoluble and relatively unavailable for uptake by plants. However, iron, trace minerals, and some toxic elements such as aluminum become more available at low pH. A major concern about acid rain is the possible increased absorption of these toxic elements by plants.

High soil pH may also decrease the availability of nutrients. If the soil is more alkaline than pH 8, phosphorus, iron, and many trace minerals become insoluble and unavailable for plant uptake.

The availability of nitrogen, one of plants' three key nutrients, is influenced by pH conditions as well. Much of the nitrogen that plants eventually use is bound within organic matter, and the conversion of this bound nitrogen to forms available to plants is accomplished by several species of bacteria living in the soil. When the soil's pH drops below 5.5, the activity of these bacteria is inhibited, and little nitrogen is available to the plants.

The usual pH range of soils is from about 4 to about 8. Over millennia, rocks and minerals decompose and slowly release large amounts of potassium, calcium, magnesium, and other alkaline nutrients. In the more humid eastern tallgrass prairie region more ample rainfall has removed some of these elements from the soil. In the more arid areas of the Great Plains, however, more intense evaporation and scantier rainfall have led to accu-

pH PREFERENCES

Species	Page	pH Range
Meadow beauty	154	4–5
Wood lily	114	4–6
Birdsfoot violet	100	4.5–6
Pasture rose	110	4.5–6
Prairie phlox	102	4.5–6.5
Butterfly weed	144	4.5–6.5
Culver's root	116	4.5–6.7
Silky aster	164	5–6.5
Wine cup	96	5–7
Queen-of-the-prairie	120	5–7
False dragonhead	156	5–7
Prairie smoke	98	5–7.5
Closed gentian	160	5–7.5
Wild bergamot	148	5–7.5
Bluebonnet	94	5–8
Wild columbine	104	5–8
Purple prairie clover	146	5.3–6.5
New England aster	162	5.3–7
Gayfeather	128	5.3–7
Canada anemone	106	6–7
American bellflower	112	6–7
Pasqueflower	92	6–8
Lance-leaved coreopsis *	134	4.5–7.7
Snow-on-the-mountain	140	4.5–7.7
Leadplant	142	4.5–7.7
Blanketflower	150	4.5–7.7
Missouri evening primrose	136	4.5–7.7
Black-eyed Susan	124	4.5–7.7
Compass plant	118	4.5–7.7
Nodding wild onion	126	4.5–7.7
Purple coneflower	130	4.5–7.7
Rattlesnake master	122	4.5–7.7
Showy tick trefoil	158	5–7.7
Mexican hat	138	6–8

*This and the following species appear to have no strong pH preferences.

mulation of these nutrients and the production of alkaline or even saline soils in some locations. As a result the soils of the region show great variability, ranging from acidic to alkaline with pH values substantially above 7. Poorly designed or poorly operated irrigation systems further contribute to increased salinity in the West by bringing additional salts to the soil surface, making the growth of many plants difficult.

Local soil acidity/alkalinity conditions may also vary because of differences in bedrock geology or vegetation. In general, limestone or marble bedrock produces mildly alkaline soils, and granite bedrock produces acidic soils.

Certain species of plants may also increase the acidity of the soil through the addition of organic matter with a low pH. Coniferous forests are noted for their acidic soils. The dead foliage of pines, spruce, fir, as well as oaks and heath plants, deposited on top of the soil, further acidifies the soil as it decomposes. In cool, wet areas, the growth of mosses may also create locally the acidic conditions typical of regions with needle-leaved forests.

Some species of wildflowers are relatively insensitive to soil acidity/alkalinity conditions, while others survive only over a narrow pH range. Most often pH preferences are more related to the balance of various nutrients required by particular species, or to changes in the biological activity of soil organisms, rather than to acidity or alkalinity itself. On page 53 is a guide to the pH preferences of those species of wildflowers that have specific soil pH requirements. It is often difficult to grow species close together if they have vastly different pH requirements. It is best to grow acid-loving species such as birdsfoot violet in a different section of the garden than species that prefer alkaline soils.

HOW TO MEASURE pH

Before deciding which wildflowers to cultivate and where to plant them, it is essential to know something about the pH of your soils. The measurement is actually quite simple, and a number of commercial products are readily available from most garden suppliers. The pH is measured by taking samples of soil from the root zone at several different spots in the garden. Using a plastic spoon, place the soil in a small plastic or glass vial, and add an equal volume of water. Shake or stir the sample to mix the soil and water thoroughly, and allow the soil to settle. The pH of the liquid in the top of the vial can then be determined by any one of several means.

The least expensive way to measure pH is with "indicator paper," which can be purchased in short strips or long rolls. This is like litmus paper, but rather than merely showing you whether a solution is acid or alkaline, it produces a range of colors to indicate the pH value. Just stick the strip of paper into the liquid extracted from the soil and compare the color of the dampened paper to the reference chart provided.

A slightly more accurate method, although usually more expensive, is the use of indicator solutions, which are frequently sold in pH kits. A small amount of the liquid extracted from the soil-and-water mix is placed in a ceramic dish, and a few drops of indicator solution are added. As with the indicator papers, the color produced is compared to a pH reference chart.

You can also measure pH with a meter. One type of pH meter operates without batteries and measures pH based on the conductivity of the moistened soil. This type of pH meter is neither more accurate nor faster than the color-indicator methods that use solutions or paper. All provide a rough, but useful, estimate of soil pH.

The most accurate measurements of soil pH use electronic meters with one or several electrodes. These instruments are quite expensive and are used by soil-testing laboratories for determining soil pH. Most state Agricultural Experiment Stations, usually located at land-grant universities, will test soil samples for a nominal charge. To arrange for such pH testing, contact your state's land-grant university or your county's Agricultural Extension Service agent.

CHANGING THE pH OF SOILS

You may find that the pH of your soil does not suit a particular species, even though all other environmental conditions seem perfect. The acidity or alkalinity of soils can be altered to a limited extent through the addition of various soil amendments. It may take several years to change a soil's pH permanently, however, so be patient.

Pine needles can be added to garden soils to lower the pH. If none of these is locally available, peat moss also works well in acidifying soils. Powdered gypsum (calcium sulfate) or sulfur powder can be used to lower soil pH, but these should be used with caution, because they act more rapidly than do the organic materials.

Ground limestone is the amendment of choice to raise the pH of the soil. Medium-ground limestone may give better long-term results than very coarse limestone (which may be slow to neutralize soil acids) or very fine limestone (which may be lost too quickly from the soil). Wood ashes can also be used, but keep in mind that they are more concentrated than limestone and may even "burn" wildflowers if too much is applied.

After measuring the pH, add the soil amendment, taking care to mix thoroughly and incorporate it uniformly in the top 6 to 12 inches of soil.

Spread the amendment thinly on the ground, and work it into the soil with a spading fork or shovel. Then add another layer, mixing it into the soil. If you do not mix the amendment evenly you may find pockets of soil with enormously different pH values. Moisten the soil, and then allow it to rest for a day or so before again measuring the pH at several spots. Repeat the process until you have the desired pH conditions.

A very rough rule of thumb is that for a 100-square-foot area of most soils it takes about 2 to 6 pounds of limestone to raise the pH one unit, and 2½ to 7 pounds of gypsum or ½ to 2 pounds of sulfur to lower the pH one unit. Clay soils require more of an amendment to change the pH; sandy soils, less.

It is strongly recommended that organic matter acidifiers be used before resorting to gypsum or sulfur. It is better to change the pH of the soil slowly than to overdo it one way and then the other.

After the appropriate pH is attained, check it periodically. Since the natural processes at work in your garden will be altering the pH through rainfall, bacterial activity, the uptake of nutrients by plants, and climatic factors, you may occasionally have to make further additions of soil amendments. With wildflowers in place, be especially careful to add the amendments in small amounts directly on the surface of the soil, and work them in with minimal disturbance of the plants' roots.

A WORD ABOUT WEEDS AND PESTS

While it might not be obvious at first glance, healthy soil is full of living organisms. It is being continually shaped through the activity of bacteria, fungi, and tiny insect-like animals too small to be seen with the unaided eye, in addition to earthworms, insects, and even mammals that are visible at times. The use of synthetic chemical pesticides, insecticides, herbicides, and fungicides often disrupts the ecological balances within the soil and should be avoided. It is far better to use mechanical means or biological controls that are specific to the pest needing control.

Wildflowers growing in their natural habitats are obviously well adapted for survival under the prevailing local conditions. Gardening, however, involves disturbing the soil and modifying the moisture and, often, light conditions. These changes frequently invite unwelcome and unwanted plants — weeds.

Many of the worst weeds, such as squirreltail grass (*Hordeum jubatum*), lambsquarters (*Chenopodium album*), Bermuda grass (*Cynodon dactylon*), Russian thistle (*Salsola kali*), pigweeds (*Amaranthus* species), yellow nut-sedge

(*Cyperus esculentus*), Johnson grass (*Sorgum halepense*), quack grass (*Agropyron repens*), Saint Johnswort (*Hypericum perforatum*), mouse-ear chickweed (*Cerastium vulgatum*), field bindweed (*Convolvulus arvensis*), and dandelion (*Taraxacum officinale*), have their origins in Europe or Asia and have found a new home to their liking in prairie regions. Not all weeds, however, are imports from overseas. Downy sunflower (*Helianthus mollis*) is a native prairie plant that has spread from where it has been cultivated. It is known to chemically kill other wildflowers as it grows, forming fairy rings. Other native species such as tall goldenrod (*Solidago altissima*) and Canada goldenrod (*S. canadensis*) can be persistent and aggressive when growing in tallgrass prairies.

In contrast to many of the desirable native wildflowers, weeds tend to grow quickly, spread aggressively, and set loose copious quantities of highly mobile seeds. Often weeds will accomplish these feats so quickly that they produce many generations in the time it takes to produce a single generation of desired wildflowers. The seeds of weeds tend to be long-lived and may remain dormant for many years, buried in the soil, just waiting for the proper conditions to germinate. Studies have shown that the seeds of some weeds can remain dormant yet capable of germinating for more than forty years. Typically, there are hundreds of weed seeds beneath each square yard of soil surface. Gardening activity frequently brings the weed seeds to the surface and provides ideal conditions for them to thrive.

Weeds are thus inevitable, but do not despair, and do not resort to the use of herbicides! Many wildflowers are particularly sensitive to the effects of herbicides, so weeding by hand is the only real choice. You will find that a modest investment of time spent weeding while your wildflowers are first becoming established will pay large dividends. Even natural gardens may need some weeding during the first several years. Once the plants are well established and holding their ground, weeds will have a more difficult time invading, and weeding will be less necessary.

You will find from time to time that various insects will visit your wildflowers, and while some of these may be there for an attractive meal, they usually have an abundance of natural predators that will keep their populations in check so that minimal damage occurs. Some wildflowers, like lupines and violets, may look a bit tattered by the end of the season, because butterfly larvae have chewed holes in the leaves. Usually the plants have suffered little, and the use of pesticides is unwarranted, especially if you are trying to attract butterflies, bees, or even hummingbirds to the garden. The use of pesticides is also to be avoided because many wildflowers are pollinated by insects, and without the pollinators, there is no fruit and seed production.

If aphids become a problem because their naturally occurring biological control agents are lacking, try controlling them with insecticidal soaps.

When establishing or maintaining a wildflower garden, slugs, household pets, ground squirrels, gophers, rabbits, mice, birds, and, in rural areas, deer may be more of a problem than insects are. To keep rodents from digging up your lily bulbs, cover them with large-mesh hardware cloth or fine-mesh chicken wire. Trapping and removal of gophers and ground squirrels may be necessary if you, your wildflowers, and these wildlife species cannot reach an accommodation. If dogs, cats, or deer become a nuisance, fencing may be the only reasonable solution. Large, robust seedlings, which have been started in flats and transplanted, may be more resistant to animal attack than are tender seedlings just emerging from the soil. Sometimes, what appears to be indiscriminate eating of wildflowers by mammals actually increases their growth. Many species of prairie grasses and wildflowers grow more vigorously after being moderately grazed upon by deer, buffalo, or jack-rabbits. If wildlife persist in decimating a particular species, however, try planting another, less enticing one.

Slugs and snails are more of a problem in the Prairie Peninsula than elsewhere, and they relish certain species of wildflowers, especially those in the lily family. They feed at night when the humidity is high, and can do considerable damage by chewing and stripping leaves. Slugs and snails can be easily and effectively controlled by hand picking, or if you find that approach offensive, by setting out dishes filled with stale beer. The shallow tubs in which whipped cream cheese or margarine are packaged make ideal traps. Make a "rain protector" for the trap by poking 3 holes in the lid in a triangular pattern and insert a plastic soda straw in each. Trim the straws so the lid rests an inch above the rim of the tub. Fill the tubs three-quarters full with beer and set them about the garden. The snails and slugs much prefer beer to your wildflowers, and once swimming in the brew they drown. Every several days, especially after heavy rains, you may have to dispose of the contents and replenish the beer.

Wildflower Propagation

One of the pleasures of growing wildflowers is the opportunity to propagate them and thereby increase their numbers in your garden. As has already been pointed out, digging wildflowers from their native environments is not only unethical, but also frequently illegal. The best way to obtain wildflowers for your garden is to purchase seeds, plants, or planting stock from reputable suppliers who sell nursery-propagated material (see Appendix A). Once your wildflowers are established, they can serve as stock for further propagation for your garden.

SEEDS   Seeds are by far the cheapest way to propagate large numbers of wildflowers, even though some perennials grown from seeds may take a long time before they are mature enough to flower. Usually seeds are collected when the fruits are mature. Many species have seed dispersal mechanisms that may make it difficult to find plants with the fruits present when you want to harvest them. One way to capture the seeds before they are released from the plant is to cut a foot-long section of a discarded nylon stocking and make a sleeve, tying off one end with a string or twisted wire closure. Slip the sleeve over the developing fruit after the flower petals have withered, but before the fruit is fully ripe. Firmly but gently tie the open end closed so that the seeds can't fall to the ground, being careful not to crush or break the stem in the process. When the fruits are fully ripe, snip the stem just below the nylon bag, put it in a labeled paper sack, and bring it indoors for further processing.

Some seeds should be planted fresh and not allowed to dry out, or germination will be delayed. Other seeds will not germinate immediately and have to undergo a process of "after-ripening" before they are ready to sprout. Seeds of fleshy fruits should generally be separated from the pulp prior to storage or planting. If seeds are not the kind that need to be planted immediately and you desire to store them for a while, allow them to air-dry for several weeks and then separate the seeds from the dried remains of the fruit. Gently crushing the dried fruits on a large sheet of white paper will usually release the seeds, which should then be separated from the chaff. The chaff can be removed either by blowing gently across the paper or, if seeds are small enough, by sifting through a strainer. Store the cleaned seeds in small manila coin envelopes, zip-closure bags, or 35mm film canisters.

The seeds of some species will remain dormant unless they undergo certain specific treatments — chilling, scratching of their seed coats, exposure to light or darkness, heating by fire, or a combination of these treatments. The treatments required to germinate specific seeds are detailed on the descriptive pages following this chapter. These treatments fall into four categories: seed chilling, or stratification; seed-coat scratching, or scarification; heat treatments; light or dark treatment.

Stratification. Some plants living in the interior of North America have evolved seeds that are dormant the first fall after they have been produced. This adaptation prevents tender seedlings from coming up and facing freezing temperatures when they would be only a month or so old. Breaking dormancy requires the seeds to be subjected to a period of cold temperatures (stratification), followed by a period of warm temperatures — as in the natural progression of seasons. Usually a temperature of only 40 degrees F is sufficient to break dormancy or enhance germination. The length of stratification varies widely among different species. Some seeds germinate more successfully if they are stratified under moist conditions in addition to the cold temperatures.

The easiest way to stratify seeds is to plant the seeds outdoors in the fall and let Nature do it for you. Seeds can be planted directly in the garden where desired or in flats that are left outdoors. If you do not desire to plant the seeds in the fall, place the container or envelope of seeds under refrigeration for the appropriate period of time. If moist stratification is required, the seeds can be placed in damp sphagnum moss or rolled up in lightly dampened paper towels and placed in an airtight container or zip-closure plastic bag for the duration of the stratification.

Scarification. In order for seeds to germinate they have to take up water and oxygen from the outside environment through the outer covering of the seed, called the seed coat. Some native species, especially those in the bean family, have seed coats so tough that water and oxygen cannot enter. These seeds remain dormant until the seed coat is scratched, or scarified. This occurs naturally when seeds are moved around in the soil, especially following heavy rainstorms, but in the home garden better results are obtained if the seeds are scarified by the gardener before planting. However, if you are planting large areas or restoring a prairie, scarify only half of the seeds before sowing to allow a staggered germination of those species with thick seed coats.

The easiest way to scarify medium-size seeds is to rub the seeds between two sheets of medium-grit sandpaper. You don't want to rub them so hard that you pulverize the seeds, just hard enough to scratch up the surface so that moisture can penetrate to the seed inside. Large seeds can be scarified by nicking the seed coat with a sharp pocket knife.

Heat Treatments. Some seeds germinate better after being submerged in hot water prior to planting. Place the seeds in a jar and fill it halfway with tap water that is hot to the touch, but not scalding. Allow the seeds to remain in the water as it cools overnight. The seeds can then be planted the next day.

Light or Dark Treatments. A few species of wildflowers have seeds that are either stimulated or inhibited by light. If the seeds are stimulated by light they should be planted shallowly, so sunlight penetrating through the surface of the soil can have its desired effect. If the seeds are inhibited by light, they should be planted at sufficient depth to prevent light from slowing germination.

PLANTING TECHNIQUES   One of the most efficient ways to propagate wildflowers from seed is to use flats or nursery beds for rearing seedlings for the first year or until they become established. The advantage of flats is that you can transplant seedlings to holding beds and maintain an optimum density of plants more easily than if you plant the seed directly in the desired location. Also, some species have seed that is slow to germinate, and it may take several years for all the viable seeds that were planted to produce seedlings. The soil can be kept in the flats until the seeds have had sufficient time to germinate completely.

If you have only a few seeds, small pots can be used for raising seedlings. If the species is one that thrives in slightly acidic conditions, peat pots are a real convenience. When the seedlings are sturdy they can be transplanted to a nursery bed, where they can grow without competition from other plants, or to permanent locations. Be careful not to disturb the roots or to break off the shoots when removing the seedlings and soil from pots. If you are using peat pots, simply tear off the bottom of the pot and plant the container with its contents so that the surface level of the soil is the same as that inside the pot. (Unlike many gardeners, I tear off the bottom of the peat pot, because I have found the plant makes better contact with the soil that way.)

Soil Mixes and Potting. The soil in which a seed germinates and the seedling starts out is every bit as important as that in which the adult plant grows. A potting soil should have both good drainage and good water-holding capacity. While commercially formulated starting mixes are available from home and garden centers, you can make an inexpensive but effective mix by adding one part milled sphagnum to one part washed builder's sand. The resulting mix is weed-free and sterile. One convenient way to start seeds is to use 4½-by-6¼-inch plastic flats that are 2½ inches deep. Fill the flat to the top with the potting mix and then tamp down the surface, with the bottom of another flat, so that the soil surface is just below the rim. Set the seeds on the soil surface, and then cover them with the appropriate depth of additional soil. Moisten the soil with a fine sprinkle, and cover the top of the flat with plastic wrap to help conserve soil moisture. Leave the plastic on the flats until the seeds germinate and the tops of the seedlings are just pushing against the film.

Plugs and Sods. An effective way to grow live plants for transplanting to meadows and prairies is to produce wildflower plugs and sods. Plugs are individual live plants that have been grown in small pots or special trays. They can be efficiently transplanted into meadows or gardens because of their compact, dense mass of roots. They are most easily produced in special plug trays available through greenhouse supply companies and larger garden centers. These trays have cavities up to 2 inches in diameter and 2 inches deep with gently tapering sides so that the plugs can be easily removed.

To produce wildflower plugs, use the larger trays with 2-inch openings, and fill the cavities with potting mix as you would other pots or flats. Allow the seedlings to develop until the roots fully bind the soil in the cavities, a process that may take most of a growing season for some species. Water the plugs by periodically setting the entire tray in a shallow pan and allowing the water to be drawn up from the bottom. The wildflowers can be transplanted into the garden or meadow when a gentle tug at the base of the plant's stem pulls the entire plug, soil and all, out of the cavity.

Wildflower sods are like plugs, only larger. Sods can be made with a number of different wildflowers and grasses grown densely together in flats. You then transplant the entire contents of the flat into a meadow or garden. One way to make sods easier to handle is to line the flat with cheesecloth before adding the potting soil. The seeds are then planted in the soil, and as the seedlings mature their roots will penetrate the cloth liner. When it is time to transplant the sod, you can lift it out of the flat by pulling on the cheesecloth. Once in the ground, the roots of the sod plants will quickly grow through the cheesecloth and after about a year the cloth will simply decompose.

A Special Note on Legumes. Members of the bean family often require the presence of special microorganisms, known as rhizobia, in the soil to ensure their survival. These microbes lead a symbiotic existence with these plants, inhabiting nodules formed on the root systems and producing nitrogen compounds that the plants eventually use. Not all soils have abundant populations of these necessary microbes. If you have difficulty in propagating leguminous wildflowers, like leadplant, purple prairie clover, and bluebonnets, you may need to purchase a commercially produced "inoculant" and add it to the soil when you plant the seeds. Different species require different strains of microbial inoculants, so the addition of "pea" or "soybean" inoculants would not necessarily be effective for wildflowers. Make sure you get the right strain of rhizobia for the species you plan to cultivate.

Rhizobia inoculants can be ordered directly from the *Nitragin Division of LiphaTech, Inc., 3101 W. Custer Avenue, Milwaukee, WI 53209*, or from *Kalo, Inc., P.O. Box 12567, Columbus, OH 43212*. You will need to indicate the scientific name of the species to be inoculated and the amount of seed you intend to treat. It may take two to four weeks for these companies to prepare special rhizobia if they are not in stock.

ROOTSTOCK DIVISIONS

One of the quickest ways to propagate perennials is by rootstock division. Rootstocks are best dug up and divided while the plant is dormant. In general, perennials that flower in the spring can be most successfully divided in the fall, and those that flower in the summer or fall are best divided in the early spring. For those species like birdsfoot violet whose shoots wither and enter dormancy before the end of the growing season, the location of the plants should be marked with a stake so that the rootstocks can be found later in the fall for propagation.

Regardless of the type of rootstock (see illustration on page 41) the principal technique is quite similar (see illustration on page 64). With a sharp knife (a pocket knife will do splendidly), cut the rootstock so that the divided pieces have at least one vegetative bud or "eye" attached. Since of the

Rootstock propagation.

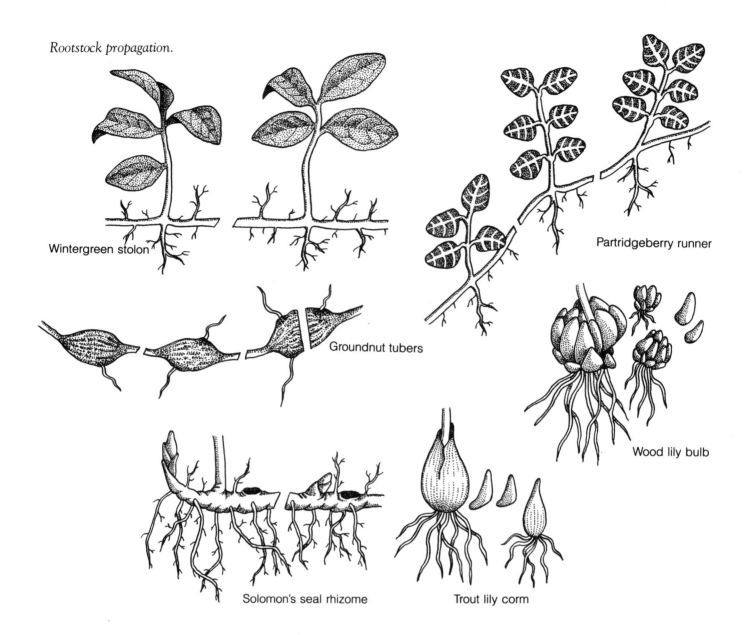

Wintergreen stolon

Partridgeberry runner

Groundnut tubers

Wood lily bulb

Solomon's seal rhizome

Trout lily corm

resulting plant will be determined to a large extent by the size of the divided piece, don't make the divisions too small (unless you want lots of tiny plants).

Runners and stolons are easily divided by cutting the horizontal stem between adjacent rooted plants, which can then be dug up and transplanted when dormant. The division of tubers is also easily accomplished. Cut tubers into pieces, each with a bud or two, and plant them with the buds pointing up (the way you would plant pieces of potato). New shoots and roots will be produced as the plant draws upon the energy reserves of the tuber flesh. Rhizomes similarly can be divided into pieces, each with buds and associated roots. Replant the segments at the appropriate depth and spacing.

Corms and bulbs of perennial wildflowers can be divided in a manner similar to other garden perennials. The small offsets that develop on the sides of mature corms and bulbs can be removed with a knife during the dormant season and planted at the appropriate depth. These cormlets and bulblets will usually take several years to develop into plants capable of flowering. If not cut off the parent rootstock, these offsets eventually mature into large, densely crowded plants that will benefit from being divided and given wider spacing.

The fleshy scales of bulbs such as lilies can be divided and planted like seeds in flats to produce large quantities of "seedlings." Break off the individual scales from dormant bulbs, and in a flat containing potting soil mixture, plant them just below the soil surface, with the tips of the scales pointing upward. Provide light shade and keep the soil moist, but not overly wet, until the resulting small plants are sturdy enough to transplant into a nursery bed or permanent location.

After replanting the rootstock divisions be especially careful not to overwater the soil. Although the soil should be prevented from thoroughly drying out, wet soils may invite problems. Rootstocks have carbohydrate-rich stores of energy that the plant draws upon during its period of most rapid growth. If the soil is too wet, bacterial and fungal rots may attack the newly divided rootstock pieces and even kill the plants. For this reason, it is a good idea to plant rootstock divisions in a nursery or holding bed that has well-drained soil, and to transplant the stock when dormant the following year.

STEM CUTTINGS   Another successful way to propagate some perennials is to make cuttings of stems. These cuttings should be made when the shoots are growing vigorously and are most successful if the shoot lacks flower buds. The best time to make a cutting is when the plant has been well watered, by rain or artificial irrigation, especially in the early morning before the sun evaporates the water from the leaf surfaces.

Before making the cuttings prepare a flat with a mixture of coarse compost or sphagnum moss and builder's sand (don't use beach sand from the ocean, as the salt might kill the cuttings). Moisten the soil, poke holes 2 to 3 inches deep and 5 inches apart with your little finger, and take the flat to the garden. Select succulent stems that snap crisply when doubled over. Cut 6-inch pieces of rapidly growing shoots by making a diagonal slice through the stem with a razor blade. To encourage root formation, remove flower buds and leaves from the bottom 6 inches of the stem. Gently place the cutting into the hole and firmly press the soil around the base to assure good contact with the cutting. Then moisten the soil again.

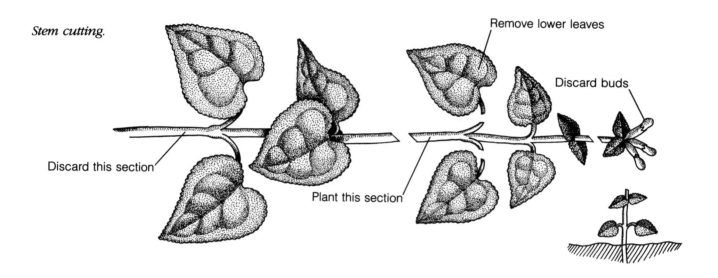

Stem cutting.

Remove lower leaves

Discard buds

Discard this section

Plant this section

Since the cuttings initially have no root systems, it is difficult for them to take up water. It is essential to keep the flats in the shade with the soil moist but not wet. Soils that are too wet will prevent oxygen from getting to the developing roots and will also encourage rotting diseases. Protect the cuttings from the effects of drying winds, and mist the plants if the humidity is low. To attain ideal humidity control, put the entire flat in a large, clear polyethylene bag (available from janitorial supply companies), and tie off the opening. Another idea is to use a clear plastic garment bag to create a mini-greenhouse for starting cuttings. Allow the cuttings to remain in the flat until they go into dormancy at the end of the growing season, and then transplant them to holding beds or permanent locations.

Whether by collecting your own seeds or by dividing or cutting live plants, wildflower propagation can give you satisfactions beyond the considerable cost savings. Many perennials should be divided every several years, and they respond to this treatment by flowering more abundantly and adding even greater beauty to the garden. You can use the surplus divisions to enlarge your plantings, give them to other wildflower enthusiasts, or use them as material for container gardens. Perhaps one of the most important benefits of propagating plants yourself is the increased familiarity with wildflowers you gain in the process.

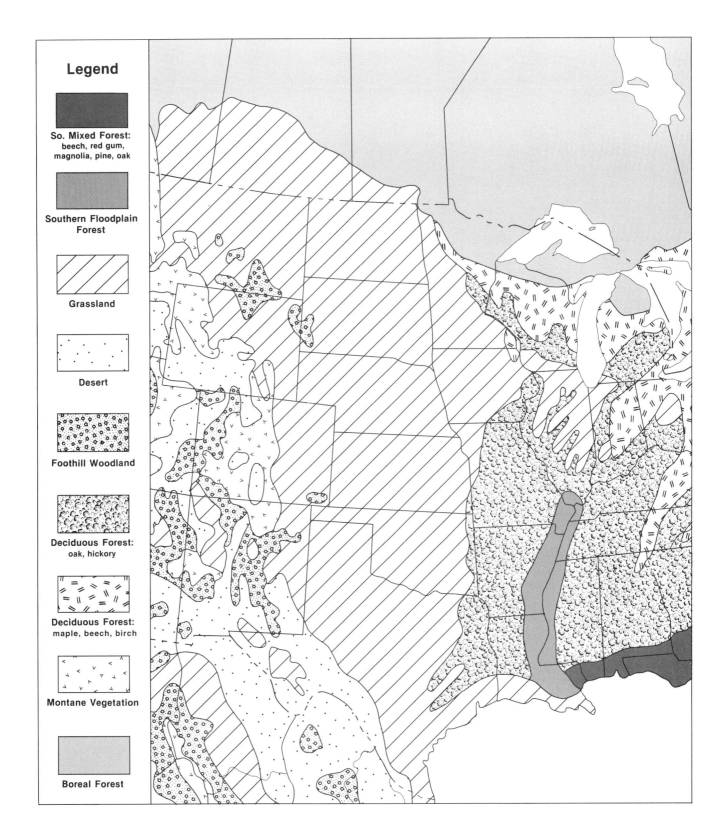

Legend

So. Mixed Forest:
beech, red gum,
magnolia, pine, oak

Southern Floodplain
Forest

Grassland

Desert

Foothill Woodland

Deciduous Forest:
oak, hickory

Deciduous Forest:
maple, beech, birch

Montane Vegetation

Boreal Forest

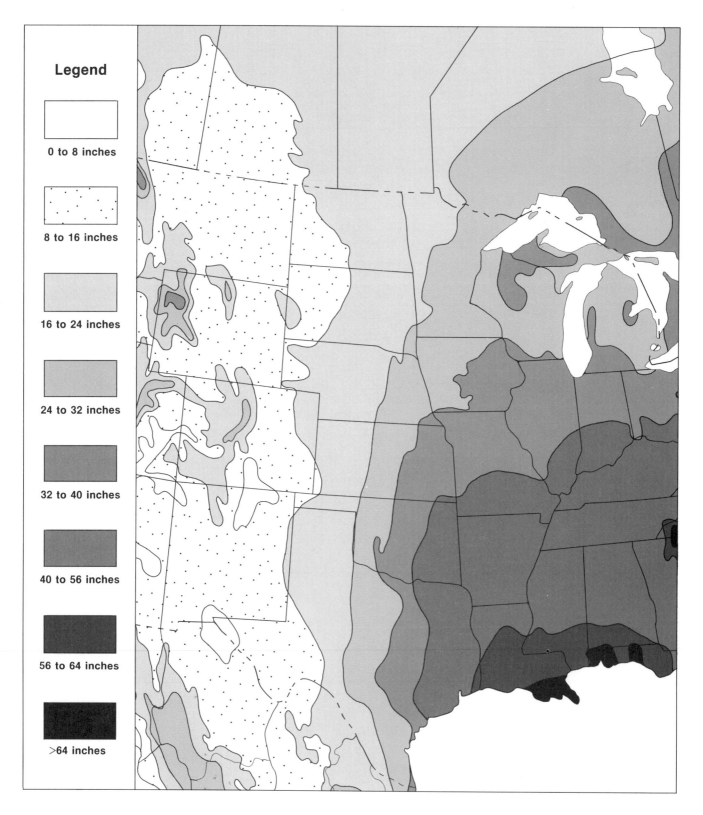

Legend

0 to 8 inches

8 to 16 inches

16 to 24 inches

24 to 32 inches

32 to 40 inches

40 to 56 inches

56 to 64 inches

>64 inches

LENGTH OF FROST-FREE PERIOD IN CENTRAL NORTH AMERICA

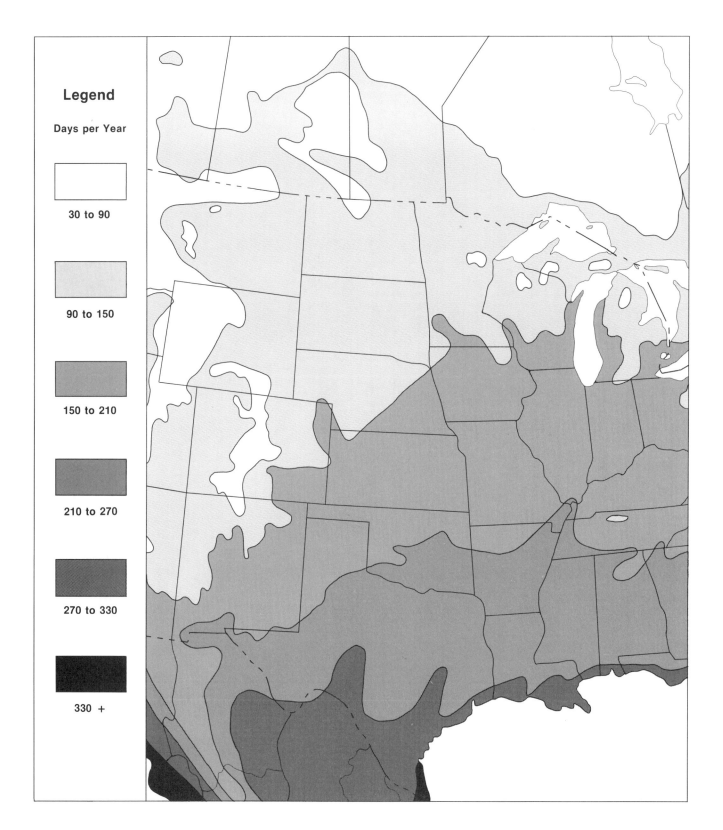

Legend

Days per Year

30 to 90

90 to 150

150 to 210

210 to 270

270 to 330

330 +

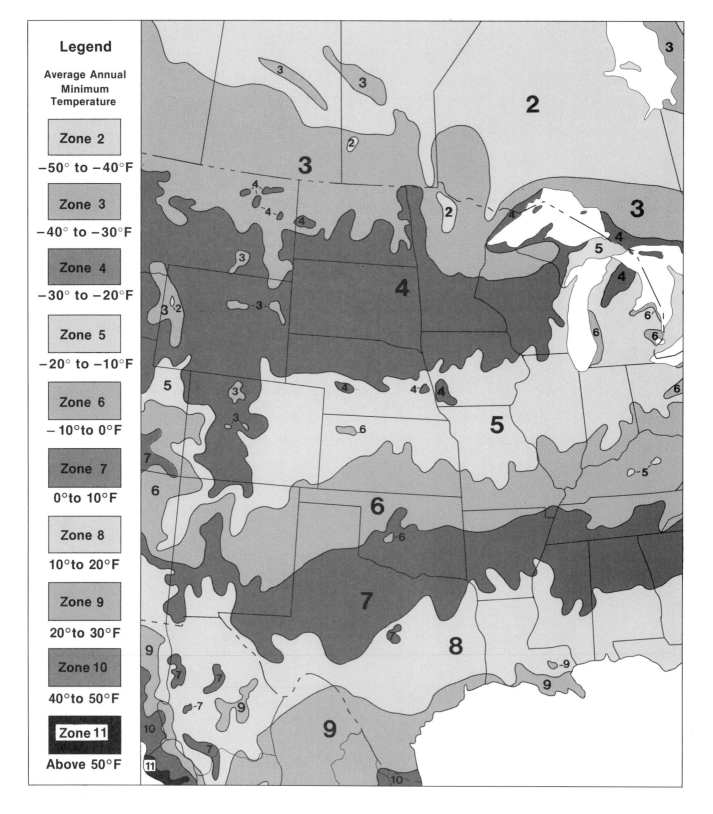

PART II

A Gallery of Midwestern Wildflowers

Pasqueflower is one of the earliest spring wildflowers. Its clusters of fuzzy fruits are borne atop a short stem. (See page 92.)

The white patches on **bluebonnet** flowers turn magenta with age. Vast areas of Texas plains are covered by this state flower, seen growing with Indian paintbrush. (See page 94.)

Winecup, with its sprawling stems, fills portions of the Great Plains with claret in the spring. (See page 96.)

The pink budlike flowers of **prairie smoke** produce wispy heads of plumed fruits. (See page 98.)

Birdsfoot violet has the largest flowers of any native violet. Its name refers to the shape of its leaves. (See page 100.)

The fuzzy stems of **prairie phlox** bear showy clusters of small, delicate pink flowers that resemble garden phlox, but appear in late spring. (See page 102.)

Wild columbine flowers produce a sweet nectar that attracts bees and hummingbirds. (See page 104.)

The unequal-sized petal-like sepals of **Canada anemone** surround its golden stamens and pistils. (See page 106.)

The simple elegance of **pasture rose** in midsummer gives way in late summer to pleasing hip fruits. (See page 110.)

The flowers of **American bellflower** are flattened, not bell-shaped, with a graceful, S-shaped style in the center. (See page 112.)

Although **wood lily** flowers point upwards toward the sky, gaps between the petals and sepals allow rainwater to drain. (See page 114.)

The exquisite candelabra spikes of pink or white **Culver's root** flowers attract bees. (See page 116.)

Compass plant leaves are arranged vertically and frequently point north-south. The yellow flowers are borne near the top of a very tall stem. (See page 118.)

The majestic spray of **queen-of-the-prairie** flowers stands above the attractively lobed foliage. (See page 120.)

Photograph by Neil Diboll

Atop the yucca-leaved stems of **rattlesnake master** are globular clusters of small, whitish flowers. (See page 122.)

One of the most adaptable of prairie plants, **black-eyed Susan** displays a ring of yellow stamens in the center of its brown disk during midsummer. (See page 124.)

The clusters of fragrant, light pink flowers of **nodding wild onion** bend toward the ground. (See page 126.)

Lavender wands of **gayfeather** flowers sway in the summer winds on tallgrass prairies. (See page 128.)

Equally at home in moist prairies and garden beds, **purple coneflower** has drooping lavender florets that accent its spiny central disk. (See page 130.)

The rich golden flowers of **lance-leaved core-opsis** are borne atop long stems. (See page 134.)

The large pale yellow flowers of **Missouri evening primrose** open in the evening and then turn orange as they wilt the next after-noon. (See page 136.)

Mexican hat comes in either yellow or red forms, both with a brown column at the center of the flower head. (See page 138.)

Grown more frequently for its variegated foliage than for its small white flowers, **snow-on-the-mountain** is native to dry prairies. (See page 140.)

The semi-woody stems of **lead-plant** bear slender clusters of tiny purple flowers with golden stamens. (See page 142.)

Purple prairie clover flowers progress as a lavender ring from the bottom to the top of the flower head. (See page 146.)

Butterfly weed's flattened clusters of light to deep orange flowers are one of the most striking sights in North American prairies. (See page 144.)

Wild bergamot has irregular lavender flowers clustered atop its square stems. (See page 148.)

Daisylike red and yellow **blanketflowers** cover portions of the northern Great Plains with summer-long color. (See page 150.)

The magenta flowers of **meadow beauty** produce coppery, urn-shaped fruits in the early fall. (See page 154.)

Showy clusters of pink flowers make **false dragonhead** an excellent cut flower. (See page 156.)

Showy tick trefoil's lavender-blue, pealike flowers produce a fuzzy pod that breaks into sections when ripe. (See page 158.)

Although **closed gentian** flowers always appear to be in the bud, they are successfully pollinated by bumblebees (left). (See page 160.)

The lavender and yellow flowers of **silky aster** contrast with its small silvery leaves. (See page 164.)

New England aster has large clusters of beautiful purple and gold flowers that attract butterflies and honey bees. (See page 162.)

PART III

Species of Wildflowers

The following pages give detailed information about 34 species of wildflowers. In general the plants are presented in order of their dates of flowering, from spring to summer to fall. The summer-blooming wildflowers, however, have been subdivided into two groups: those of wet or moist habitats, and those of dry or well-drained sites. Often, species found in one group can grow as companions with those of another group. Each section is introduced by general comments, a wildflower garden plan, and suggestions of additional species not in this edition of *The Wildflower Gardener's Guide* that make appropriate companions. Further information on these companions can be found in *A Garden of Wildflowers* and other books listed in Appendix D.

Each wildflower is listed by its most frequently used common name, its Latin scientific name, and other common English, Spanish, and French names. The individual wildflower description starts with general information about the species and its ecology. A discussion of culture and growth requirements follows, with specific directions for the plant's propagation. A few companions that grow under similar conditions are listed.

Each species is illustrated. A scale shows the approximate size of the plant, and a quick reference box shows plant family, flower color, flowering time, growth cycle (annual, biennial, or perennial), habitats where the species naturally occurs, and hardiness zones where it can be grown. The map shows the wildflower's native distribution, but most species can be grown over a much wider area.

Spring Prairie Species

Some of the species presented in this section appear as the last snow disappears in the spring, and others persist into the early summer. Some grow on dry sites and others prefer moist soils.

Spring is a time to remove mulches from the garden and to plan burning of established meadows and prairies. In general it is best to burn meadows and tallgrass prairies in the early spring when the dead grass tops are dry and before new green growth has appeared.

A great variety of native plants are available to supplement the species presented in this section. **Pink evening primrose** (*Oenothera speciosa*), a perennial growing in masses in open fields and along roadsides in eastern and central Texas, is easily propagated by seed. **Scarlet paintbrush** (*Castilleja indivisa*), a native annual wildflower of Texas, is one of the few species within that genus that is easily grown from seed. Unlike other species of paintbrush, it can survive without developing parasitic relationships with the roots of other plants, but it flowers more abundantly when it does. It should be planted in mixtures with other species such as **bluebonnet, firewheel** (*Gaillardia pulchella*), a more brilliantly colored annual relative of **blanket-flower**, and **coreopsis** (*Coreopsis tinctoria*), an annual relative of lance-leaved coreopsis that has yellow flowers with deep red bases and maroon disk flowers.

Wild geranium (*Geranium maculatum*) is a 2-foot-high hardy perennial with attractive blue to lavender 5-petaled flowers. It grows in moist prairies and eastern woodland gaps and can be propagated from either rootstock divisions or seed. **Eastern shooting star** (*Dodecatheon media*) grows in the same habitats and is best propagated from divisions of its roots. Its white to pink flowers look like miniature cyclamen. Other spring wildflowers of moist prairies and meadows include **bluets** (*Houstonia caerulea* or *Hedyotis nigricans*), with tidy, light blue, cross-shaped flowers arising from low (6-inch) clumps of wiry stems, and **larger blue flag** (*Iris versicolor*), a relative of the garden iris flowering in late spring on wet northern prairies and along roadsides.

Spring prairie garden.

A. June grass
B. Porcupine needlegrass
C. Wine cup
D. Wild columbine
E. Prairie phlox
F. June grass
G. Western wheatgrass
H. Canada anemone
I. Prairie smoke
J. Bluebonnet
K. Pasqueflower
L. Birdsfoot violet

On drier sites in northern tallgrass prairies try **hairy puccoon** (*Lithospermum croceum*). It has delightful rich golden yellow flowers and fuzzy leaves covered with soft hairs, and can be propagated most easily from root cuttings. A purple dye can be extracted from its roots. Another species for better-drained sites is **wild lupine** (*Lupinus perennis*), whose light violet-blue flowers are every bit as attractive as domestic cultivars. A member of the bean family, it is best propagated from seeds that are first scarified and then inoculated with rhizobia if needed.

Also consider native woody plants that are showy in the spring. **Shadbush** (*Amelanchier alnifolia*) grows to 6-8 feet tall with lovely white 5-petaled flowers in early spring. Later it has red, berrylike fruits that attract birds or can be eaten by humans. **Redbud** (*Cercis canadensis*) is another small tree that should be planted where soils are moist. Its clusters of red-pink flowers are a delightful complement to spring wildflowers.

PASQUEFLOWER

Anemone patens

(Prairie smoke, windflower)

A harbinger of spring in the North American prairies and tundra, the pasque-flower blooms are often seen in the matted remains of the previous year's foliage and dried grasses soon after the snow disappears. They are low plants rarely exceeding 6 inches in height. Long, silky hairs cover the finely divided, deeply lobed leaves and give the plant a silvery sheen. The leaves arise from a brown root crown and expand after the flower is open. The solitary, 2-3-inch flowers have 5 to 7 pointed petallike sepals, which range in color from lavender to pale blue to white, and surround the many golden stamens and pistils in the center of the flower. The long plumes of seedlike fruits give rise to one of pasqueflower's common names, prairie smoke. Pasqueflower's root system is fibrous and possesses enormous regenerative capacity. If the top is damaged during the growing season, subterranean buds are activated and send up new shoots. Both the roots and foliage contain an acrid, alkaloid substance, anemonine, which is poisonous to livestock. Even though poisonous in high doses, Native Americans used pasqueflower for the treatment of rheumatism.

CULTURE

This hardy perennial grows well in full sun to very light shade, and has most of its growth during the coolness of the spring and fall. Pasqueflower requires a well-drained soil, and once established can tolerate fairly dry conditions during the summer by becoming dormant. Sandy loams are perfect; the pH should be close to neutral, between 6 and 8.

PROPAGATION

Pasqueflower is best propagated from seed. The seeds benefit from a short period of cold, damp stratification, but will germinate without the treatment. This plant is difficult to establish from seed sown directly into dense grass, but can easily be raised in a nursery bed for the first year and then transplanted to the desired location. In the fall, place mature seeds in flats filled with sand or sandy loam. Cover the seeds with 1/8 inch of sand, cover with mulch, keep moist, and leave out for the winter. Remove the mulch in the early spring. Stratified seeds planted in the spring will germinate in 1 to 2 weeks, and will reach 3-4 inches by summer. Keep the seedlings under nursery conditions for the first year. Mulch well each fall and remove some of the mulch in the spring. Seedlings usually take 2 to 3 years to mature and flower. Alternatively, propagate by divisions or cuttings of the roots made in the early spring or late fall. Root segments should be several inches long, planted 1 inch deep, and kept moist until young plants emerge and become established.

COMPANIONS

Leadplant, butterfly weed, rattlesnake master, and lance-leaved coreopsis.

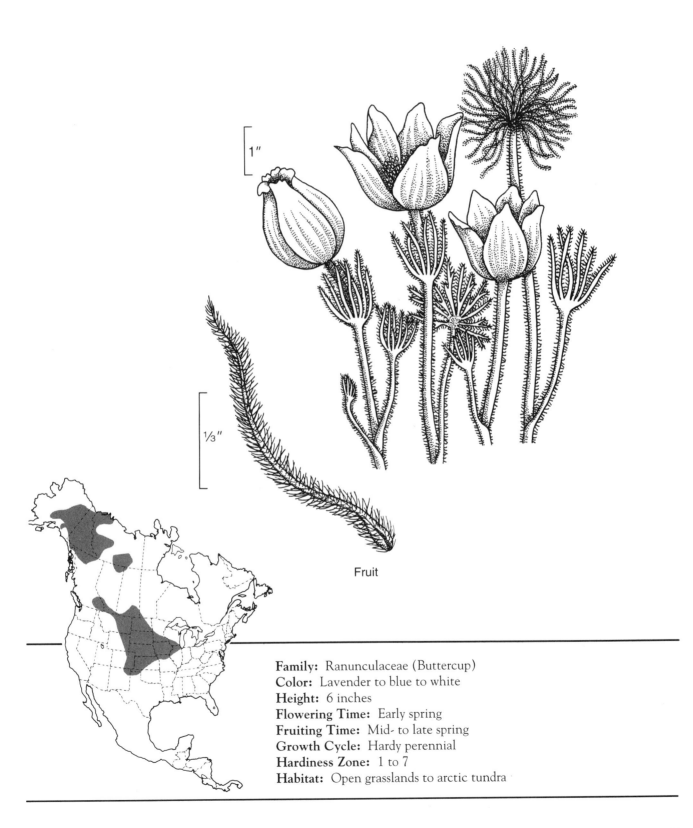

1"

1/3"

Fruit

Family: Ranunculaceae (Buttercup)
Color: Lavender to blue to white
Height: 6 inches
Flowering Time: Early spring
Fruiting Time: Mid- to late spring
Growth Cycle: Hardy perennial
Hardiness Zone: 1 to 7
Habitat: Open grasslands to arctic tundra

PASQUEFLOWER (*Anemone patens*)

BLUEBONNET

(Texas bluebonnet, buffalo clover, *el conejo*)

Of the six species of blue and white lupines that are the official state flower of Texas, this is the most widely distributed and one of the showiest. *Lupinus texensis* is also larger and has more sharply pointed leaflets and more numerous flower heads than most of the other bluebonnet species, and does not hybridize with any of them. Numerous light green, velvety, palmately compound leaves are attached to the branching 6-18-inch-high stems topped by clusters of up to 50 5-petalled flowers, the number of flowers produced depending upon growing conditions. Bees, especially bumblebees, are the main bluebonnet pollinators. When a bee lands on the deep blue, lateral wing petals and pushes down on the folded keel petals below, pollen is ejected from the anthers onto its abdomen. The bee's only reward is pollen, since the fragrant bluebonnets do not produce nectar. Bees locate flowers with fresh pollen by looking for a white or light yellow spot on the uppermost banner petal. Five to six days after a flower opens, just after stigmas have maximum receptivity, the spot turns red and bees don't bother stopping. This visual change in the appearance of flowers promotes the cross-fertilization needed for successful seed set. Each of the 2-3-inch-long pod fruits contains 1 to 8 seeds that are explosively propelled up to 12 feet as the fruit matures in the late spring. The diffuse root system has many nodules containing nitrogen-fixing rhizobium bacteria.

CULTURE
Although bluebonnets are most spectacular on the alkaline, calcareous soils of east and central Texas, they can tolerate a wide range of soil types with pH 5.0-8.0. Below pH 5.0 the rhizobia don't grow well, and should not be fertilized in any case. Bluebonnets need full sun, and will flower as long as moisture remains available in the spring. They are not eaten by cattle and horses, but sheep will nibble them down to the ground.

PROPAGATION
Bluebonnet, which grows as a winter annual or biennial, can only be propagated from seed. Sow seeds in the early fall and they will germinate with fall rains, forming rosettes that remain green over the winter while the roots grow slowly. Cool winter temperatures are needed for plants to develop properly; then flowering in the spring is rapid as the air temperature rises toward 70°F. If you are planting bluebonnets in an area where they have not previously grown, the soil may need to be inoculated with the proper rhizobium, such as Nitragin-type Lupinus Special 4. If you are planting only a small area in a garden, scarifying the seed, or soaking seeds in warm water for 3 days, will hasten germination. If you are planting a large area, scarification is not recommended, it being better to have delayed germination than to put all your eggs in one basket.

COMPANIONS
Wine cup, snow-on-the-mountain, lance-leaved coreopsis, butterfly weed, and blanketflower.

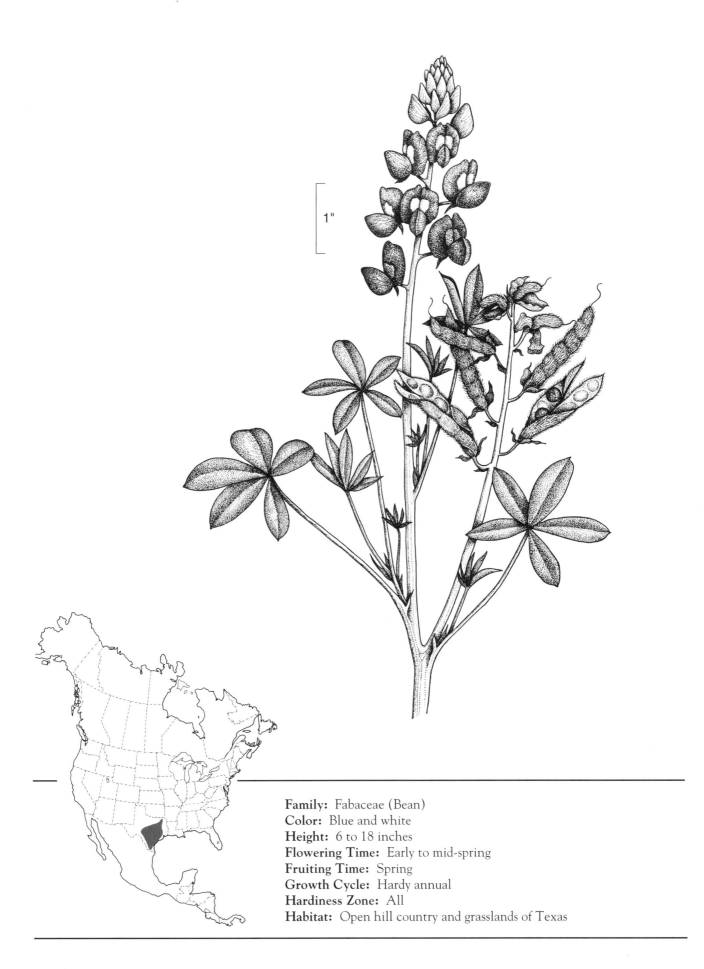

Family: Fabaceae (Bean)
Color: Blue and white
Height: 6 to 18 inches
Flowering Time: Early to mid-spring
Fruiting Time: Spring
Growth Cycle: Hardy annual
Hardiness Zone: All
Habitat: Open hill country and grasslands of Texas

BLUEBONNET *(Lupinus texensis)*

WINE CUP

(Purple poppy mallow, buffalo rose, low poppy mallow)

Callirhoë was the daughter of the river god in Greek mythology, but this plant named in her honor fills drier portions of the Great Plains with its claret-crimson flowers from spring until summer. The foot-high stems sprawl along the ground, arching upward to 2 feet with support. Rounded, hairy leaves low on the stems have 5 to 7 lobes, while toward the flowering tips they are 3-to-5-clefted. The chalice-shaped 1½-2½-inch flowers have a white spot at base of their petals. A central column is formed by a sheath of more than 100 stamens that cover the many styles with stigmas on their inner surfaces. Three leafy bracts encircle the bottom of the flower. The anthers open from the top toward the bottom releasing their short-lived pollen during the 2-3 day period before the stigmas become receptive. This pattern favors cross-pollination between different flowers, primarily by ground-nesting bees (*Diadasia afflicta*) whose main flight period coincides with wine cup's peak blooming period in the spring. The bees use pollen pellets to adorn the entrances of their nests and to provision underground chambers for their developing young.

A small proportion of plants have smaller flowers that don't produce pollen at all. Along with pollen, bees take nectar from nectaries at base of the 5 sepals. The flowers close in the evening and open in the morning, but remain permanently closed after pollination. The hollyhock-like fruits resemble small wheels of cheese. Native Americans used the large, thick, edible turnip-shaped root for food and to treat stomach disorders.

CULTURE Wine cup is an attractive, spreading, drought-resistant hardy perennial, ideal for filling in space, especially banks and rock gardens, in xeriscapes. The tops of the plants may die back in mid-summer under extreme droughty conditions, but then reappear by early fall. Grow wine cup in full sun on well-drained soils of pH 5-7. The growing season can be prolonged by removing old flowers before they set seed. During wet years in the Great Plains, keep an eye out for *Endophyllum tuberculatum* rust, and destroy infected leaves. Wine cup is hardy to zone 4, but should be mulched in areas colder than zone 5.

PROPAGATION Wine cup can most easily be grown from seed. No seed chilling treatment is needed, but scarification is essential for good germination which then occurs within a day or so. Sow seeds in early spring, scratching them lightly into the soil or ¼ inch deep in deep flats. Transplant at end of first season as seedlings become dormant, spacing 2 feet apart, with the root crowns at ground level. Plants from seed flower in the second year.

COMPANIONS Bluebonnet, snow-on-the-mountain, leadplant, butterfly weed, and black-eyed Susan.

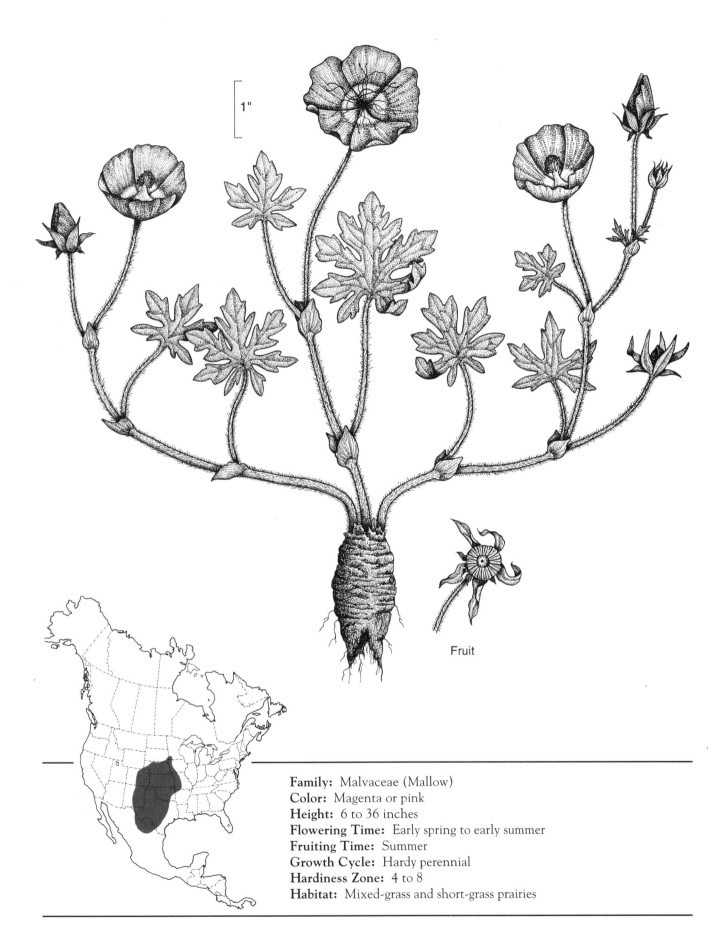

Family: Malvaceae (Mallow)
Color: Magenta or pink
Height: 6 to 36 inches
Flowering Time: Early spring to early summer
Fruiting Time: Summer
Growth Cycle: Hardy perennial
Hardiness Zone: 4 to 8
Habitat: Mixed-grass and short-grass prairies

Fruit

1"

WINE CUP *(Callirhoe involucrata)*

PRAIRIE SMOKE

Geum triflorum

(Old man's whiskers, prairie avens, torchflower)

The wispy fruits of prairie smoke look like the miniature footprints of the wind on the northern grasslands. Numerous 4-9-inch-long, ferny, light blue-green leaves covered with soft hairs arise in clumps from rootstocks of this hardy perennial. The 5 oval reddish petals surrounded by 5 purple-red sepals and elongated red bracts form bell-shaped flowers that hang in groups of three, or sometimes more, from 6-18-inch-high stems. The nodding flowers of this member of the rose family never look completely open, but are efficiently pollinated by early spring insects. The clumps of feathery, plumed, pink-gray fruits have 2-inch tails and stand erect when mature. The fruit clusters stay on the plant much of the summer, and can be dried for everlasting arrangements if collected before they are dispersed by the wind. Prairie smoke is a cool-season plant, making much of its growth in late fall through early spring. Native Americans and pioneer settlers of northern prairies and plains made an astringent tea from prairie smoke roots to treat digestive disorders and reduce fever.

CULTURE

Prairie smoke can be grown in full sun to light shade as long as moisture is available, but not excessive, during most of the growing season. An ideal rock garden plant, it thrives under a wide range of soil conditions (pH 5-7.5) from poor, gravelly, mildly acidic to alkaline soils as long as competing grasses are not too dense. Prairie smoke benefits from periodic additions of ground limestone.

PROPAGATION

Grow prairie smoke from seeds or rhizome division. Collect seeds in the late spring or early summer. No seed treatment is needed, but germination rate is low. Plant the fruits ¼-⅓ inch deep in the desired locations, or in flats, and keep moist. Prairie smoke grows slowly the first year, forms rosettes that remain green over winter, and should be transplanted from flats only after seedlings have leaves 1-2 inches long. Rootstock division is a faster way to propagate prairie smoke. Divide the rhizomes in late summer or early spring, being sure the pieces have ample new, light-colored roots. Plant them spaced 1-2 feet apart with crowns at ground level. Over time prairie smoke rhizomes continue to spread, so division every several years may be necessary.

COMPANIONS

Pasqueflower, butterfly weed, wild columbine, prairie phlox and, on mildly acid soils, birdsfoot violet.

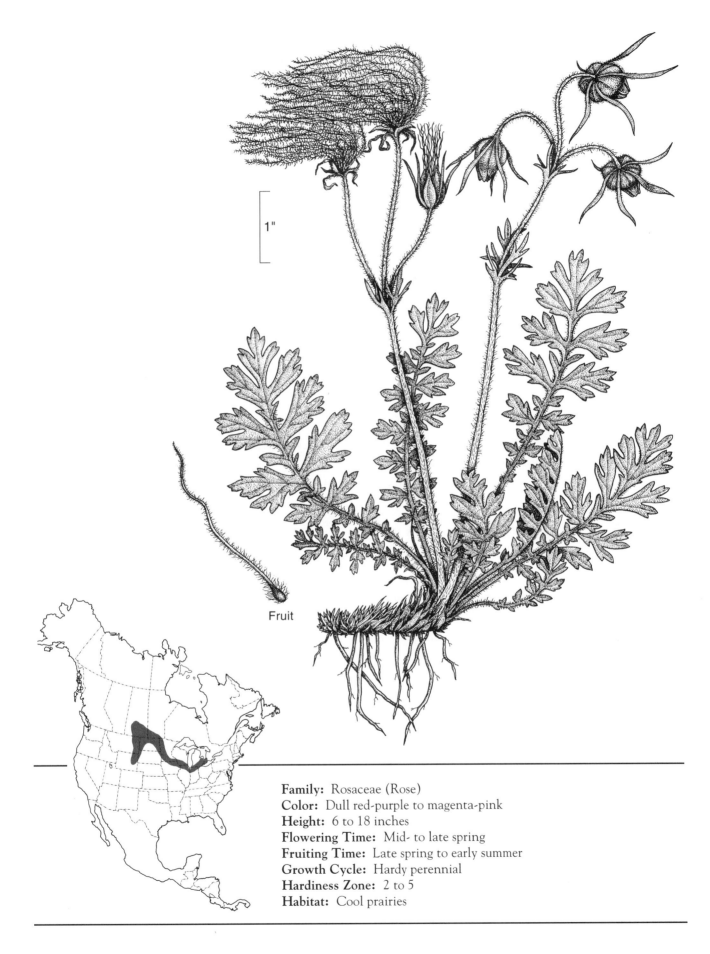

Fruit

Family: Rosaceae (Rose)
Color: Dull red-purple to magenta-pink
Height: 6 to 18 inches
Flowering Time: Mid- to late spring
Fruiting Time: Late spring to early summer
Growth Cycle: Hardy perennial
Hardiness Zone: 2 to 5
Habitat: Cool prairies

PRAIRIE SMOKE (*Geum triflorum*)

BIRDSFOOT VIOLET

(Pansy violet, _violette pédalée_)

This wildflower of dry, open prairies has the largest, showiest flowers of any North American native violet. Its common name refers to the bird's-foot shape of the 1-2-inch-wide leaves, palmately dissected into 3 to 5 lobes. The depth of leaf lobes increases as the days lengthen, the foliage usually disappearing in mid-summer to reappear in the fall with shallow lobes. Birdsfoot violet is "stemless," meaning that both leaves and flowers arise directly from the perennial rootstock. Its single, ¾-1¼-inch-broad, flat, lilac-lavender flowers on 2-6-inch stalks resemble miniature pansies. The 2 upper petals are the same color as the lower 3 petals in the northern variety _lineariloba_, but are darker purple in the southern _pedata_ variety. Although birdsfoot violet lacks the bearded tuft of hairs common with other species, it has the typical ring of 5 bright orange stamens encircling the stigma and short pistil. Solitary bees and many other insects pollinate birdsfoot violet and are rewarded by the nectar in the spur projecting from the lower petal. These violets lack the self-pollinated, petalless "cleistogamous" flowers produced late in the growing season by other viola species. Insect pollination is necessary to produce the ⅓-inch capsule fruits that are divided into 3 sections, each of which explosively ejects its contents of ¹⁄₁₆-inch, golden-tan seeds up to 15 feet away. Ants often retrieve the seeds, attracted to an oily nub of tissue on the seed known as an "elaiosome," and carry them farther from the parent plant. The erect rhizome and roots were used by Native Americans as a mild laxative.

CULTURE

Birdsfoot violet is a bit more finicky than other violets, but well worth the trouble. It grows best in full or filtered sunlight on sandy, even gravelly, well-drained, acidic (pH 4.5- 6.0) soil. An ideal plant for a sunny rock garden, it is prone to rotting if the soil is too wet. It is not a strong competitor with other plants, so keep it free of weeds and protected from rabbits at first. Give it an over-winter mulch if grown in the garden without the protection of grasses.

PROPAGATION

This wildflower is most easily grown from seed, which should be collected in the brief period after it turns from white to brown and before the capsules explode. Remove the elaiosomes and plant them immediately ¼-inch deep in the desired location or in flats left out for the winter. For spring seeding, keep the seeds moist and give them a short period of stratification (1 month at 40°F). Plants from seed produce flowers the second year. Rootstock divisions can be made in the early spring by cutting the rhizome lengthwise, being sure each section has well-developed buds and roots. Replant the pieces, spaced 6-12 inches apart, with the buds just below the soil surface.

COMPANIONS

Pasqueflower, lance-leaved coreopsis, purple prairie clover, prairie smoke, and wine cup.

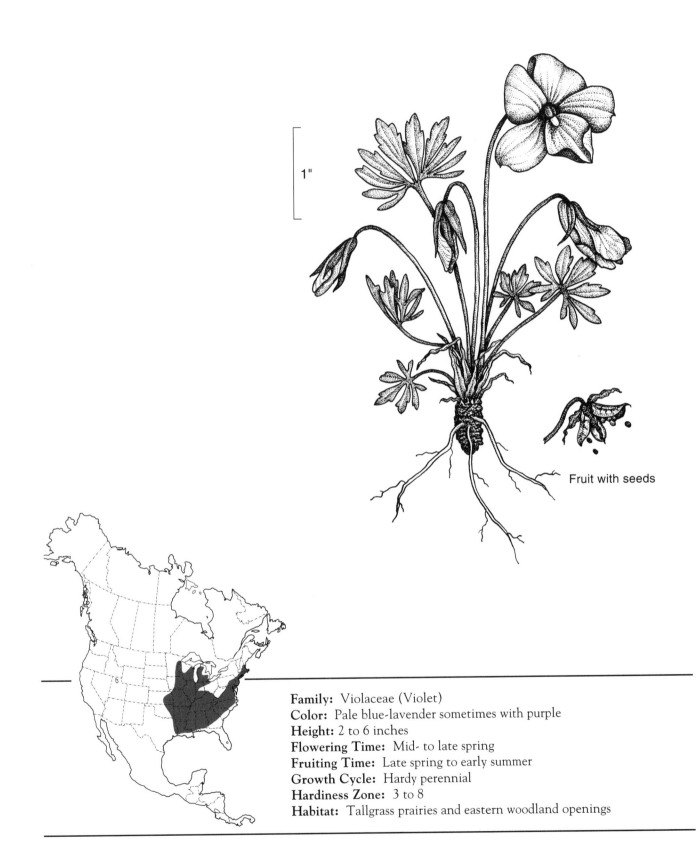

1"

Fruit with seeds

Family: Violaceae (Violet)
Color: Pale blue-lavender sometimes with purple
Height: 2 to 6 inches
Flowering Time: Mid- to late spring
Fruiting Time: Late spring to early summer
Growth Cycle: Hardy perennial
Hardiness Zone: 3 to 8
Habitat: Tallgrass prairies and eastern woodland openings

BIRDSFOOT VIOLET (*Viola pedata*)

PRAIRIE PHLOX

(Downy phlox, *phlox pubescent*)

This downy and delicate relative of the garden phlox graces eastern prairies and open dry woods in late spring and early summer. The 8-30-inch-tall stems attach at their brittle bases to the perennial taproot. The slender stems and the clasping pairs of narrow, sharply pointed 3-inch leaves are covered with soft hairs, described by the Latin name *pilosa*. Several subspecies of prairie phlox are distinguished by differences in leaf shape and amount of hairiness. The ¾-inch, round-lobed flowers have 5 petals joined at the base into an elongate trumpet with a darker throat. The clusters of lavender, light pink, or even white, fragrant flowers have anthers that shed pollen several days before the stigmas can receive it, thus encouraging cross-pollination by butterflies, hawkmoths, and even hummingbirds. The small capsule fruits explosively eject their 2 to 3 seeds when they are mature. During dry summers prairie phlox growing in grasslands may die back to the roots, but then reappear the following spring.

CULTURE
: Grow prairie phlox in full sun on sandy, well-drained, slightly to moderately acidic (pH 4.5-6.5) loams. They may be shorter-lived in the garden than when growing in their native tallgrass prairies. This perennial is hardy to zone 4. At first it may need to be protected from deer.

PROPAGATION
: Prairie phlox can be propagated from seed, stem cuttings, or root division. Since the fruits open abruptly when ripe, save the seed by tying a mesh bag around the developing fruits after the flowers have withered. Germination is unpredictable, but enhanced by a short cold stratification (1 week at 30°F). Scratch seeds gently into bare soil in the desired location or plant in the fall ¼ inch deep in flats that are left out over the winter. Transplant the seedlings after the first growing season. Some plants from seed may flower the first year, but most wait until the second. Make 6-inch stem cuttings in late spring, set in sand-filled flats, keep moist (but not wet), and move rooted cuttings to permanent locations in the late summer or early fall after the tops have withered. Root divisions are best made in the fall after leaves have reappeared. Space the divisions 1 foot apart, setting the crowns at soil level.

COMPANIONS
: Lance-leaved coreopsis, black-eyed Susan, snow-on-the-mountain, prairie smoke, and nodding wild onion.

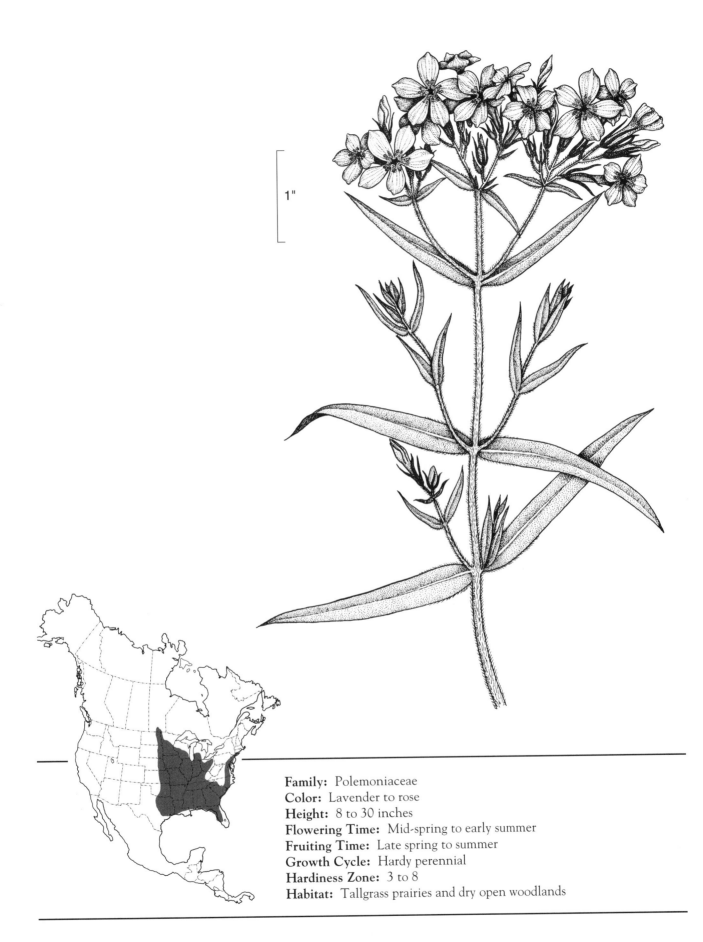

Family: Polemoniaceae
Color: Lavender to rose
Height: 8 to 30 inches
Flowering Time: Mid-spring to early summer
Fruiting Time: Late spring to summer
Growth Cycle: Hardy perennial
Hardiness Zone: 3 to 8
Habitat: Tallgrass prairies and dry open woodlands

PRAIRIE PHLOX *(Phlox pilosa)*

WILD COLUMBINE

Aquilegia canadensis

(Eastern columbine, meetinghouses, *gants de Notre Dame*)

The wild columbine is one of the easiest and most beautiful plants to grow in a native plant garden. A slender, hardy perennial, it reaches up to 2 feet in height. The attractive rounded, compound leaves are a dull grayish green and are divided into threes. The showy, nodding flowers, up to 2 inches across, are borne atop leafy stems and have 5 spurred scarlet petals covering the yellow centers. The French name means "Our Lady's gloves," referring to the flower's 5 "fingers," and the common name "meetinghouses" refers to the congregation of spurs in the center. Inside the spurs are drops of sweet nectar, extracted by bumblebees as they hang upside-down pollinating the flowers. Hummingbirds also frequent the flowers. Some naturally occurring varieties of wild columbine have salmon, pink, or yellow flowers. The fruit is a 5-chambered capsule that becomes erect as it matures and then opens, flinging away the many small, glossy, black seeds as the plant sways in the wind. The gnarled rootstocks tend to be deep seated. Native Americans used wild columbine seeds, roots, and leaves (all of which contain alkaloid compounds) to treat stomach disorders and as a diuretic.

CULTURE

This is an ideal plant for moist prairies as well as rocky slopes and a variety of shade conditions from full sun to full shade. Though frequently found growing in limestone-rich soils, it can be successfully grown on alkaline to moderately acid soils, with pH between 5 and 8. Seedlings need moisture to become established, but the deep rootstock of mature plants enables the eastern columbine to endure dry spells well. An attractive plant for rock gardens, especially where the winters are relatively mild and the foliage remains green.

PROPAGATION

Wild columbine is most easily propagated from seed, because mature rootstocks are difficult to divide and transplant. For seeds to germinate properly they must be stratified in moist soil for 3 to 4 weeks at 40°F or below. Germination will then occur in 3 to 4 weeks if seeds are held at 70-80°F temperatures. Clear a small area where you want the plants to become established, and gently scratch the seed into the soil with a garden rake. Cover the area with a light mulch of compost. Alternatively, in the fall, sow seeds ¼ inch deep in flats, cover with a thin layer of light soil and mulch, then leave outdoors for the winter. After seedlings have become sturdy the following spring, they may be carefully transplanted to permanent locations. Plants will usually produce flowers the second year. Once established, columbine will self-seed readily and requires little further care.

COMPANIONS

Nodding wild onion, Canada anemone, prairie smoke, and birdsfoot violet.

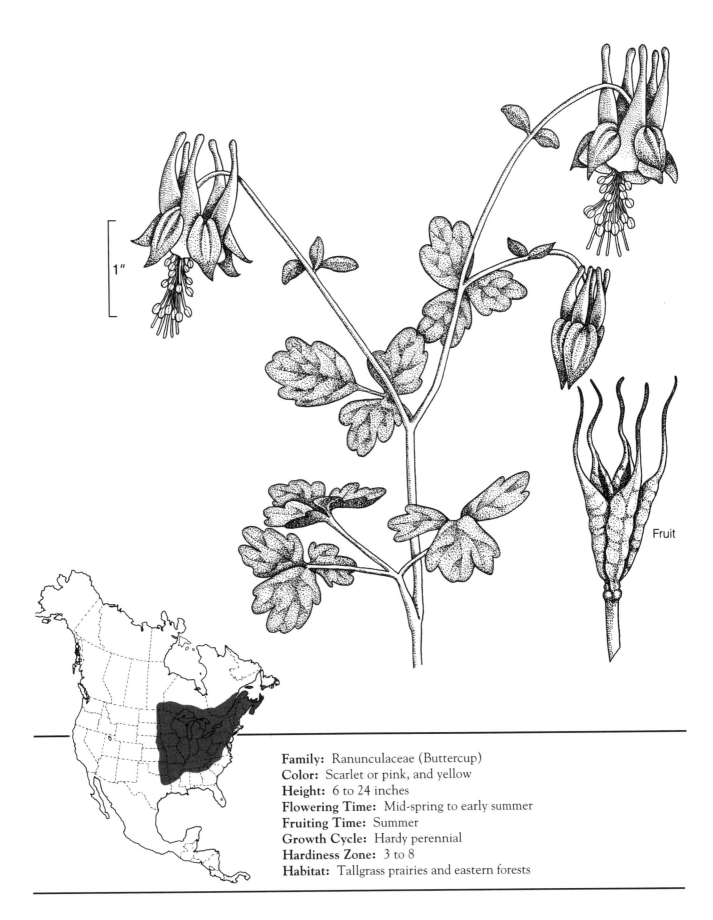

Family: Ranunculaceae (Buttercup)
Color: Scarlet or pink, and yellow
Height: 6 to 24 inches
Flowering Time: Mid-spring to early summer
Fruiting Time: Summer
Growth Cycle: Hardy perennial
Hardiness Zone: 3 to 8
Habitat: Tallgrass prairies and eastern forests

Fruit

1″

WILD COLUMBINE (*Aquilegia canadensis*)

CANADA ANEMONE

Anemone canadensis

(Anemone du Canada)

This is one of the easiest of the northern prairie wildflowers to grow and an excellent plant to fill in open or even partially shaded areas. Canada anemone, a member of the buttercup family, is a hardy perennial which grows 1 to 2 feet tall. The flower stems appear to have grown through the pairs of stalkless leaves. The long-stemmed single flowers have 5 white, unequal-sized petal-like sepals surrounding the rich yellow stamens and pistils. When the pollen is ripe and ready to be released, the sepals protect the anthers by closing at night and on cloudy days. Bees and syrphid flies pollinate the 1-2- inch flowers of Canada anemone. Burrlike clusters of flattened, ¼-inch fruits with long beaks are produced by mid-summer. The plant's extensive root system was used medicinally by Native Americans.

CULTURE   Although Canada anemone grows best in open, sunny locations it can be grown in partial shade as well. It grows most robustly in soils with moderate moisture and neutral conditions (pH 6-7), but is not at all choosy about soils and can even be found growing along roadsides. When Canada anemone is grown in the garden, it will often quickly crowd out other wildflowers and attempt to escape. It is usually prudent to confine the plants with 6-inch-wide plastic or metal strips buried just at the soil surface. Canada anemone is much less aggressive when grown in prairies, meadows, in dryish soils, or in partial shade. As clumps of anemone become crowded, flowering may decrease. If this occurs, divide the plants in the fall.

PROPAGATION   Canada anemone has no difficulty propagating itself once established. To increase this species further, divide the rhizomes in the early spring or fall when plants are dormant. Each piece of rhizome should be several inches long and have good roots and buds visible. Plant the segments a foot apart and no more than ½ inch deep with the bud just at the soil surface. Seeds should be gathered when mature in the summer and planted where you wish the plant to become established. Usually the seedlings will mature and produce flowers within two years.

COMPANIONS   In prairies and meadows, butterfly weed, pasture rose, wild columbine, black-eyed Susans, along with bunch grasses. In the garden grow it alone!

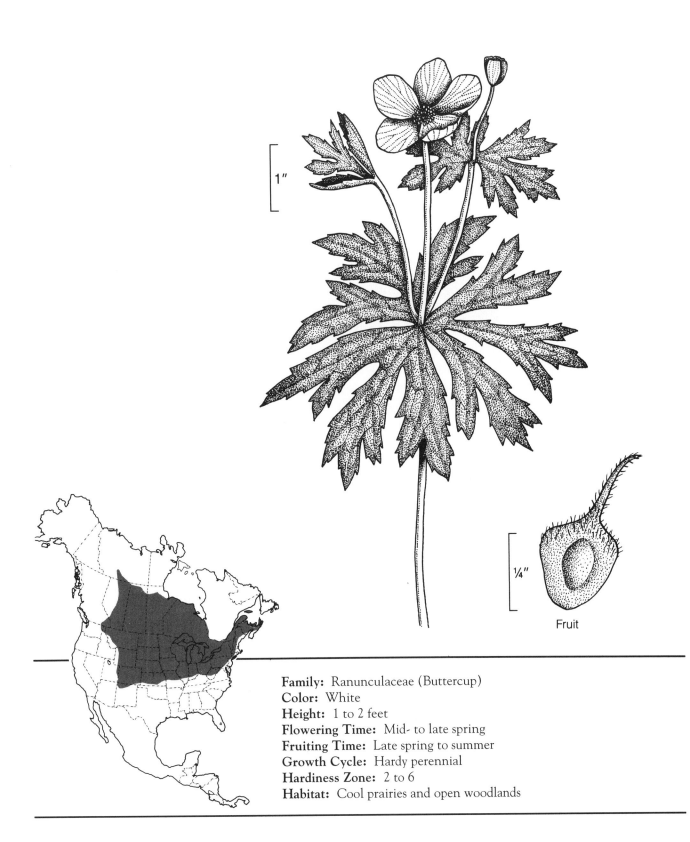

1"

¼"

Fruit

Family: Ranunculaceae (Buttercup)
Color: White
Height: 1 to 2 feet
Flowering Time: Mid- to late spring
Fruiting Time: Late spring to summer
Growth Cycle: Hardy perennial
Hardiness Zone: 2 to 6
Habitat: Cool prairies and open woodlands

CANADA ANEMONE (*Anemone canadensis*)

SUMMER SPECIES OF MOIST PRAIRIES

Summer in the tallgrass and mixed-grass prairies brings waves of yellow, orange, and lavender as flowering reaches its peak. The summer color palette can be enriched by adding other native species, most of which can survive the drying winds and droughts that periodically sweep the region.

A variety of soil and moisture conditions exists within the moist tallgrass prairie region, so take advantage of the different habitats when planning wildflower meadows and prairie restorations. Trees, shrubs, and vines are also effective additions to moist prairie landscapes when planted where they don't shade the grasses and wildflowers.

For the wettest areas consider **turkscap lily** (*Lilium superbum*), with its clusters of pendant yellow-orange flowers hanging from 2-4-foot-high stems, or **red milkweed** (*Asclepias incarnata*), which has rounded clusters of rose-pink or red-violet flowers and can be propagated from seed. **Fireweed** (*Epilobium angustifolium*) grows in cool northern prairies, filling recently burned grasslands with tall spires of magenta flowers in the summer, and filling the early autumn air with its light, plumed seeds. Wet meadows in the southern tallgrass prairie region are ideal for **Oswego tea** (*Monarda didyma*), a scarlet version of wild bergamot that attracts hummingbirds, butterflies, and bees.

The off-white to lavender flowers of **prairie larkspur** (*Delphinium virescens*) grace the tallgrass prairie in early summer. This relative of the garden larkspur is easily propagated from seed. **Spiderwort** (*Tradescantia ohiensis*) has clusters of rich, deep blue, 3-petaled flowers. Each flower lasts only a day, but the many stems produce flowers from late spring through the summer. **Wild quinine** (*Parthenium integrifolium*), which is found growing even into the shortgrass prairies and eastern woodlands, has clusters of knotty white flower heads atop 2-4-foot-high stems. **White false indigo** (*Baptisia leucantha*) has white, pealike flowers that produce beanlike pod fruit. Its seeds need chilling before they will germinate.

Woody plants are also natural additions to moist prairie gardens, but care should be used in planting them where they will neither invade the grassland

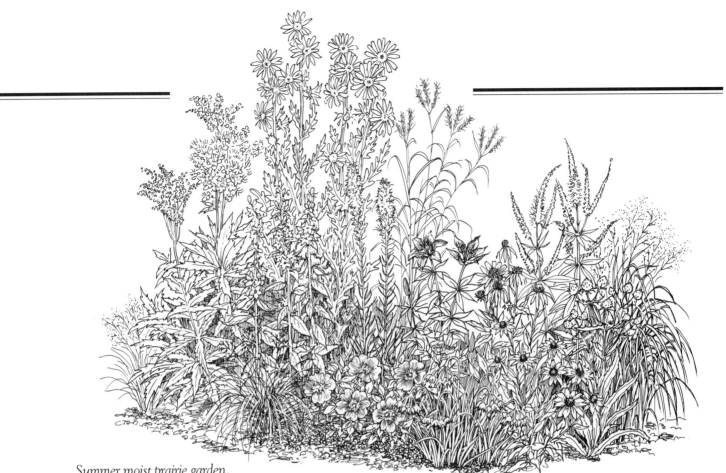

Summer moist prairie garden.

A. Queen-of-the-prairie
B. Compass plant
C. Big bluestem
D. Culver's root
E. American bellflower
F. Gayfeather
G. Wood lily
H. Purple coneflower
I. Rattlesnake master
J. Switch grass
K. Prairie dropseed
L. Pasture rose
M. Nodding wild onion
N. Black-eyed Susan

nor be harmed by fire or mowing if these techniques are used to maintain the landscape. **Indigo bush** (*Amorpha fruticosa*) is a close relative of lead-plant, having similar-looking purple flowers with golden anthers. It differs from its short, dry-site relative by growing in wet or moist soils, to a height of 10-20 feet under ideal conditions. **New Jersey tea** (*Ceanothus americanus*), an attractive low shrub (1-3 feet high), has clusters of frothy white flowers at the ends of its branches. **Trumpet creeper** (*Campsis radicans*) is a woody vine that grows on the margins of tallgrass prairies and woodland openings. Its clusters of 2 to 8 large (3-inch) trumpet-shaped red-orange flowers attract hummingbirds.

Native trees can provide welcome shade and attractive accent to the edges of prairies and meadows, especially when planted in clusters and around buildings. **Shagbark hickory** (*Carya ovata*) is hardy to zone 4. It has broad, dark green, compound leaves and bark that forms long, thin, flaky strips. Species of catalpa have large heart-shaped leaves, flower in the early summer, and produce elongated seed pods by autumn. Both the **southern catalpa** (*Catalpa bignonioides*) and the **northern catalpa** (*Catalpa speciosa*) are hardy, but should be planted where their falling flowers, which create a bit of a mess, aren't a problem. **Red cedar** (*Juniperus virginiana*) is a superb small tree that grows through much of the eastern and southeastern prairies. Its dark, compressed evergreen foliage and pale blue, pungent fruits make it ideal, especially in limestone-rich soils.

PASTURE ROSE
Rosa carolina

(Prairie rose, Carolina rose, *rosier de Caroline*)

A low (1-3-foot-high) shrub with single, upright stems arising from spreading underground stolons, this relative of fancy garden roses is a simple yet elegant addition to borders or meadows. The straight thorns of pasture rose are scattered sparsely along its stem. Fragrant, 2-inch flowers are borne singly or in small groups, and have 5 pale pink petals encircling a ring of numerous, bright yellow stamens. Pasture rose does not produce nectar, but pollinating insects such as bumblebees and syrphid flies harvest copious amounts of pollen as a reward for visiting the flowers. The fruit, a ⅓-inch hip, turns from dark green to bright red as it matures. The hip contains several bony, tan, ⅛-inch seeds, and remains on the plant during the winter or until eaten by birds. The seeds surviving the passage through a bird's digestive system have an excellent germination rate. The hips, long used for making tea and jam, are a rich source of vitamin C.

CULTURE
While pasture rose is one of the most shade-tolerant roses, it grows best in open, sunny locations. It prefers moderately acid soils (pH 4.5-6), which are moist but well-drained. Once established, pasture rose can tolerate fairly dry soils. This perennial requires relatively little care and is hardy to zone 4.

PROPAGATION
Pasture rose can be propagated by seed, cuttings, and stolon division. Separate and transplant the stems arising from the underground stolons in the late fall or early spring. Divide with a sharp spade, being sure each division has vigorous roots, and replant with the rootcrown just at the soil surface. Make greenwood or softwood cuttings in the early spring after vigorous shoot growth has just started. Cut 6-7-inch pieces, plant 3 inches deep in sand, keep moist (but not too wet), and provide shade. Replant in a permanent location after the stem loses its leaves in the fall. Collect seeds as soon as the hips have turned red in the late summer or early fall. Do not allow them to dry out or germination may be difficult. Remove the seed from the pulpy hip and plant thickly ¼ inch deep in a flat containing a mixture of sand and peat moss. Seeds require stratification (3 months at 40°F) and may benefit from scarification. Leave the flats outside for the winter. Germination may be slow, so leave the flat out a second winter before you become discouraged and recycle the soil. Transplant the seedlings when they become several inches high and have well-developed root systems. It usually takes the seedlings 3 to 4 years to reach the flowering stage. Once established, they will spread by stolon extension.

COMPANIONS
Gayfeather, butterfly weed, black-eyed Susan, New England aster, and wood lily.

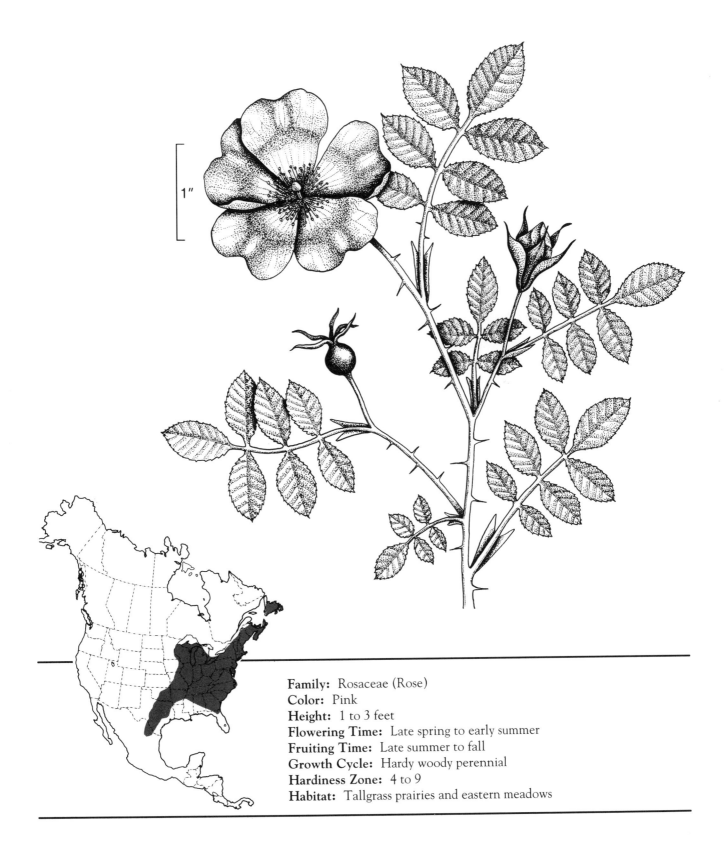

Family: Rosaceae (Rose)
Color: Pink
Height: 1 to 3 feet
Flowering Time: Late spring to early summer
Fruiting Time: Late summer to fall
Growth Cycle: Hardy woody perennial
Hardiness Zone: 4 to 9
Habitat: Tallgrass prairies and eastern meadows

PASTURE ROSE (*Rosa carolina*)

AMERICAN BELLFLOWER

Campanula americana

(Tall bellflower, American bluebell, *campanule d'Amerique*)

American bellflower is a relative of the garden species of bluebells and campanulas, but lacks bell-shaped flowers. Instead, this stately wildflower has flat, 5-petaled flowers arising from the axils of leafy bracts scattered along the top foot or 2 of the unbranched stem. The lowest flowers are the first to open, and blooming then progresses up the stem. The 1-inch flowers are a lovely light blue with a white ring in the center and a long style, curved in a subtle S-shape. Honeybees and bumblebees gather pollen from the 5 anthers, which mature several days before the stigma is receptive, thereby ensuring cross pollination. The bellfower fruit is a capsule with a hole at the tip. When the fruit is fully ripe the seeds are flung from the capsule as the 2-6-foot-high stem sways in the wind. The seeds are elliptical, dark brown, and only $1/16$ inch long. The leaves, lance-shaped with toothed edges, decrease in size up the stem. American bellflower shoots and leaves have a high oil content and are rich in a natural rubber.

CULTURE   Grow American bellflower in full sun to partial shade. No special soil conditions are required, although it grows best in moist soils that are rich in organic matter and slightly acidic (pH 6-7). American bellflower requires exposure to cold winter temperatures in order to flower the following summer, a trait that limits the southern distribution of the species.

PROPAGATION   Plant the small seeds in the fall or spring; American bellflower behaves as an annual or biennial depending upon when the seeds are sown. Seeds planted in the fall will overwinter as seedlings and flower the next summer under the influence of long days. Seeds planted in the spring will behave as biennials, requiring winter cold to produce flowers the following summer. Germination is stimulated by exposure to light, so barely scratch them into the surface of bare mineral soil. The seeds require no chilling treatment and germination should occur a week or two after the seeds are planted. Keep the soil moist until the seedlings become established.

COMPANIONS   Showy tick trefoil, queen-of-the-prairie, purple coneflower, and wood lily.

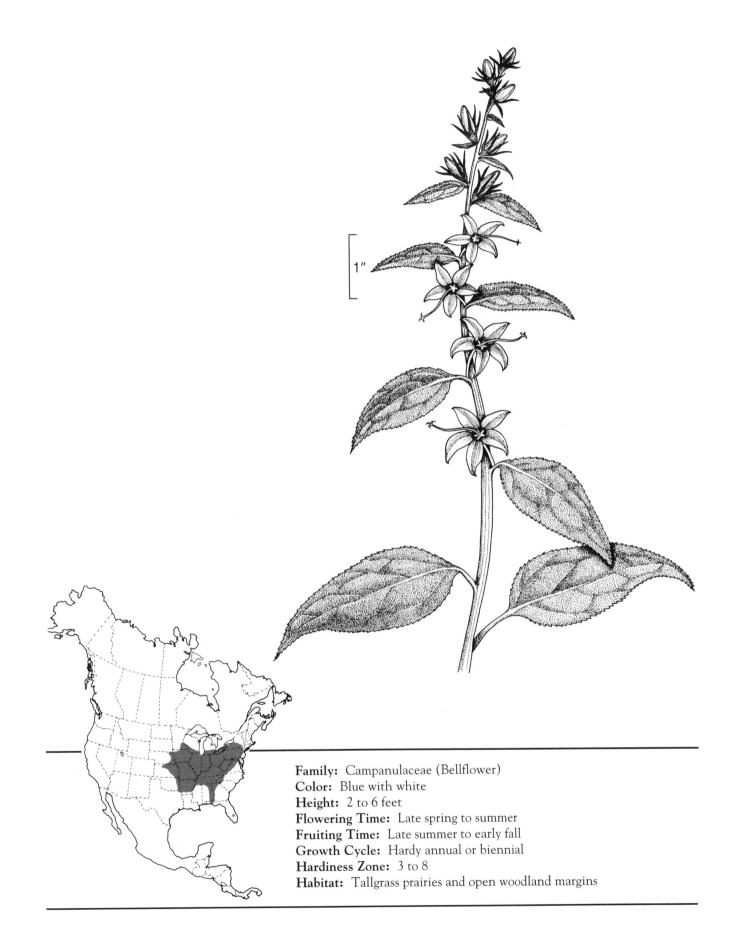

Family: Campanulaceae (Bellflower)
Color: Blue with white
Height: 2 to 6 feet
Flowering Time: Late spring to summer
Fruiting Time: Late summer to early fall
Growth Cycle: Hardy annual or biennial
Hardiness Zone: 3 to 8
Habitat: Tallgrass prairies and open woodland margins

1"

AMERICAN BELLFLOWER (*Campanula americana*)   113

WOOD LILY

Lilium philadelphicum
(L. umbellatum)

(Wild red lily, flame lily, *lis de Philadelphie*)

This flamboyant lily grows across North American grasslands and in open gaps in eastern woodlands. One of the few lily species whose flowers point upward, wood lilies have spaces between the bases of the petals and the sepals, which allow rainwater to drain out. The 6 large brown anthers open and release pollen in dry weather but close when it rains. Flower colors range from bright red in the West to orange in the East, but all varieties have purple spots on the petals and petallike sepals. As the flowers age, their colors subtly fade. Flowers occur singly or in clusters atop an 8-36-inch stem. In the western prairie variety the leaves are scattered along the stem, while in the eastern variety they are arranged in whorls around the stem. The roots of this hardy perennial arise from a deep-seated, white, scaly bulb an inch or so in diameter. New bulbs are formed at the sides of the mature bulb each year. The fruit of the wood lily is a 1-2-inch capsule with densely packed, flat, ¼-inch seeds with papery wings.

CULTURE
While one variety of wood lily will grow in relatively dry prairies, other varieties grow in swamps. One of the most drought-tolerant lily species, it generally grows best in well-drained soils. Although wood lilies do grow in the light shade of open woodlands, they should be planted where they can get full sun for at least part of the day. They do best in moderately acidic (pH 4-6), humus-rich soils.

PROPAGATION
Since there are different regional varieties of this species, use a reputable supplier as close to home as possible when first purchasing this species. Propagation is easiest from divisions of the scaly bulb, which can be dug as soon as the lily goes into dormancy (foliage turns yellow) and the seed is ripe in the late summer. Be careful when digging the bulbs not to damage the roots of the mature plant. The small offset bulbs can be divided, planted about 3 inches deep, and mulched, or individual bulb scales of the mature bulb can be separated and planted ½ inch deep in flats filled with light sandy soil mixed with peat moss and left out over winter. Flats may need to be protected from digging rodents with hardware cloth. When plants become dormant the next year, transplant the small bulbs 3 inches deep in the desired location. In several years they will reach maturity and flower. Plant seeds in outdoor flats, keeping the seedbed moist, but not wet. The seeds will generally germinate in the fall, overwinter as tiny bulbs, and resume growth the following spring. Transplant the small bulbs when they are dormant the following late summer. Seedlings from seeds will generally produce a single leaf the first year and take 3 to 5 years to reach maturity and flower. Since cross-pollination is necessary for wood lily to produce seeds, plant several bulbs in your garden.

COMPANIONS
Gayfeather, rattlesnake master, queen-of-the-prairie, pasture rose, and asters.

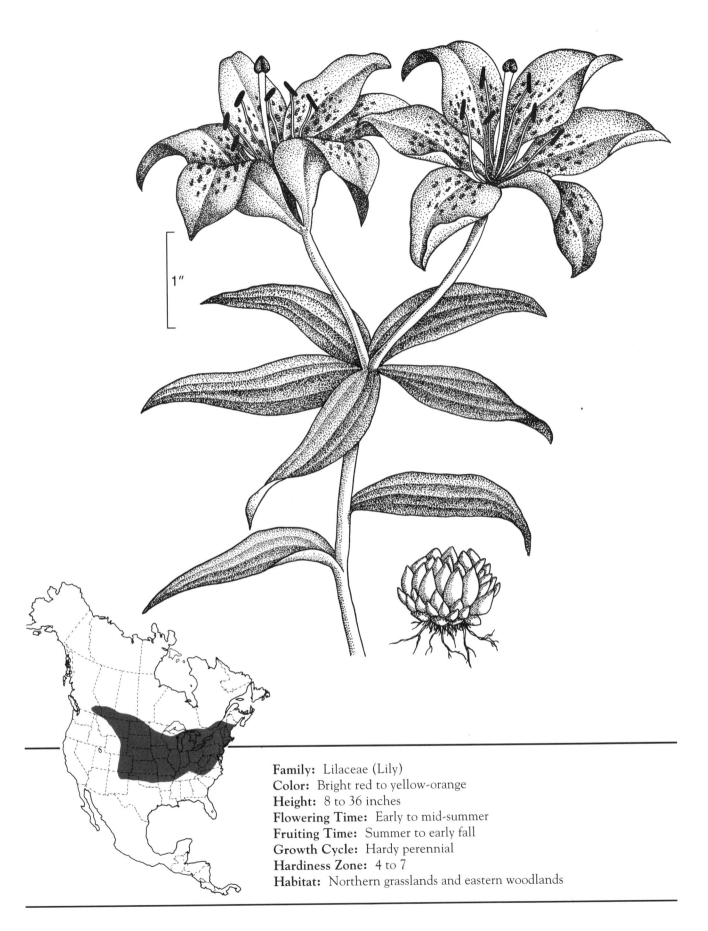

Family: Lilaceae (Lily)
Color: Bright red to yellow-orange
Height: 8 to 36 inches
Flowering Time: Early to mid-summer
Fruiting Time: Summer to early fall
Growth Cycle: Hardy perennial
Hardiness Zone: 4 to 7
Habitat: Northern grasslands and eastern woodlands

WOOD LILY (*Lilium philadelphicum*)

CULVER'S ROOT

Veronicastrum virginicum

(Culver's physic, Bowman's root, *veronicastre de virginie*)

The common names of this plant refer to the medicinal use of the roots which allegedly were prescribed by a Doctor Culver. The roots contain leptandrin, a potent cathartic and emetic, and Native Americans used this plant as a remedy for several ailments. The unbranched stems grow 2-6 feet tall and are topped by several spikes of densely clustered white or lavender flowers. Each of the tiny, trumpet-shaped flowers has 4 lobes beyond which extend 2 stamens. The total effect is of a candelabra of tapering bottle brushes. Bees are a primary pollinator of Culver's root and find the sweet nectar a rich reward. The flowering season is quite long, and Culver's root makes an excellent cut flower. The fruits are small, 2-celled capsules containing many minute seeds. The dark green leaves are sharply toothed and arranged in whorls of 3 to 9 around the stem. The yellow roots are fibrous and extensive.

CULTURE

Culver's root is an easy plant to establish in tallgrass prairies and moist meadows, as well as an ideal hardy perennial for cultivation in gardens, since it is so adaptable. It grows well in full sun or in locations with moderate shade. Any soil with average to damp moisture conditions will do, and Culver's root is quite indifferent to soil acidity conditions (pH 4.5-7). It does grow best where there is ample organic matter in the soil, so annual additions of compost may be beneficial. With age, Culver's root tends to form clumps, but is not overly aggressive.

PROPAGATION

While Culver's root can be propagated by seed and stem cuttings, it is most effectively propagated by root division. Divide roots in the late fall or early spring while the plants are dormant. Cut the rootstock into segments, each of which should have a bud. Set the pieces about a foot apart with the bud just at the soil surface, and mulch for the winter. Stem cuttings should be made in the early summer. Plant 6-inch stem sections 3 inches deep in sand, keep the cuttings moist, and provide shade for the first growing season. Transplant them to permanent locations in the fall. It typically takes three years for cuttings to mature and flower. Seeds can also be scratched into the surface of the soil in the desired location or in flats left outdoors over the winter. As with cuttings, propagation by seed is slower than by root division.

COMPANIONS

Queen-of-the-prairie, pasture rose, gayfeather, American bellflower, and wood lily.

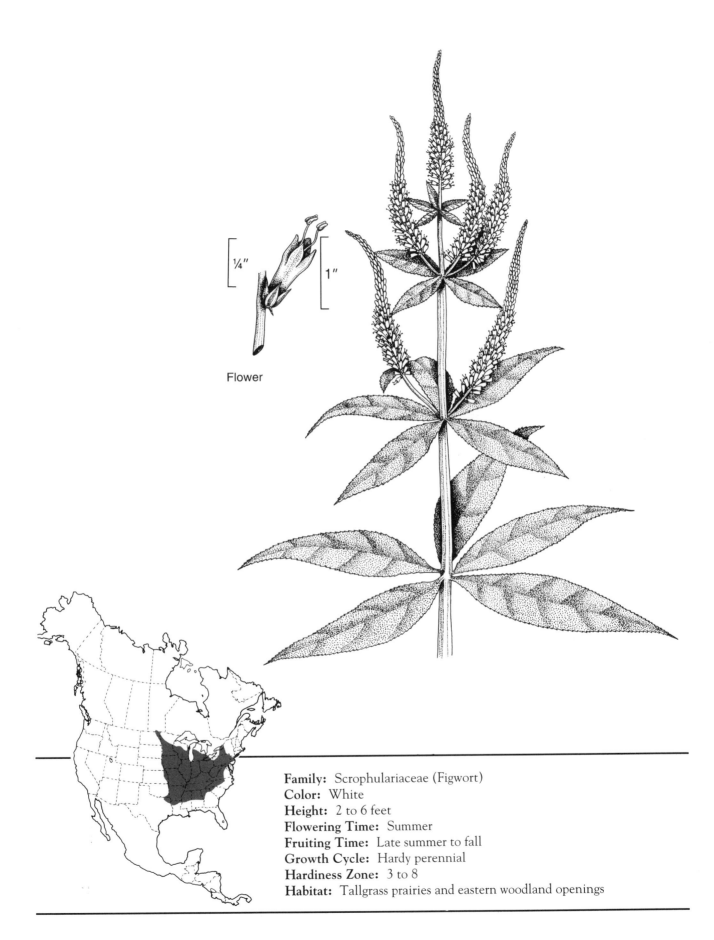

Flower

¼"   1"

Family: Scrophulariaceae (Figwort)
Color: White
Height: 2 to 6 feet
Flowering Time: Summer
Fruiting Time: Late summer to fall
Growth Cycle: Hardy perennial
Hardiness Zone: 3 to 8
Habitat: Tallgrass prairies and eastern woodland openings

CULVER'S ROOT (*Veronicastrum virginicum*)

COMPASS PLANT

Silphium laciniatum

(Rosinweed)

The handsome, yellow, sunflowerlike flowers of this magnificent 3-12-foot-high plant of tallgrass prairies and grasslands are rivaled only by its unusual foliage. The deeply cut, angularly-lobed, clasping, hairy leaves are oriented vertically rather than horizontally, and the lower ones may approach 2 feet in length. The leaf blades usually point north and south, thereby avoiding the heat of the noonday sun and earning the plant its common name. The upper stem exudes a sticky, aromatic pitch, the origin of the common name rosinweed, which was chewed like gum by Native Americans and prairie pioneers. Scattered along the top half of the bristly, resinous stem are 2-5-inch flower heads, with 20 to 30 long yellow ray flowers surrounding the 1-inch yellow discs. Flowering progresses downward from the top of the stem, and the blooming season may last up to 2 months. The relatively large (½-inch-long) seeds, covered with tough seed coats, are favored by birds and small mammals. Compass plant has a large, woody taproot which may reach down 15 feet.

CULTURE   Compass plant requires a lot of open space to grow in, and with time it may form clumps. Full sun is the only specific requirement of this easily cultivated hardy perennial. Once established it is adaptable to a wide variety of soil and moisture conditions. Some protection of young plants from deer may be necessary as this wildflower is becoming established.

PROPAGATION   The easiest way to propagate compass plant is by seed. Germination requires damp stratification (2 months at 40°F), and is enhanced by scarification. To scarify the seed, nick the seed coat with a sharp knife prior to planting. In the fall, plant the seeds ⅓-½ inch deep in a deep flat and leave outdoors over the winter. Germination is rapid (2 weeks) when temperatures near 70°F in the spring. Transplant the seedlings when they are several inches tall. Alternatively, the seeds can be planted in permanent locations in the fall, but it is advisable to clear away the roots of competing grasses to give the seedlings a chance to become established. The first year the seedlings have but a single leaf, and it will take 2 to 3 years for the plants to mature and produce flowers.

COMPANIONS   Purple coneflower, rattlesnake master, purple prairie clover, showy tick trefoil, and New England aster.

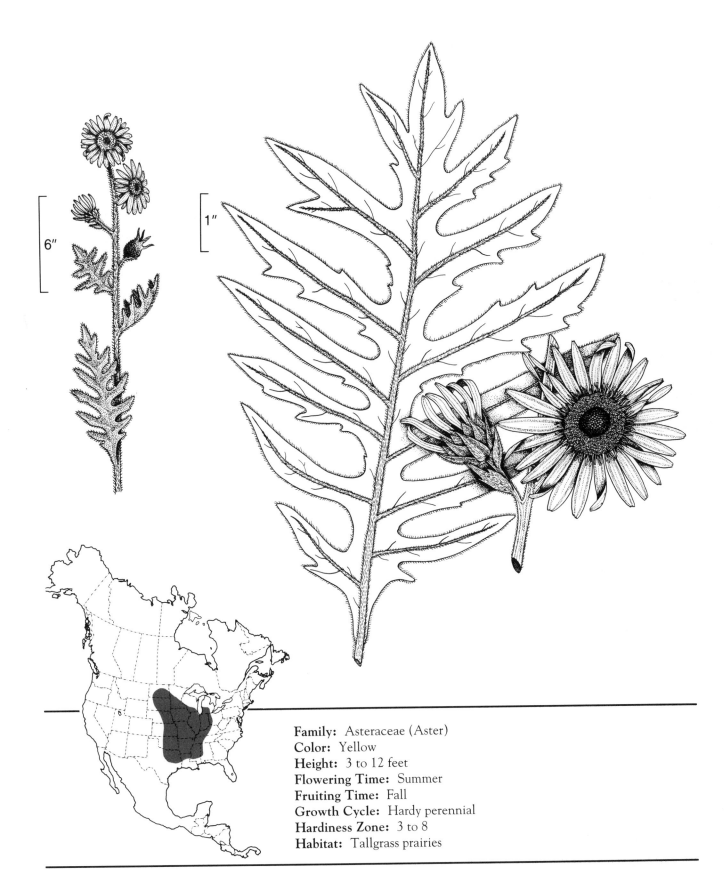

Family: Asteraceae (Aster)
Color: Yellow
Height: 3 to 12 feet
Flowering Time: Summer
Fruiting Time: Fall
Growth Cycle: Hardy perennial
Hardiness Zone: 3 to 8
Habitat: Tallgrass prairies

COMPASS PLANT (*Silphium laciniatum*)

QUEEN-OF-THE-PRAIRIE

Filipendula rubra

(Meadow-sweet, *filipendule rouge, reine des prés*)

This regal pink native was cultivated in the gardens of early settlers of the tallgrass prairie. Queen-of-the-prairie is a robust hardy perennial, typically growing 3-5 feet high, with attractive foliage. The large (up to 3-foot-long), smooth, deeply cut leaves have 7 to 9 pointed lobes with toothed edges and are attached alternately on the branched stem. The crowning glory of this wildflower is its showy, flat-topped sprays of small, pink, fragrant blossoms, swaying in early summer breezes. The buds emerge like clusters of pink barley pearls and open into ⅓-inch flowers with numerous stamens that give the blossoms a frothy appearance. The spirea-like flowers are short-lived after cutting, but the small, tight clusters of 1-seeded fruits that mature in the early fall can be dried and used in everlasting arrangements. The rhizome rootstock gradually spreads, sending up new shoots and roots. Native Americans of the plains used this plant to treat skin disorders, its shoots being rich in tannin, an astringent compound, and salicylic acid, an analgesic.

CULTURE Queen-of-the-prairie needs year-round moisture and is ideal for margins of ponds or moist meadows, but should not be planted in standing water. It grows best in rich soils of pH 5-7, and benefits from additions of compost. Although it grows in light shade to full sun, filtered sunlight is best for starting young plants. Once established, this perennial is hardy to zone 4, and requires little maintenance.

PROPAGATION Queen-of-the-prairie is best increased by rootstock division, although propagation from seeds and stem cuttings is possible. In the early spring or fall divide the mature plants by cutting the rhizomes that connect the shoots, being sure the pieces have well-developed buds and sturdy roots. Replant the rhizome pieces horizontally 2 inches deep and spaced 1-2 feet apart. Large divisions will flower the next year, but smaller ones may wait until the second year. Divide large, mature plants every 3 to 4 years. To propagate from seed, collect fruits in the late summer or early fall when tops of plants turn gray. Plant the cleaned seeds directly in the desired location by gently scratching them into the soil. The seeds have low viability and should be sown densely. It takes at least 2 years for plants from seed to reach flowering size. Plant fall-collected seeds in spring after cold-damp stratification (40°F for 2 months). Stem cuttings should be made in mid-spring before flower buds appear. Follow the directions for cuttings on page 65, planting them in permanent locations when small plants are dormant in the fall.

COMPANIONS New England aster, rattlesnake master, American bellflower, gayfeather, Culver's root, and wood lily.

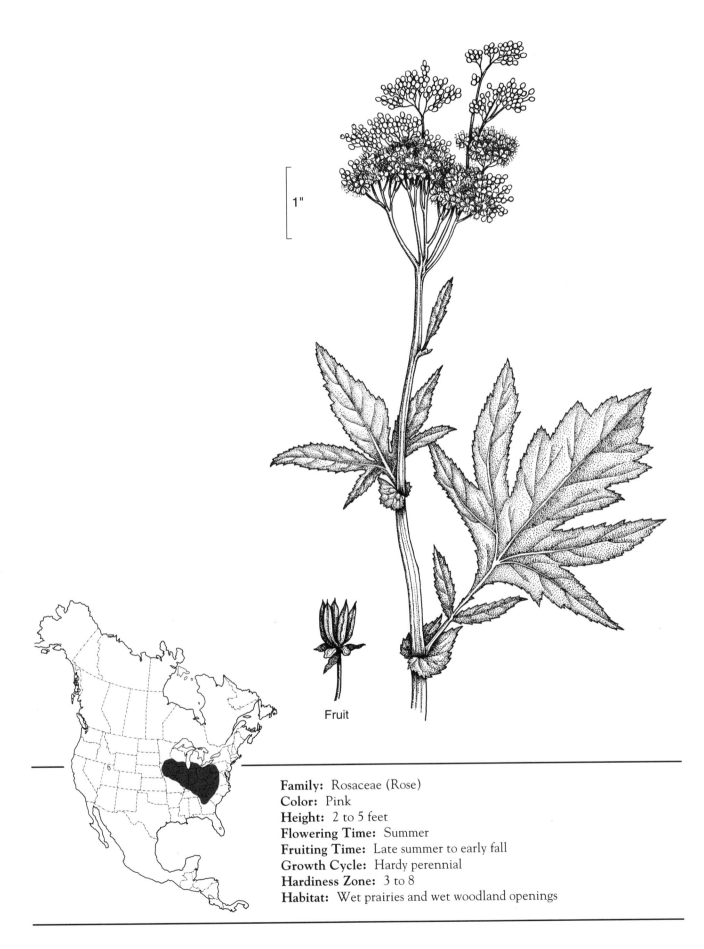

Fruit

Family: Rosaceae (Rose)
Color: Pink
Height: 2 to 5 feet
Flowering Time: Summer
Fruiting Time: Late summer to early fall
Growth Cycle: Hardy perennial
Hardiness Zone: 3 to 8
Habitat: Wet prairies and wet woodland openings

QUEEN-OF-THE-PRAIRIE (*Filipendula rubra*)

RATTLESNAKE MASTER

Eryngium yuccifolium

(Button snakeroot, yucca-leaf eryngo, *éryngie à feuilles de Yucca*)

Don't be fooled by the name of this unlikely member of the parsley family —
although Native Americans used it as a remedy for a variety of ailments,
rattlesnake master has no proven medicinal value in treating snake bites and
little relation to rattlesnakes at all. Scattered along the stiff, unbranched, 1-
6-foot stem are tough, linear, blue-green, yucca-like leaves with soft, spiny
edges. These may reach 3 feet in length, but become considerably shorter
toward the flowers. Native Americans used fibers from the leaves to make rope.
The individual flowers are quite small but cluster into globular heads ¾-1 inch
in diameter, borne on irregularly branching stems near the top of the plant. The
5 greenish white petals are easily overlooked without magnification. The
flowers have a sweet aroma that attracts various insect pollinators, especially
bees. After the petals fade and the seed head turns brown, the small fruits
remain attached to the flower head, and the ¼-inch seeds retain their sharp
scales.

CULTURE   Rattlesnake master is a hardy perennial of prairies and woodland clearings and
should be planted where there is ample sunlight. It grows best in moist, well-
drained soils, but once established, it will tolerate a range of moisture conditions
from dry to periodically wet. Not too particular about soil acidity conditions,
it requires little care except for protection of the young leaves from being eaten
by rabbits and deer as they emerge in the spring.

PROPAGATION   Usually rattlesnake master is propagated by seed, although mature plants
divided in either the early spring or late fall will flower the first year. Collect
the seed in the fall and plant directly where desired or ¼ inch deep in flats
containing moist, well-drained soil. Since the seeds need damp stratification
(2 months at 40°F) for germination, leave the flats outdoors over winter. Allow
the seedlings to grow for one season in the flats or transplant them carefully to
a nursery bed for one year before transplanting them to permanent locations.
Some of the plants from seed will flower the first year, but most will flower the
second. Once established, they will hold their own and self seed abundantly.

COMPANIONS   Gayfeather, Culver's root, wood lily, black-eyed Susan, and queen-of-the-
prairie.

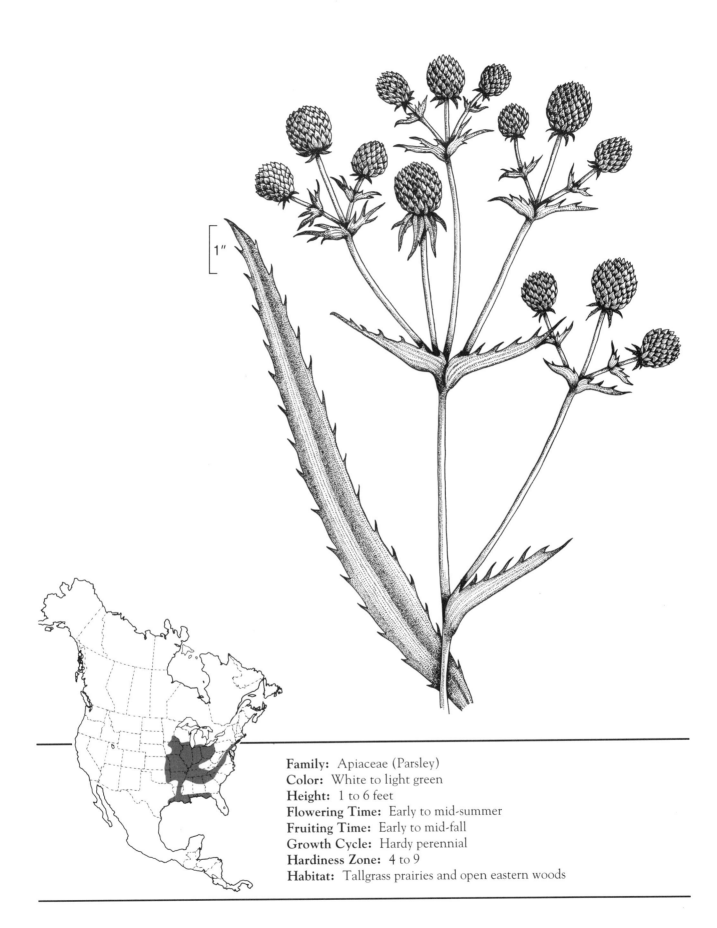

Family: Apiaceae (Parsley)
Color: White to light green
Height: 1 to 6 feet
Flowering Time: Early to mid-summer
Fruiting Time: Early to mid-fall
Growth Cycle: Hardy perennial
Hardiness Zone: 4 to 9
Habitat: Tallgrass prairies and open eastern woods

RATTLESNAKE MASTER (*Eryngium yuccifolium*)

BLACK-EYED SUSAN

Rudbeckia hirta
(R. serotina)

(Brown-eyed Susan, *rudbeckie hérissée, rudbeckie tardive*)

Black-eyed Susan's first flowering signifies that summer has arrived, and its last flowering, that summer is gone. Originally a native perennial of the Midwest and Lake States, black-eyed Susan reportedly expanded its range after its seeds were accidentally shipped to the East with clover seeds and planted in farm fields. The 1-3-foot-high stems and scattered 4-inch-long leaves are covered with short, bristly hairs. The 2-3-inch flower heads are borne on relatively long stalks, making the black-eyed Susan an attractive cut flower. The individual flowers are of two kinds and cluster together in the flower head, as is characteristic of members of the aster family. In the center is a hemispherical disc of tiny chocolate-brown flowers, surrounded by 10 to 20 petallike, inch-long, golden-yellow ray flowers which are sometimes darker at their bases. The roots of this plant tend to be fibrous and may become extensive. Antibacterial and antifungal compounds have been extracted from this wildflower which was used by Native Americans to make a tea for curing colds.

CULTURE

Although black-eyed Susan is a plant of sunny habitats, it can tolerate light shading. It is quite indifferent to soil conditions and will do well in dry, infertile soils if there is sufficient moisture for it to become established. It grows exceptionally well under cultivation and may become somewhat aggressive if given abundant sun, moisture, and nutrients.

PROPAGATION

Propagation of black-eyed Susan from seed is easy, but it is difficult to divide the root system successfully. The $\frac{1}{5}$-inch-long black seeds require stratification for germination (3 months at 40°F). Sow them about $\frac{1}{3}$ inch deep in loamy soil as soon as they are ripe in the summer or early fall. Germination takes place in the spring after about 2 weeks of temperatures between 65 and 75°F. If started early, black-eyed Susan can be grown as an annual. Many plants will flower the first year and nearly all will flower the second year. First-year plants tend to continue flowering later into the fall than second-year plants, so you can extend the flowering season by planting some new seed each spring. Since black-eyed Susan sometimes grows as a biennial, you may want to plant seeds two years in a row anyway. Seeds can also be sown is flats, left out over winter, and transplanted the following spring after the seedlings have become sturdy. Once established, they self-seed well.

COMPANIONS

Purple coneflower, New England aster, butterfly weed, wild bergamot, Culver's root, false dragonhead, and many others.

SUMMER SPECIES OF MOIST PRAIRIES

Family: Asteraceae (Aster)
Color: Golden yellow with brown
Height: 1 to 3 feet
Flowering Time: Summer to early fall
Fruiting Time: Late summer to fall
Growth Cycle: Hardy annual, biennial, perennial
Hardiness Zone: 3 to 9
Habitat: Tallgrass prairies and eastern meadows

BLACK-EYED SUSAN (*Rudbeckia hirta*)

NODDING WILD ONION   *Allium cernuum*

(*Ail penché, chigagou*)

The wild onion adds a touch of light lavender to moist prairies during mid-summer. The French explorer Robert de La Salle allegedly marked the Algonquin name for this plant, *chigagou*, on an early map of the southwest shore of Lake Michigan, and the settlement that eventually developed there took on the name "Chicago." The soft, grasslike leaves and 1-2-foot-high flower stalk arise from bulbs, which look like miniature versions of their cultivated relative. The stem bends over so that the flowers, borne in a cluster at the top, nod toward the ground. Individual flowers have 3 petals and 3 petallike sepals, all of which are joined together at their bases. They range in color from white to pink to lavender. The top of the stem becomes erect as the 3-part capsule fruits mature, containing black, ⅛-inch seeds. All parts of this plant, including the leaves and seeds, have a pleasant, pungent oniony scent.

CULTURE

Nodding wild onion grows best in open, moist habitats with neutral-to-alkaline soils, especially those with abundant organic matter. With little care, nodding wild onion is easy to grow in the garden. It will also naturalize effectively in meadows and prairies, if the grass is not too thick.

PROPAGATION

This plant can be easily propagated by seed or by bulb division. Plant the seeds, when ripe in the fall, ¼ inch deep in soil that is free from competing plants and relatively rich in organic matter. Seeds germinate best if scarified by rubbing between sanding blocks. If planted in flats, they should be left out over winter, since the seed from at least the northern part of its range requires cold, moist stratification for proper germination. Seed from the southern part of its range may not require such treatment. Transplant the small bulbs at the end of the first summer, and they will flower the second summer. The offset bulblets, which form around the base of the larger bulbs, can be divided in the fall and planted ½-1 inch deep. These are most effectively planted in small groups. Some of these bulblets will produce flowers the next summer and many will the following year.

COMPANIONS

Pasture rose, purple coneflower, prairie phlox, Culver's root, and false dragon-head.

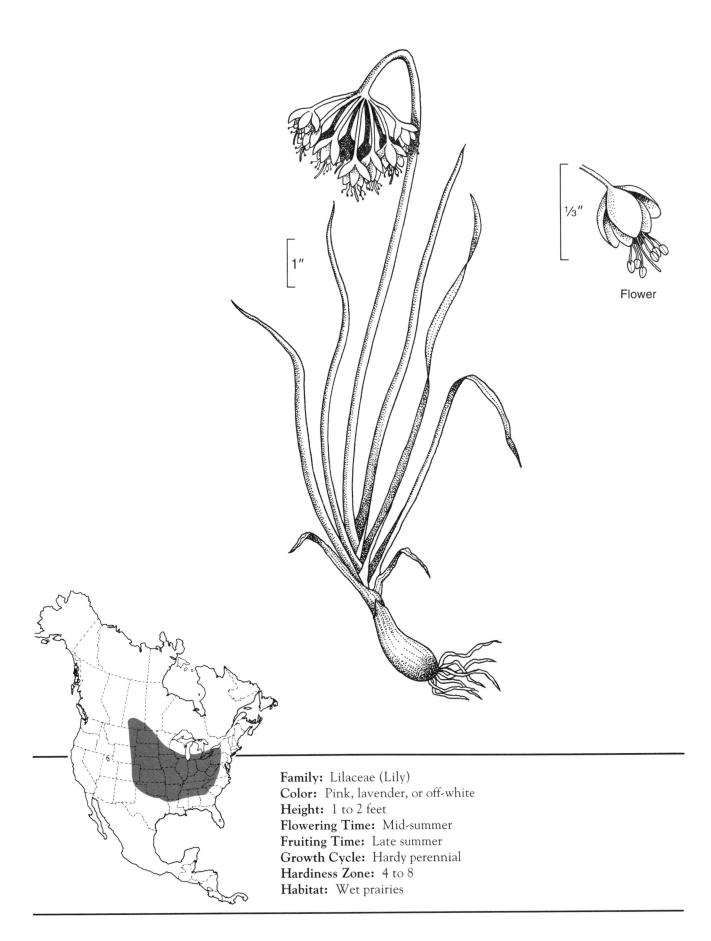

1"

⅓"

Flower

Family: Lilaceae (Lily)
Color: Pink, lavender, or off-white
Height: 1 to 2 feet
Flowering Time: Mid-summer
Fruiting Time: Late summer
Growth Cycle: Hardy perennial
Hardiness Zone: 4 to 8
Habitat: Wet prairies

NODDING WILD ONION (*Allium cernuum*)

GAYFEATHER

Liatris pycnostachya

(Prairie blazing star, thick-spike gayfeather, button snakeroot)

The graceful lavender spikes of gayfeather sway in the summer winds of the prairies of the North American heartland. One of its other common names, button snakeroot (no relation to the button snakeroot on page 128), refers to the showy display of flower heads crowded onto a 6-12-inch spike atop an unbranched, 1-5-foot stem. The flower heads have 5 to 7 individual flowers, each with 5 long, slender, pointed petals, and bloom first at the top of the stem and then progress toward the bottom. Bumblebees, attracted to the dense flower clusters, are the primary pollinating agent. The hairy stems are closely covered with 4-inch, fuzzy, grasslike leaves, usually drooping at their tips. The seeds are ⅙ inch long with tufts of hairs at their tips, while the root system is an inch-long bulbous corm with fibrous roots. Gayfeather and its close relatives were used by Native Americans to treat kidney diseases and have long been cultivated in European gardens as bedding plants and for cut flowers.

CULTURE
Although this long-blooming hardy perennial is drought resistant, it grows best in soils that are moist, well drained, and slightly acid to neutral (pH 5.5-7). Gayfeather can be planted in full sun or with sun for most of the day. Provide a thick over-winter mulch in regions colder than hardiness zone 5, removing most in the early spring. In the garden, this species sometimes requires staking, but when grown in prairie and meadows, it requires little attention since the grasses keep the spikes from leaning over. Gayfeather sometimes requires protection from rabbits when young plants are becoming established or new shoots are emerging in the spring.

PROPAGATION
Gayfeather can be propagated by seed or division of the corm. Seed propagation tends to be preferable, but the seeds require moist stratification (3 months at 40°F) in order to germinate. Harvest seeds when spikes are tan. Nick the seeds with a sharp knife and plant them in the fall about ¼ inch deep in flats filled with a mixture of sandy loam and compost. Leave outdoors for the winter, and the seeds will germinate after 2 to 4 weeks of warm weather in the spring. The seedlings should be left in the flat for the first growing season since the newly formed roots are quite fragile. Transplant the young corms that form by the first fall to a nursery bed or a permanent location. Many will produce flowering plants the next summer, and all should flower the third year. Spring is the best time to divide the corms in regions colder than hardiness zone 6 since they are sensitive to frost heaving. Divide the corm vertically into pieces, each with at least one bud. Plant the divisions vertically, spaced 1-2 feet apart, with the buds 2 inches below the soil surface.

COMPANIONS
Culver's root, rattlesnake master, queen-of-the-prairie, wood lily, and meadow beauty.

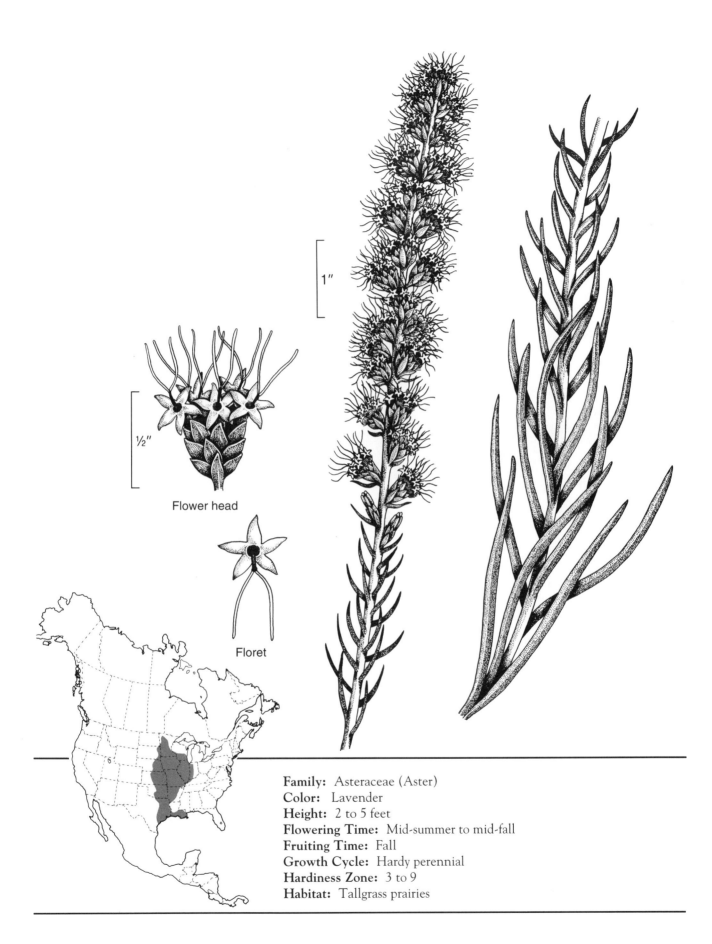

1"

½"

Flower head

Floret

Family: Asteraceae (Aster)
Color: Lavender
Height: 2 to 5 feet
Flowering Time: Mid-summer to mid-fall
Fruiting Time: Fall
Growth Cycle: Hardy perennial
Hardiness Zone: 3 to 9
Habitat: Tallgrass prairies

GAYFEATHER *(Liatris pycnostachya)*

PURPLE CONEFLOWER

Echinacea purpurea

(Black sampson, red sunflower, *échinacée pourpre*)

Although purple coneflower is frequently listed in flower seed catalogs around the world it is native to the prairies of the Midwest and the open woods of the southeastern U.S. The smooth 2-5-foot-high stems have scattered, rough, 3-8-inch, toothed leaves that become smaller and narrower toward the top of the plant. Purple coneflower is an excellent cut flower, since the single flower heads are borne on long stems and are long-lasting. The 2-4-inch flower heads have 12 to 20 dull-purple to crimson ray flowers with drooping petals. The spiny, golden-purple disc flowers covering the ½-1-inch domed disc give this plant its scientific name *Echinacea* from the Greek word for "hedgehog" and "sea-urchin." The 4-sided, ⅛-inch seeds, shaped like small pyramids, remain attached to the disc and form a "seed head" after the ray flowers have withered. This hardy perennial is a veritable pharmacy. Its thick, black, edible roots contain the compound echinolone, which increases the body's resistance to infection and shows promise in medical treatments to reduce tumors. Tinctures of the root have long been used in folk medicine as a remedy for corns, and Native Americans used the plant to treat a range of ailments, from toothaches to snake bites.

CULTURE   Grow purple coneflower in the full sun or very light shade. It is not particularly choosy about soil conditions and will even tolerate dry soils, although it does best where the soil is moderately moist but well-drained, and rich in humus.

PROPAGATION   This plant can be propagated by seed or root division. Collect the mature discs in the fall and break them open to extract the seeds. Sow seeds ¼ inch deep in permanent locations or in flats that should be left out over winter. After moist stratification, germination occurs in about 2 weeks at 70-75°F. If flats are used, transplant the seedlings after the first growing season. Generally the plants start to flower the second year, but if started early they sometimes flower the first summer. Make root divisions in the early spring, and plant divided root sections with the buds just barely under the soil surface.

COMPANIONS   Black-eyed Susan, lance-leaved coreopsis, compass plant, butterfly weed, and American bellflower.

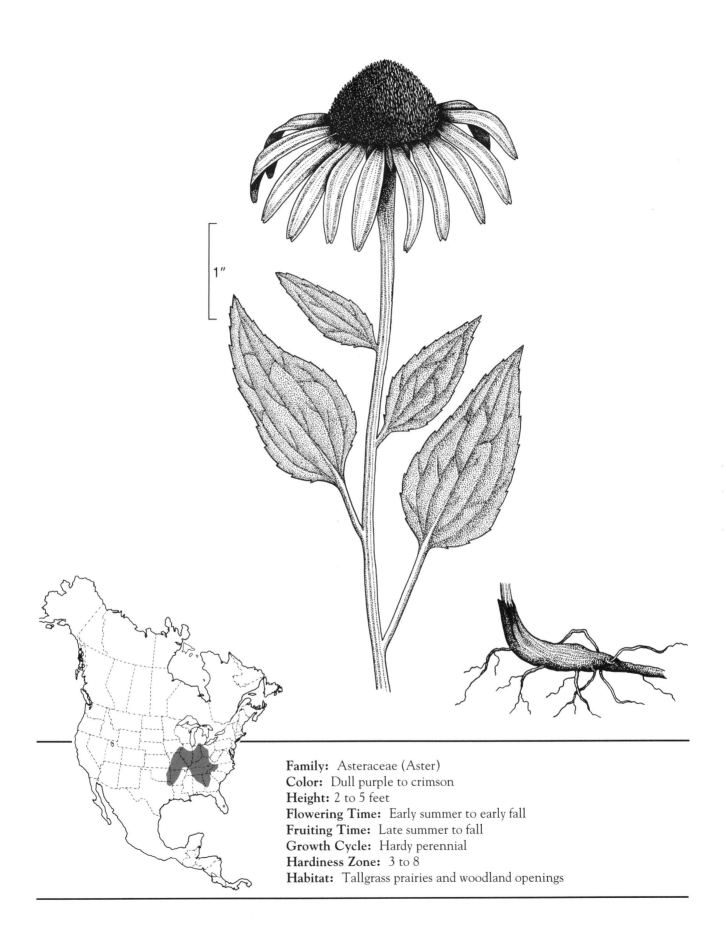

Family: Asteraceae (Aster)
Color: Dull purple to crimson
Height: 2 to 5 feet
Flowering Time: Early summer to early fall
Fruiting Time: Late summer to fall
Growth Cycle: Hardy perennial
Hardiness Zone: 3 to 8
Habitat: Tallgrass prairies and woodland openings

PURPLE CONEFLOWER *(Echinacea purpurea)*

SUMMER SPECIES OF DRY PRAIRIES

The summer-flowering plants presented in this section grow on well-drained soils in the Central Lowlands or Great Plains regions. Since they are adapted to drought conditions they are all excellent candidates for use in xeriscapes as well in restoring shortgrass and mixed-grass prairies or dry meadows.

The wildflowers in this section can be augmented with other natives such as **harebell** (*Campanula rotundifolia*), a wide-ranging species with delicate pendant light blue bell-shaped flowers borne atop masses of thin foot-high stems with hairlike foliage. Another possibility is **blue flax** (*Linum lewisii*), a perennial of the Great Plains and foothills of the Rockies. It has 3-foot-high stems with powder blue flowers and dark green foliage.

White prairie clover (*Petalostemum candidum*) is a natural complement to purple prairie clover and is propagated by the same methods. You may need to inoculate the soil with rhizobia (see page 63) to establish this species or other legumes like **Goat's rue** (*Tephrosia virginiana*). Goat's rue is a foot-high perennial whose pealike flowers have white or light yellow banner petals and bright pink wing and keel petals streaked with purple. It grows on sandy soils in the tallgrass prairie region.

Sandy soils are also ideal sites in which to plant **Rocky Mountain beeplant** (*Cleome serrulata*) a native annual that looks like a pink to lavender version of the garden spider-flower. The prairie gentian or **Texas bluebell** (*Eustoma grandiflorum*) grows as an annual or biennial from seeds planted in winter or previous fall. It starts blooming in summer and its purple-blue, cup-shaped flowers with bright golden pistils may continue to appear well into autumn. **Scarlet globe mallow** (*Sphaeralcea coccinia*) is a drought-tolerant, foot-high perennial with apricot flowers resembling miniature hollyhocks and attractive powdery light blue-gray foliage. It has a deep taproot and should be propagated from seed.

Do not forget shrubs and small trees, some of which are quite drought resistant, when planning dry prairie landscapes. **Skunkbush sumac** (*Rhus trilobata*) is a small shrub with attractive red fruit, a dense, compact form, and 3-leaved foliage that emits a somewhat pungent odor when crushed. **Fra-**

Summer dry prairie garden.

A. Side oats grama
B. Purple prairie clover
C. Snow-on-the-mountian
D. Blanketflower
E. Leadplant
F. Blue grama grass
G. Side-oats grama
H. Butterfly weed
I. Wild bergamot
J. Mexican hat
K. Lance-leaved coreopsis
L. Missouri evening primrose
M. Blue grama grass
N. Indian ricegrass

grant sumac (*Rhus aromatica*), a close relative, has a similar shape and foliage with a more pleasant aroma.

Numerous shrubs native to the Rocky Mountain foothills grow well in xeriscape gardens. The dense semi-evergreen foliage of the 3-8-foot-high **Apache plume** (*Fallugia paradoxa*) turns coppery in the fall. Its single white roselike flower blooms in the spring and produces showy pink plumelike fruits by the summer. It should be planted in the full sun, can withstand considerable drought, and is an excellent plant for controlling erosion. **Sagebrush** (*Artemisia tridentata*) can grow even higher and can be used as an effective background screen since it has small, dense branches covered with ½-inch-long, hairy, gray, aromatic leaves. Smaller subspecies are also available if your garden has limited space. Another drought-resistant woody plant is **winterfat** (*Ceratoides lanata*), a low-growing shrub that tends to spread with age. Both the fruits and leaf surfaces of this 12-18-inch-high shrub are covered with wooly white hairs, making it seem to glow in the sun.

LANCE-LEAVED COREOPSIS

Coreopsis lanceolata

(Sand coreopsis, tickseed, *coréopsis lanceolée*)

The lance-leaved coreopsis is probably the most common coreopsis of the North American prairies. It has long been used as a garden plant and has escaped from cultivation throughout much of eastern North America. A member of the aster family, this hardy perennial grows 8-24 inches tall. The smooth, infrequently branched stems become leafy near the ground. The leaves, as one would expect from its common name, are lance-shaped and sometimes have two additional deep, thin lobes at their bases. Blooming begins in the late spring as days near their maximum length. The 2-inch, daisylike, yellow flowers are borne on long, smooth, slender stems which make this species an excellent cut flower. The 8 ray flowers are a rich yellow with 4 rounded lobes at their tips, while the disc flowers are slightly darker. The 1/8-inch-long seeds are flat with narrow wings projecting to the side and two short spines extending from the tip. The seed's resemblance to a tick has given this plant one of its common names, tickseed. Compounds in the leaves of lance-leaved coreopsis act as natural insecticides by slowing the development of insect eggs and larvae, while the flowers have a chemical agent that kills nematode worms.

CULTURE

Lance-leaved coreopsis requires full sunlight but will grow on moist or dry soils and can tolerate fairly droughty conditions, making it an excellent choice for xeriscaping. It is also tolerant of a wide range of soil acidities. Under cultivation it requires little care.

PROPAGATION

This plant is easy to propagate by either seed or root division. The seeds, which do not require a chilling treatment, can be planted 1/8-1/4 inch deep in the spring or fall. Germination usually takes place after 2 to 3 weeks of warm weather in the spring (7 to 10 days at 70°F) and is stimulated by light. As seedlings are becoming established, they should be thinned to 8-12 inches apart. A few plants may flower the first year, but most will flower the second. Mature plants can be divided easily in the early spring or fall. Divide the roots so that each piece has at least one bud, and plant the sections with the buds 1 inch below the soil surface, spaced a foot apart.

COMPANIONS

Leadplant, butterfly weed, showy tick trefoil, snow-on-the-mountain, and silky aster.

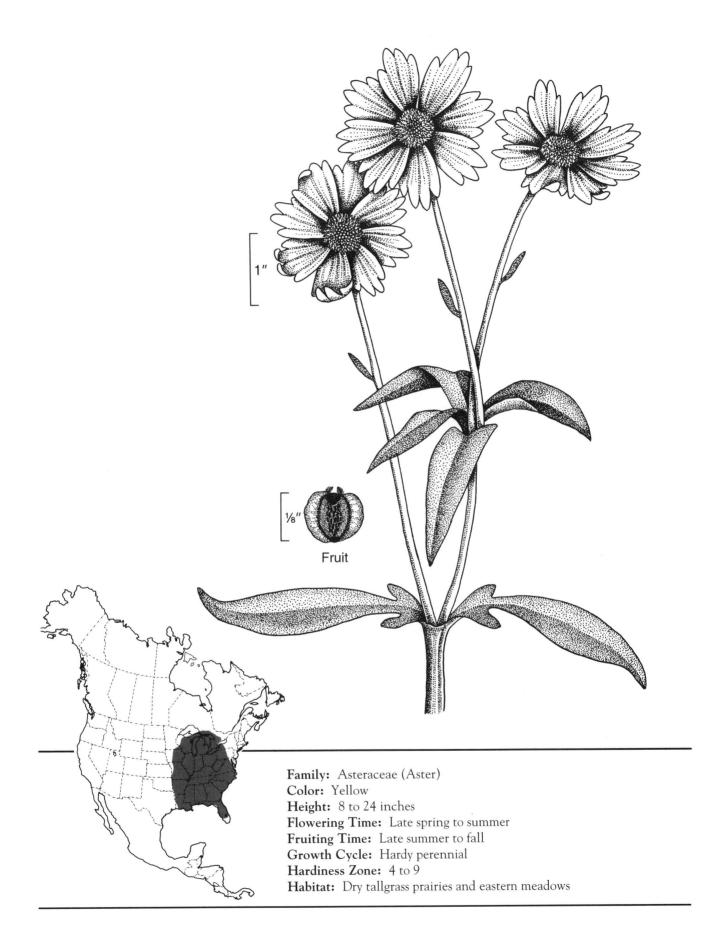

1"

1/8"

Fruit

Family: Asteraceae (Aster)
Color: Yellow
Height: 8 to 24 inches
Flowering Time: Late spring to summer
Fruiting Time: Late summer to fall
Growth Cycle: Hardy perennial
Hardiness Zone: 4 to 9
Habitat: Dry tallgrass prairies and eastern meadows

LANCE-LEAVED COREOPSIS (*Coreopsis lanceolata*)

MISSOURI EVENING PRIMROSE   *Oenothera missouriensis*

(Ozark sundrops, glade lily, Missouri primrose)

A relative of garden sundrops (*Oenothera fruticosa*), Missouri evening primrose is considerably shorter (8-10 inches high) and has larger (3-6-inch), showier flowers. The short, hairy stems are densely covered with 5-inch-long, thick, narrow, lance-shaped leaves, and the erect flower buds are spotted with red. Brilliant yellow, 4-petaled flowers droop somewhat as they open in the evening, and fade the next day. As with other members of the evening primrose family, this species has 8 stamens and a 4-part, cross-shaped stigma. The slender style is surrounded by the green calyx tube, which is so long (2-5 inches) it might be mistaken for the flower stalk. The fruit is a large (2-3-inch), ovaloid, 4-winged pod with many small seeds. Missouri evening primroses have deep taproots.

CULTURE   Missouri evening primrose requires full sun and little water. These preferences combined with its low stature and showy flowers make it excellent for rock gardens or for the moister areas of xeriscapes. It grows in rocky, gravelly, and sandy soils with good to excessive drainage, and in the slightly acidic to slightly alkaline soils typical of gardens. The Missouri evening primrose is a perennial hardy to zone 4.

PROPAGATION   This plant can easily be propagated from seed or stem cuttings, though the taproot makes root divisions tricky. Since Missouri evening primrose is difficult to transplant, it is best to scratch the seeds gently into the surface of the soil where plants are desired. The seeds don't require stratification in order to germinate and can be planted in either spring or fall. Plants from seed will generally flower in 2 years. An alternative method of propagation is to make stem cuttings in the early summer. Place the cut segments in moist sand and keep the soil damp, but not wet. Carefully transplant to a permanent location when the plants become dormant in the fall.

COMPANIONS   Mexican hat, blanketflower, butterfly weed, purple prairie clover, and lance-leaved coreopsis.

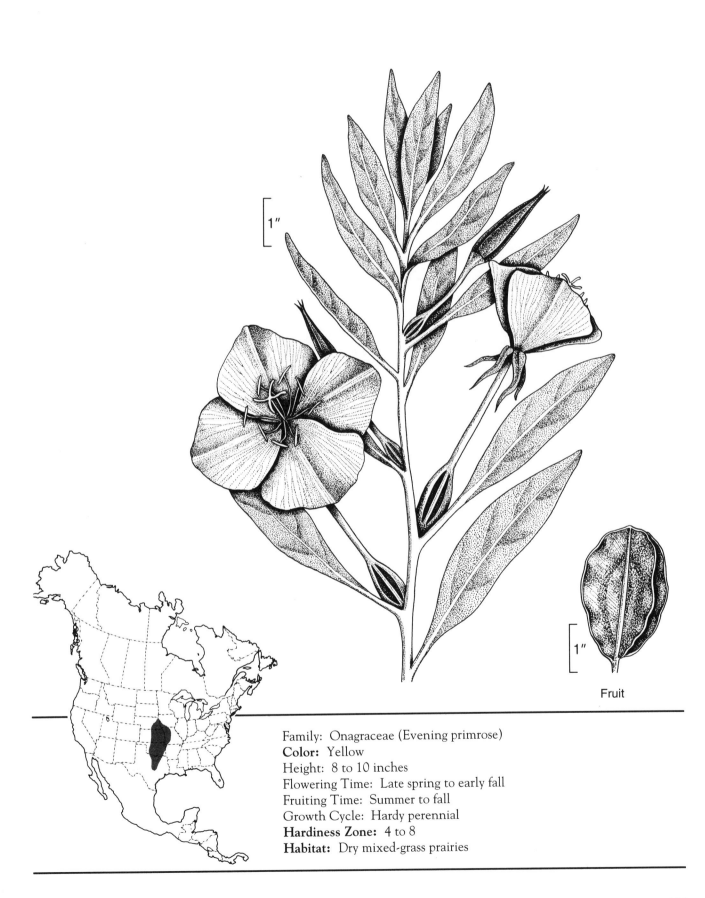

Family: Onagraceae (Evening primrose)
Color: Yellow
Height: 8 to 10 inches
Flowering Time: Late spring to early fall
Fruiting Time: Summer to fall
Growth Cycle: Hardy perennial
Hardiness Zone: 4 to 8
Habitat: Dry mixed-grass prairies

Fruit

MISSOURI EVENING PRIMROSE (*Oenothera missouriensis*)

MEXICAN HAT

Ratibida columnifera
(*R. columnaris*, *Lepachys columnaris*)

(Red Mexican hat, upright coneflower, prairie coneflower)

The central brown discs of this member of the aster family protrude ½-2½ inches beyond the drooping ray flowers, making the 1-3-inch flower heads resemble sombreros. As the dark purple, tubular flowers start blooming from the bases of the discs, the hats even appear to have hatbands. This hardy perennial has branched 1½-3-foot-high shoots with feathery, deeply cleft leaves on the lower portion of the stem, often with short, stiff bristles. Flowering begins in the long days of late spring and continues until fall. The 3 to 7 flowers are borne on leafless stems, making the Mexican hat an excellent cut flower. Ray flowers may be entirely yellow or yellow with red bases, the latter form often called red Mexican hat. Dakota skipper butterflies (*Hesperia dacotae*) use Mexican hat as a nectar source even though it conceals camouflaged predators such as ambush bugs (*Phymata*) and flower spiders (*Misumena vatia*). The seedlike ⅛-inch fruit has fringe on one edge and two teeth projecting from one end. The root system is a diffuse taproot. Although confusion can arise from the many common names associated with the two different color forms of Mexican hat and the frequent listing of the plant as *Ratibida columnaris* or *Lepachys columnaris* in seed catalogs, they are all one species.

CULTURE

Grow Mexican hat in full sun on well-drained soils. It prefers soils that are slightly acidic to alkaline (pH 6-8), but is adaptable to normal garden conditions. Once established, this superb prairie plant requires little water, being quite drought tolerant, and can withstand competition from other wildflowers and grasses. It is an excellent choice for xeriscaping.

PROPAGATION

This is one of the easiest wildflowers to propagate from seed, either in the desired location or in flats for future transplanting. In the fall or spring plant the seeds ¼ inch deep in sandy loam or sandy soil. Unstratified seeds will germinate, but the best results are obtained if seeds are chilled at 40°F for 9 weeks, then germinated at 80°F. Germination is rapid once temperatures are warm. Seedlings need moisture while becoming established. Mexican hat can be grown as an annual if the growing season is long enough, or started indoors in late winter and transplanted 8-12 inches apart in the spring. Plants from seed usually bloom the second year. In hardiness zone 5 and colder regions, give Mexican hat a good overwinter mulch, and remove it in the spring.

COMPANIONS

Blanketflower, butterfly weed, lance-leaved coreopsis, purple prairie clover, and Missouri evening primrose.

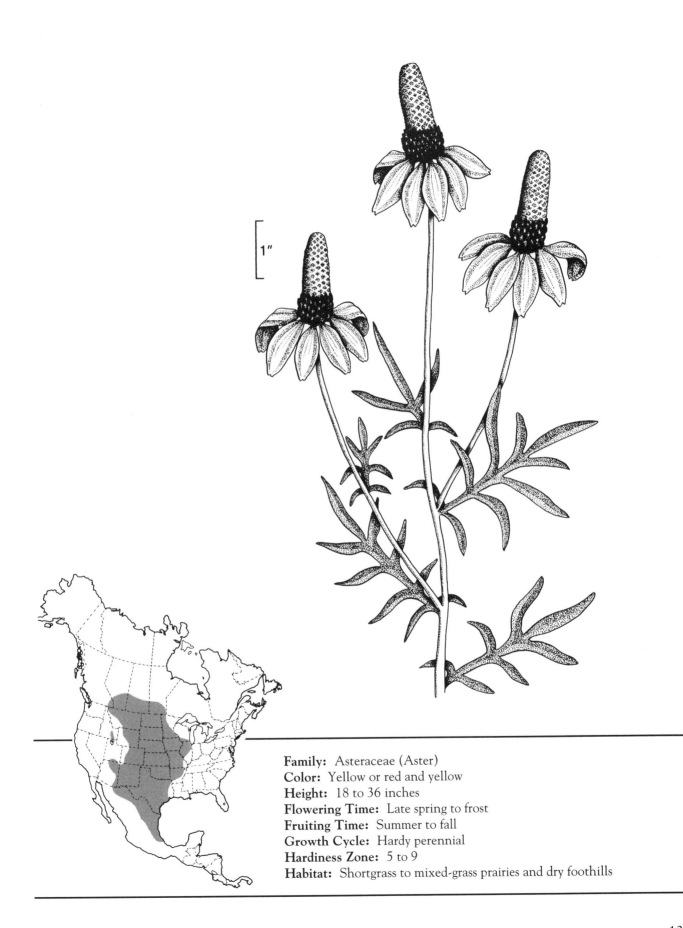

Family: Asteraceae (Aster)
Color: Yellow or red and yellow
Height: 18 to 36 inches
Flowering Time: Late spring to frost
Fruiting Time: Summer to fall
Growth Cycle: Hardy perennial
Hardiness Zone: 5 to 9
Habitat: Shortgrass to mixed-grass prairies and dry foothills

MEXICAN HAT (*Ratibida columnifera*)

Snow-on-the-Mountain

Euphorbia marginata

(Mountain snow, variegated spurge, *euphorbe marginée*)

This plant's common name "snow-on-the-mountain" probably refers to the white flowers at the top of its 1-3-foot stems, or perhaps to its white-margined leaves, but it definitely is not a reference to the native habitat of this annual of the Great Plains. It is grown as much for its attractive foliage as for its flowers. The 1-3-inch-long leaves clasp the stem and may be light green, variegated, or entirely white. Obviously only some of the leaves can be white, otherwise the plant would be unable to photosynthesize. The erect, many-branched stems are softly fuzzy and frequently reddish toward the base. Both stem and leaves exude a white, milky sap when injured. The sap contains euphorbon, a substance that is an emetic and purgative if taken internally and causes dermatitis if gotten on the skin. This plant also accumulates selenium, a substance toxic to livestock, if present in the soil. Snow-on-the-mountain is best planted, therefore, where its foliage won't be eaten by livestock or disturbed by children running after baseballs. Do not use it as a cut flower. The small flowers, each with 5 petallike bracts, are borne in showy clusters at the top of the stem. The hairy, green, ¼-inch fruit has three lobes and contains several ⅛-inch, rough-surfaced seeds.

CULTURE

This hardy annual is easy to cultivate and can be grown in nearly any garden soil, moist or dry, as long as it is in a sunny spot. It is easier to establish in shortgrass prairies and meadows with bunchgrasses than where tall grasses form a continuous sod.

PROPAGATION

Plant seeds in the spring or fall in the desired location, ⅛-¼ inch deep. In established prairies clear a spot about a foot in diameter before planting the seeds.

COMPANIONS

Silky aster, purple prairie clover, blanketflower, Mexican hat, and lance-leaved coreopsis.

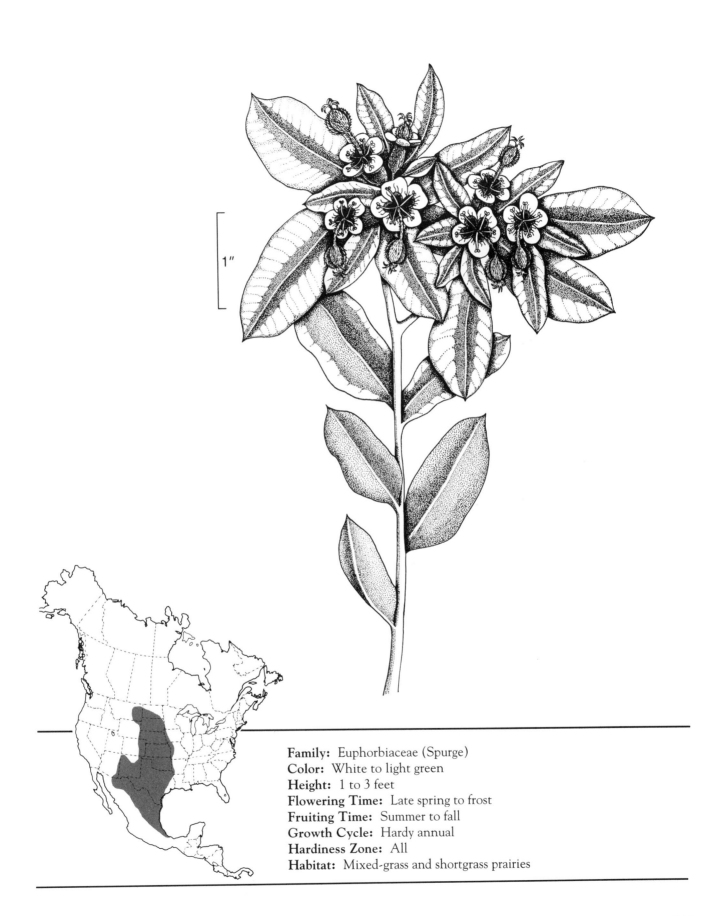

Family: Euphorbiaceae (Spurge)
Color: White to light green
Height: 1 to 3 feet
Flowering Time: Late spring to frost
Fruiting Time: Summer to fall
Growth Cycle: Hardy annual
Hardiness Zone: All
Habitat: Mixed-grass and shortgrass prairies

SNOW-ON-THE-MOUNTAIN (*Euphorbia marginata*)

LEADPLANT

Amorpha canescens

(*Amorphe*)

Leadplant is a hardy, semi-woody perennial inhabiting virgin tallgrass prairies. Its ½-inch-long compound leaflets are densely covered by short, wooly hairs giving the foliage a grayish color and its common name. The small flowers are clustered together in 4-6-inch spikes atop the robust 2-3-foot stems. Although leadplant is a member of the pea family, its violet-gray flowers don't look pealike. The flowers have a single petal from which the golden-yellow stamens protrude. The fruits are small, fuzzy, beanlike pods containing a couple of seeds. Leadplant has a deep, branching taproot, which gives it an advantage in dry prairies, especially those periodically swept by fires, and typically has increased growth and flowering for several years following burning. Native Americans made tea and smoked the foliage.

CULTURE

Leadplant should be cultivated in open sunny locations with only light shade at most. It does best in relatively dry, well-drained soils with moderate amounts of humus. Like other members of the pea family, leadplant has nitrogen-fixing microorganisms that attach to its roots. If the proper microorganisms are not present in the soil when you first plant seeds of leadplant, a commercially available soil inoculant should speed their establishment, and eventually the nitrogen content of the soil around the plant will increase. If inoculation of seeds is needed, use Amorpha-type rhizobia (Nitragin type-EL). Do not apply artificial nitrogen fertilizers because they retard the establishment of rhizobia. Leadplant is hardy as far north as zone 4, and half-hardy in colder regions.

PROPAGATION

Leadplant is usually propagated by seed, although making greenwood cuttings of the young stems is also possible. The seeds should be scarified to allow water to enter. Since the plant requires cold winter temperatures for its seeds to germinate, seed planted in regions warmer than zone 8 should be artificially stratified first (10 weeks of damp stratification at 40°F). Plant the scarified seeds ⅓ inch deep in a nursery bed or deep flat filled with sandy loam mixed with compost. If planted in the fall and left in place during winter, the seeds will germinate over several weeks in the spring when temperatures reach 65-70°F. Allow the seedlings to grow the first year in a nursery bed or flat, and then transplant them in the fall to permanent locations. The buds at the top of the root should be set about 2 inches below the soil surface. If the top of the plant is accidentally damaged, the root will usually resprout. Once established, leadplant requires little care, but it takes about 4 years for the plants to reach maturity and flower.

COMPANIONS

Butterfly weed, pasqueflower, purple prairie clover, lance-leaved coreopsis, showy tick trefoil, and Mexican hat.

142

SUMMER SPECIES OF DRY PRAIRIES

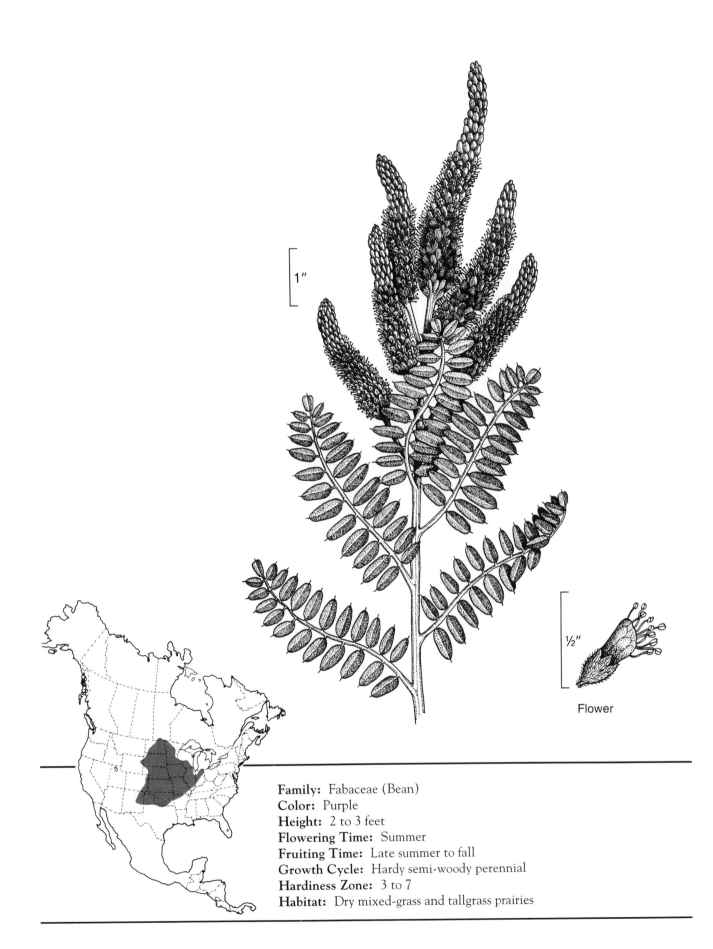

Family: Fabaceae (Bean)
Color: Purple
Height: 2 to 3 feet
Flowering Time: Summer
Fruiting Time: Late summer to fall
Growth Cycle: Hardy semi-woody perennial
Hardiness Zone: 3 to 7
Habitat: Dry mixed-grass and tallgrass prairies

LEADPLANT (*Amorpha canescens*)

143

BUTTERFLY WEED

Asclepias tuberosa

(Orange milkweed, butterfly plant, pleurisy root, *asclépiade tubéreuse*)

The orange, flat-topped clusters of butterfly weed flowers are one of the most striking summer sights in North American prairies. Unlike many of its relatives in the milkweed family, this hardy perennial has rough hairy leaves and stems, scattered rather than paired leaves, and an absence of white, milky sap. The 3-5-inch clusters of yellow-orange to red-orange flowers are near the top of the 1-3-foot high stems. The fused petals of butterfly weed form a crown with 5 projecting horns, between which is a mass of sticky pollen that attaches to the feet of insects visiting the fragrant flowers. Usually fewer than 1 flower in 100 matures into a fruit, a long pod containing typically flat milkweed seeds, with tufts of long, silky hairs to catch the wind. The root, a large tuberous rhizome with smaller fibrous roots, may become enormous with age. Native Americans and European settlers used the fragrant, brittle roots both for food and as a remedy for pleurisy and other lung diseases, thus the common name pleurisy root.

CULTURE

Plant butterfly weed in sunny locations with well-drained soils. A sandy loam is ideal, and once established the plant endures drought well. Butterfly weed is adaptable to soils ranging between pH 4.5 and 6.5. Cutting the first flower clusters of the summer will provide elegant flowers, prolong the flowering season, and give the plant a pleasant shrubby appearance. Butterfly weed is hardy to zone 3, but protect it in winter in regions colder than zone 6.

PROPAGATION

Butterfly weed can be propagated by both seed and root cuttings. Plant fresh seeds in the early fall, ½ inch deep in deep flats filled with sandy loam, mulch lightly, and leave out over winter. Germination is enhanced by moist stratification (3 months at 40°F). Seedlings will quickly germinate in spring when air temperatures rise above 75°F. They will quickly develop taproots and should not be transplanted to permanent locations until they are dormant in the fall. Some of the plants from seed will bloom the second year. Cuttings of the tuberous rhizome can be made in the fall or early spring. Cut 2-inch sections of the rhizome, each with at least one bud, and plant them 2-3 feet apart with buds 2 inches below the soil surface. Keep the soil slightly moist while young plants are becoming established, but do not overwater, especially in cool weather. If planting an established grassland or meadow, clear a patch 1 foot in diameter; but once established, butterfly weed will have no problems holding its ground.

COMPANIONS

Silky aster, leadplant, purple prairie clover, wild bergamot, and lance-leaved coreopsis.

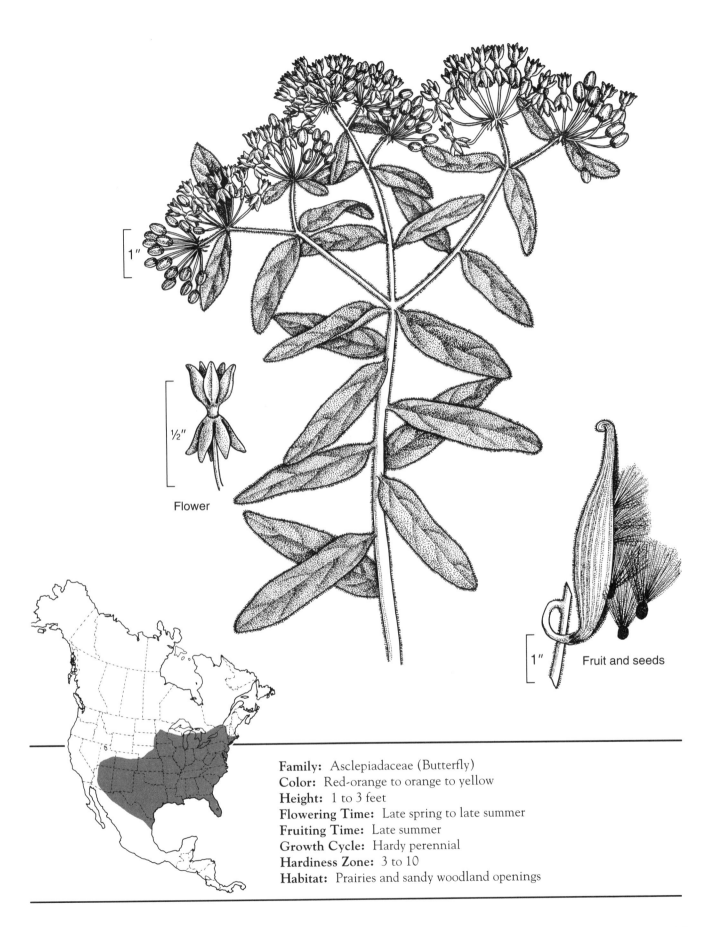

1"

½"

Flower

1"

Fruit and seeds

Family: Asclepiadaceae (Butterfly)
Color: Red-orange to orange to yellow
Height: 1 to 3 feet
Flowering Time: Late spring to late summer
Fruiting Time: Late summer
Growth Cycle: Hardy perennial
Hardiness Zone: 3 to 10
Habitat: Prairies and sandy woodland openings

BUTTERFLY WEED (*Asclepias tuberosa*)

PURPLE PRAIRIE CLOVER
Petalostemum purpureum

(Red tassel flower)

A plant of prairies and dry hills, this member of the pea family has cylindrical, densely packed, ½-2-inch flower heads perched atop 1-3-foot upright stems. Each individual ¼-inch flower has a single small rose-purple to crimson petal with 4 even smaller petals attached to it. The 5 stamens with bright yellow-orange anthers project beyond the petals. The flowers bloom in a ring around the flower head, starting at the bottom and progressing to the top. Pollination is accomplished by numerous insects ranging from bumblebees to beetles. The fruits are tiny, thin pods containing 1 or 2 small seeds. Most of the leaves, with their 3 to 5 narrow, inch-long leaflets, are at the bottom of the stem. The short, highly branched, vertical rootstock has fibrous roots with nodules inhabited by nitrogen-fixing microorganisms. With time the roots may become deep and extensive. Native Americans used a tea made from purple prairie clover as a tonic to prevent a variety of diseases.

CULTURE
Purple prairie clover should be planted in areas with full sun. An excellent xeriscaping plant, it does best on well-drained, warm soils that are slightly acidic (pH 5.5-6.5), and, once established, is quite drought resistant. Since this plant is susceptible to attack from damping-off fungus, plant it where the soil is not overly wet, and irrigate it sparingly. If inoculation is necessary in order to establish seeds in your soil, use Saintfoin-type rhizobia (Nitragin-type F).

PROPAGATION
Seeds are the best means of propagating this legume, since the root system is difficult to divide. Collect the seeds when the flower heads are dry and gray, and scarify to hasten germination by rubbing them gently between sanding blocks. Seeds can be planted ¼-½ inch deep in flats or in nursery beds during the fall or early spring. They will germinate readily with warm spring weather if their seed coats have been abraded. Seedlings should be thinned to 6 inches apart. Transplant the yearling plants in the fall to permanent locations. Plants from seed will flower the second year.

COMPANIONS
Silky aster, wild bergamot, leadplant, butterfly weed, and lance-leaved coreopsis.

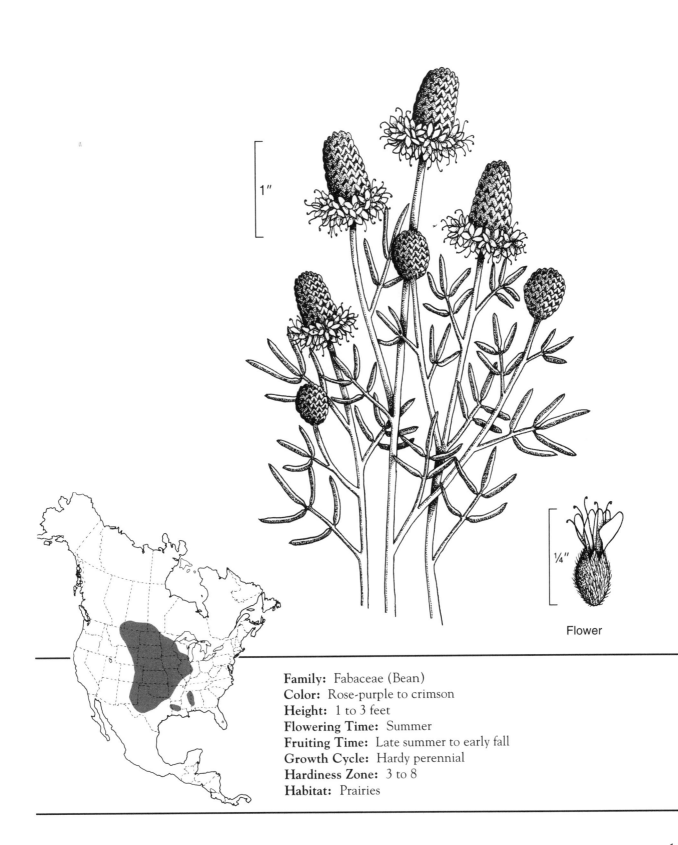

1″

¼″

Flower

Family: Fabaceae (Bean)
Color: Rose-purple to crimson
Height: 1 to 3 feet
Flowering Time: Summer
Fruiting Time: Late summer to early fall
Growth Cycle: Hardy perennial
Hardiness Zone: 3 to 8
Habitat: Prairies

PURPLE PRAIRIE CLOVER *(Petalostemum purpureum)*

WILD BERGAMOT

Monarda fistulosa

(Bee balm, horsemint, *Monarde fistuleuse*)

Wild bergamot's membership in the mint family is indicated by its familiar square stems and irregular flowers. The name wild bergamot refers to the similarity between the aromas of this plant's pungent foliage and the fruit of the bergamot orange tree of Europe. Indeed the leaves of wild bergamot have long been used for making herbal tea and as a treatment for the common cold. The genus *Monarda* is named in honor or Nicolas Monardes, an European herbalist who wrote about North American native plants in the 1500s. The fuzzy 2-4-feet-high stems bear pairs of firm, 3-inch-long, hairy, gray-green leaves and a 2-inch whorl of lilac to pink flowers in clusters at the top of the plant. The 2-lobed upper lip of the tubular, 1-inch flowers bears a tuft of hairs and arches over the 3-lobed lower lip. The long stamens and stigma protrude from the throat of the flower and arch slightly upward. The stigmas are receptive to pollen from other flowers when young, but with age can be self-fertilized. Clear-wing sphinx moths (*Hemaris thysbe*) and many species of butterflies are attracted to the flowers. The seeds are 1/16-inch elliptical nutlets.

CULTURE

Wild bergamot is a widely distributed hardy perennial that grows well in full sun to light shade. While typically found growing in prairies and dry meadows, it responds well to moisture if the soil is well drained. Wild bergamot may develop mildew on its leaves if grown in too humid a location. Soil acidity conditions (pH 5-7.5) are not as important as making sure the plants have full sun at least part of each day.

PROPAGATION

The easiest way to propagate wild bergamot is from seeds. In the fall, plant the seeds ¼ inch deep in flats or in the desired location. They can also be planted indoors in the early spring. The seeds do not require stratification, although germination may be faster if they receive a chilling treatment. The seeds germinate quickly in the spring (1 to 2 weeks) and grow rapidly, sometimes producing flowers the first year. Most of the plants from seed will flower the second year. By the end of the first season wild bergamot will start to produce multiple shoots and over time the plants may become bunchy, even crowding out other plants in their immediate vicinity. Clumps can be divided in the spring and the pieces of rhizome with buds set 1 inch deep and 1 to 2 feet apart. Avoid fall divisions since wild bergamot is susceptible to winter kill and frost-heaving of the roots.

COMPANIONS

Black-eyed Susan, silky aster, New England aster, butterfly weed, and purple prairie clover.

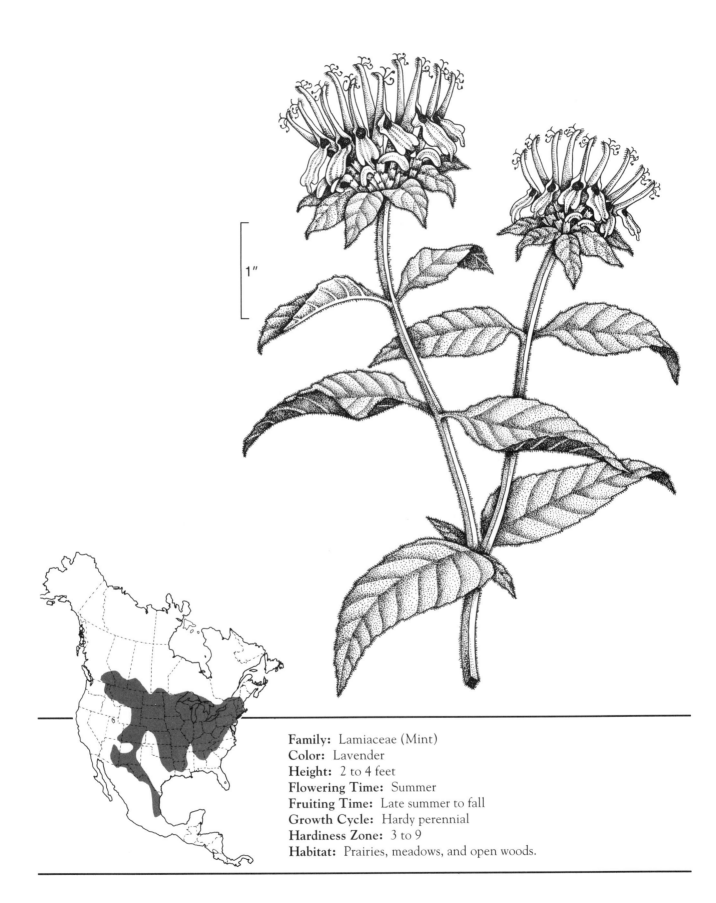

Family: Lamiaceae (Mint)
Color: Lavender
Height: 2 to 4 feet
Flowering Time: Summer
Fruiting Time: Late summer to fall
Growth Cycle: Hardy perennial
Hardiness Zone: 3 to 9
Habitat: Prairies, meadows, and open woods.

1"

WILD BERGAMOT (*Monarda fistulosa*)

BLANKETFLOWER

Gaillardia aristata

(Indian blanket, gaillardia, *gaillarde*)

This half-hardy perennial blankets parts of the northern Great Plains with yellow and red daisylike flowers all summer long. Blanketflower was first collected by the Lewis and Clark Expedition in 1806 and within a decade was being offered in European seed catalogs. The large garden blanketflower most often sold by nurseries, however, is the hybrid *Gaillardia* x *grandiflora*, the product of a series of crosses between G. *aristata* and its annual relative G. *pulchella*. Blanketflower's thick, hairy, dandelion-like leaves clasp the slender hairy stems of this erect, 2-4-foot plant. The inch-long ray flowers have yellow, 3-toothed tips and dark red to purple bases. While in the bud, the disc flowers are frequently red-orange, but as the fuzzy, 5-lobed flowers open they are generally the same color as the bases of the ray flowers. Tufts of hairs project from the tops of the ⅛-inch, conical, seedlike fruits. The plant's fuzzy hairs can cause a skin rash in people with sensitive skin.

CULTURE Blanketflower is adaptable to most sunny locations. It is not particular about soils if they are well drained. It grows best in soils with slight to moderate acidity (pH 5.0-6.5), but even tolerates alkaline conditions with soil pH of 8.0. Don't bother adding compost or other soil amendments to areas contemplated for blanketflower; it does best in infertile soils. While it is extremely hardy (to hardiness zone 3) when grown in its native dry range, it is only half-hardy in more humid eastern regions where it should be mulched heavily for the winter. Once established, blanketflower is quite drought resistant. It is an excellent choice for meadows and xeriscaping or in the cutting garden. The flowering season can be prolonged by removing withering flowers before they set seed.

PROPAGATION Blanketflower can easily be propagated by seed or root division, and softwood stem cuttings are also possible. No chilling treatment of the seed is needed; simply plant in the fall or spring ⅛-¼ inch deep in a sunny location on well-drained soil. The seeds may also be started indoors in the early spring and transplanted to permanent locations after all danger of frost has passed. Germination takes only a week or two and plants may flower by the end of the first summer. Make root divisions in the early spring. Divide the taproot vertically, being sure that each section has at least one bud and as many small lateral roots as possible. Plant sections 10-12 inches apart with the buds just at the soil surface. Since blanketflower is not a long-lived perennial, it may be necessary to divide the clumps every 2 or 3 years to keep it growing vigorously. Softwood cuttings can be made from the stems in the late spring, but seed and root division propagation are easier.

COMPANIONS Mexican hat, snow-on-the-mountain, lance-leaved coreopsis, butterfly weed, and wild bergamot.

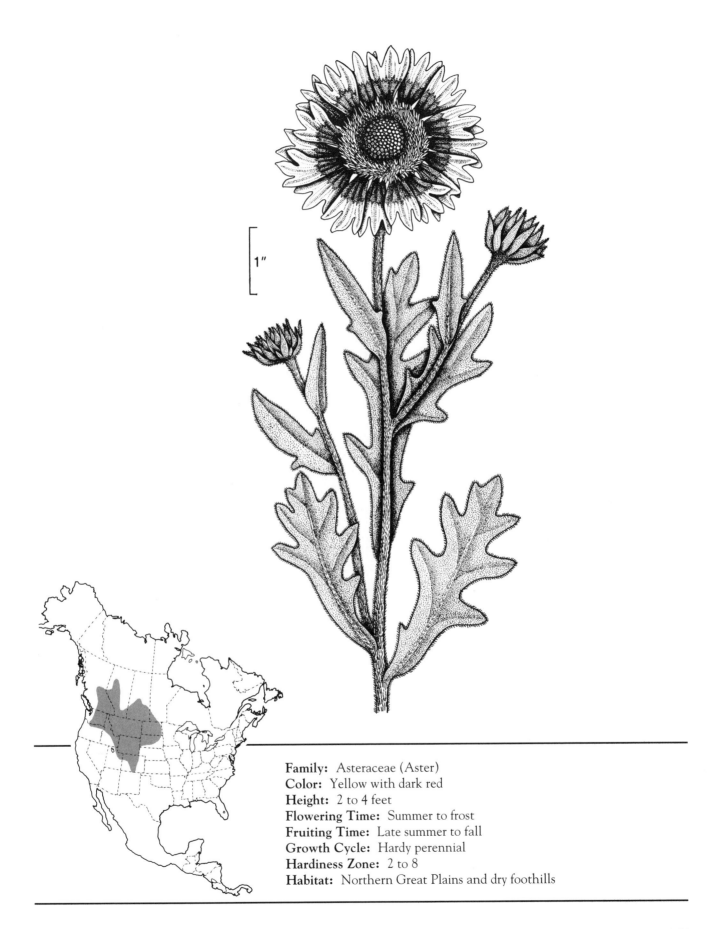

Family: Asteraceae (Aster)
Color: Yellow with dark red
Height: 2 to 4 feet
Flowering Time: Summer to frost
Fruiting Time: Late summer to fall
Growth Cycle: Hardy perennial
Hardiness Zone: 2 to 8
Habitat: Northern Great Plains and dry foothills

BLANKETFLOWER (*Gaillardia aristata*)

151

AUTUMN PRAIRIE SPECIES

In late summer and autumn, prairie grasses and wildflowers display colors drawn from a different palette. Before winter sets in the asters' last flashes of color contrast with the subtle shades of meadow beauty, closed gentian, and false dragonhead. This is also the season for the peak color of grass fruit heads and foliage, as species like little bluestem turn bright red-purple and display their feathery fruits.

In addition to the asters presented in this section, you may want to consider other species such as **heath aster** (*Aster ericoides*), which grows on a variety of soils and has small, delicate, white, densely crowded flower heads and tiny, stiff leaves. It is easily propagated from divisions of its trailing rhizome. The **azure aster** (*Aster azureus*) is a bright blue- flowered prairie species with large leaves along its stems and many tiny leaflets on its flowering branches. **Ironweed** (*Vernonia fasciculata*), a tall, tough-stemmed member of the aster family, has brilliant blue-violet flower heads with a fringy appearance.

Goldenrods are often a striking feature of autumn prairies and meadows. Their heavy pollen, which sticks to the legs and bodies of pollinating insects, is *not* the source of hay fever in the fall. These large, conspicuous wildflowers bloom at about the same time as the real culprits, the inconspicuous ragweeds, which produce highly irritating air-borne pollen. When planting goldenrods, stay away from the large, aggressive species such as **tall goldenrod** (*Solidago altissima*) and **Canada goldenrod** (*Solidago canadensis*). The pungent **sweet goldenrod** (*Solidago odora*), the compact **gray goldenrod** (*Solidago nemoralis*), and the spectacular **showy goldenrod** (*Solidago speciosa*) are much better behaved, although the latter grows quite vigorously in moist soils.

Moist meadows and prairies are ideal locations for **cardinal flower** (*Lobelia cardinalis*), a tall perennial that thrives in wet soils and has spikes of scarlet flowers that resemble cranes in flight. **Joe-Pye weed** (*Eupatorium maculatum*) grows in the same habitats and has large clusters of ragged, red-lavender flower heads.

Autumn prairie garden.

A. Little bluestem
B. Meadow beauty
C. Showy tick trefoil
D. New England aster
E. Indian grass
F. False dragonhead
G. Silky aster
H. Closed gentian
I. Little bluestem

Many trees and shrubs of grassland and prairie margins turn spectacular colors in autumn. **Smooth sumac** (*Rhus glabra*), a shrub that can grow 8-12 feet high and is excellent for erosion control, has pinnately compound leaves that turn reddish in the fall, while rusty **blackhaw viburnum** (*Viburnum rufidulum*) has brilliant red foliage and blue-black fruits that resemble clusters of tiny cherries. In the moist margins of the tallgrass prairie, the hardy pagoda or **alternate-leaved dogwood** (*Cornus alternifolia*) has foliage with hints of purple, dark blue berries, and graceful maroon twigs and branches.

Quaking aspen (*Populus tremuloides*), a tree common to the northern and western margins of prairies, reaches the peak of its beauty in the fall as its trembling green leaves turn to golden yellow and its creamy bark turns golden-green.

MEADOW BEAUTY
Rhexia virginica

(Deergrass, *rhexie de Virginie*)

An aptly named plant, this is one of the most beautiful flowers growing in moist Midwestern prairies and wet meadows in the East. The exquisite 1-1½- inch flowers cluster at the top of the stems, which have 4 ridges and vary greatly in height from 4 inches to 2½ feet. The pairs of 2-inch-long, light green leaves are bristly, especially on the upper surface. Surrounding the yellow pistil and ring of golden, curved stamens in the center of the flower are 4 rounded, rose-crimson petals, which frequently fall off by early afternoon. The fruit, a 4-part capsule resembling a small copper urn or pitcher, contains numerous tiny, coiled, snail-shaped seeds. Fine roots extend from the tuberous root system. Meadow beauty is pollinated by bees, but it can also spread by the swellings of its tuberous roots. The shoots of the plant are a favorite food of deer, giving this species the common name deergrass.

CULTURE Meadow beauty thrives in wet, acid soils. The soil should have a pH between 4 and 5, be moist or damp through most of the growing season, and have abundant organic matter. Soils that are too alkaline should be adjusted to the proper pH by adding peat moss. Plant meadow beauty in full sun to partial shade. This hardy perennial can withstand the cold, acid conditions of the boggy areas of the northeastern part of its range, but can adapt to garden conditions if proper acidity and moisture are maintained.

PROPAGATION Meadow beauty is easily propagated by seed or tuber division. Plant seeds as soon as they are ripe in late summer or early fall. Sprinkle seeds on the surface of a flat filled with a mixture of peat moss and sand, moisten, and cover with a thin layer of peat moss. Germination in the spring is enhanced by moist stratification (2 to 3 months at 40°F), so leave the flats outdoors for the winter. Be sure to keep the seedlings well watered. The newly formed tubers can be planted 1 inch deep in permanent locations in the fall. Plants from seed mature in about 2 years. Divide tubers of mature plants in the early spring or late fall, making sure that each division has at least one bud. Plant the segments a foot apart with the buds 1-1½ inches below the soil surface. Cuttings can also be made from newly growing stems, before plants flower in the early summer. Place 6-inch cuttings 3 inches deep in moist sand and provide shade. Plant the newly formed tubers in the fall after the plant has become dormant.

COMPANIONS False dragonhead, New England aster, gayfeather, and closed gentian.

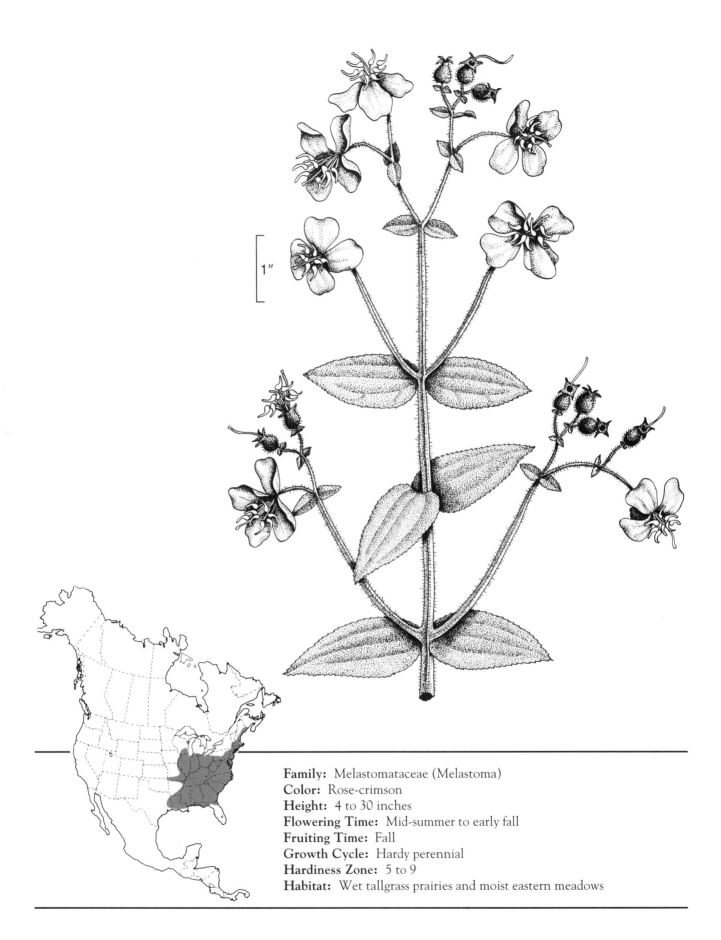

Family: Melastomataceae (Melastoma)
Color: Rose-crimson
Height: 4 to 30 inches
Flowering Time: Mid-summer to early fall
Fruiting Time: Fall
Growth Cycle: Hardy perennial
Hardiness Zone: 5 to 9
Habitat: Wet tallgrass prairies and moist eastern meadows

MEADOW BEAUTY (*Rhexia virginica*)

FALSE DRAGONHEAD

Physostegia virginiana

(Obedient plant, *Physostégie de Virginie*)

The smooth, wandlike stems of false dragonhead are frequently seen growing in clumps in moist prairies, meadows, and even open woodlands in the eastern U.S. and Canada. This member of the mint family spreads by underground stolons from which arise 2-4-foot-high stems with pairs of 3-5-inch-long, lance-shaped, sharp-toothed leaves and a terminal spike of lavender to pink flowers. The inch-long flowers have 5 triangular lobes, 2 forming an inflated upper lip and 3 forming a lower lip. False dragonhead is also called obedient plant because if its individual flowers are moved laterally, they stay put rather than springing back. The long-lasting blooms make this an excellent cut flower. The fruits are ⅛-inch dull brown nutlets. Each fall the above-ground stem dies back after flowering, but the extensive system of stolons and white fibrous roots sends up new shoots the following spring.

CULTURE This is an easy perennial to cultivate since it is relatively indifferent to soil acidity conditions (pH 5-7.5), and tolerates a variety of light conditions from full sun to half-shade. The most important factor in cultivating false dragonhead is to maintain ample soil moisture. A moist, well-drained soil rich in humus is ideal, although once established it will grow to a smaller size in dry soils. Hardy to zone 3, false dragonhead should be given a thick layer of mulch over winter in zone 4 and colder regions.

PROPAGATION False dragonhead can easily be propagated by seed and stolon division. Plant the seeds, as soon as they are ripe in the fall, ¼ inch deep in flats containing a mixture of loam and humus. The flats should be left out over winter since germination of the seeds is enhanced by damp stratification (3 months at 40°F). Germination takes place in the spring several weeks after temperatures rise into the 70°F range, and seedlings can be transplanted to permanent locations in the fall. Plants from seed will produce flowers the second year and will increase in number in subsequent years as they spread by means of stolons. The clumps that form can be divided in early spring or late fall. Cut the stolon connections with a sharp spade and replant the rootstocks 1 foot apart with the top of the crown just at the soil surface. If divided in the fall, the plants should be mulched.

COMPANIONS New England aster, closed gentian, gayfeather, Culver's root, and meadow beauty.

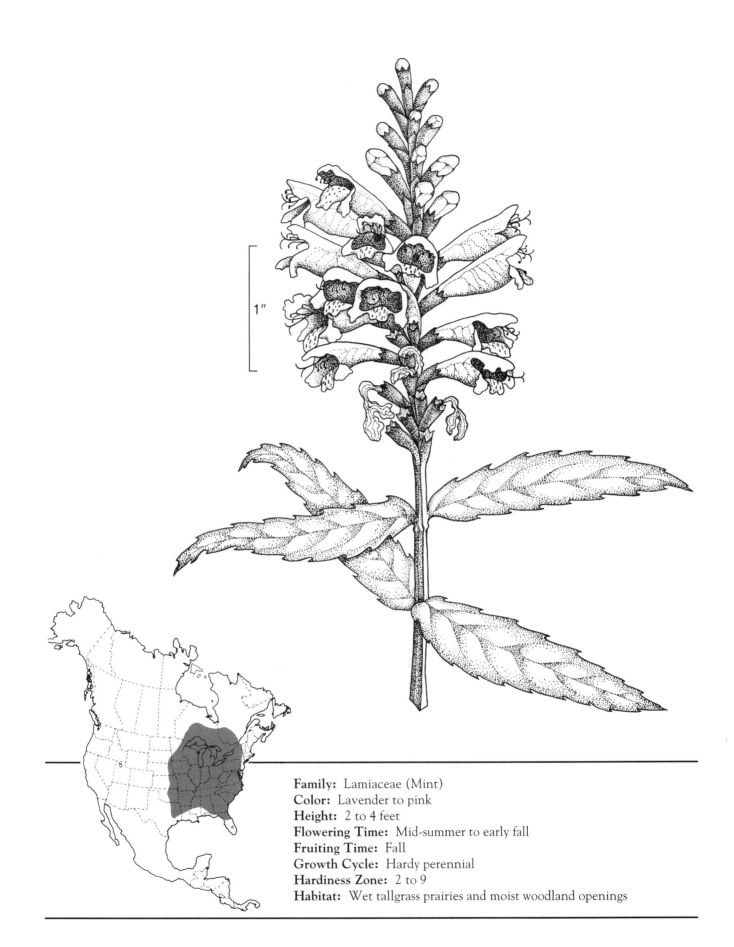

Family: Lamiaceae (Mint)
Color: Lavender to pink
Height: 2 to 4 feet
Flowering Time: Mid-summer to early fall
Fruiting Time: Fall
Growth Cycle: Hardy perennial
Hardiness Zone: 2 to 9
Habitat: Wet tallgrass prairies and moist woodland openings

FALSE DRAGONHEAD (*Physostegia virginiana*)

SHOWY TICK TREFOIL

Desmodium canadense

(Desmodie du Canada)

This is an aptly named plant of Midwestern prairies. Its clusters of flowers are among the showiest of the pea family, its seeds are reminiscent of small ticks, and each of its leaves is divided into 3 leaflets, called a trefoil. Showy tick trefoil is a robust hardy perennial with branched stems reaching 4-6 feet in height. Velvety hairs cover the stem and thick, 3-inch-long leaflets, especially toward the top of the plant. Dense clusters of up to hundreds of flowers nod at the top of the stems, the spikes looking flat-topped from a distance. Each pealike, ½-inch-long flower turns from rose-purple to blue with age. Honeybees and bumblebees are the main agents of pollination for showy tick trefoil, while caterpillars of the eastern tailed blue (*Everes comyntas*) and hoary edge (*Achalarus lyciades*) butterflies eat its foliage. At maturity, the thin-walled, velvety, 1-3-inch pod breaks between each of the 3 to 5 seeds. The pod is covered with minutely hooked bristles so that when the individual segments of the fruit break off, they cling to your clothing or to the fur of passing animals. The root system is a slender, brown, sometimes branched taproot with smaller secondary roots.

CULTURE
Showy tick trefoil grows well in any soil of moderate moisture, in full sun to light shade, and is generally indifferent to soil acidity conditions. Since it is a legume, its root nodules will fix nitrogen from the air and add it to the soil. If you have difficulty establishing showy tick trefoil, add an inoculant such as Nitragin-type EL rhizobium. Although the seedlings are sensitive to competition from dense grasses, showy tick trefoil can later become rather large and aggressive, so plant it where there is growing room.

PROPAGATION
Grow showy tick trefoil from seed. The seed does not require any chilling to germinate, but, like many of the legumes, its hard seed coat often slows the germination process by making it difficult for water to penetrate. The best way to alleviate this problem is to scarify the seeds using sandpaper or to nick the seed coat carefully with a sharp razor or knife. Plant scarified seeds ½-¾ inch deep in the spring. Seeds usually germinate in 2 to 4 weeks and make rapid growth. If planted in a garden, rather than in grassy locations, the seedlings should be thinned to an 18-inch spacing. Once established showy tick trefoil will vigorously resprout from the roots if the top is cut, but it is not easy to propagate this plant from root division. Some plants from seed may flower the first year, and most will flower the second.

COMPANIONS
Leadplant, lance-leaved coreopsis, butterfly weed, Culver's root, and closed gentian.

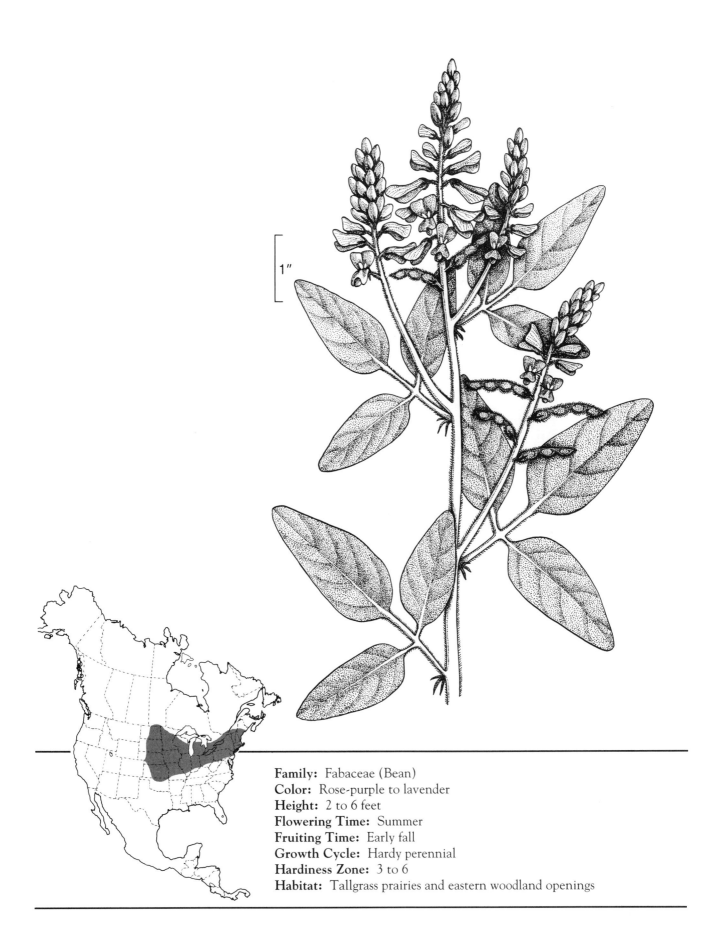

1″

Family: Fabaceae (Bean)
Color: Rose-purple to lavender
Height: 2 to 6 feet
Flowering Time: Summer
Fruiting Time: Early fall
Growth Cycle: Hardy perennial
Hardiness Zone: 3 to 6
Habitat: Tallgrass prairies and eastern woodland openings

SHOWY TICK TREFOIL (*Desmodium canadense*)

159

CLOSED GENTIAN
Gentiana andrewsii

(Bottle gentian, blind gentian, *gentiane d'Andrews*)

Not only is the closed gentian one of the easiest of the gentians to cultivate, but it has unusual and interesting flowers as well. Clusters of 2 to 5 1½-inch blossoms are borne at the bases of the upper leaves of this hardy, 1-2-foot perennial. Robust plants may have 2 whorls of flowers. The 5 petals range in color from intense navy blue to blue-violet and even white, attached to one another by petal-like pleats that form a tube. Though this tube appears to lack an opening, inspiring the plant's common names of closed, bottle, and blind gentian, pollinating insects such as bumblebees force their way into the flower with ease. Surrounded by the petals and unseen from outside the flower are 5 stamens, their anthers fused together in another tube, surrounding the 2 stigmas. The sometimes reddish stems are clasped by pairs of 2-4-inch leaves, whose size increases toward the top of the stem. The fruit of the closed gentian is a tan, papery capsule containing ⅛-inch, light tan, winged seeds. The root has a thickened crown with many white, fibrous roots extending away from it.

CULTURE   An excellent garden plant, closed gentian is adaptable to a wide variety of conditions from full sun to light shade, in soils that range from dryish to damp, and from neutral to slightly acidic (pH 5-7.5). It grows best in a sandy or even gravelly loam, rich in humus and moist throughout the growing season.

PROPAGATION   Closed gentians can be propagated either by seed or by divisions of the root crown. Divide root crowns in the fall or early spring. Cut crowns into chunks, each with at least one bud, and plant the sections 1 foot apart with the buds at the top of the crown about 1 inch below the soil surface. Mice love to eat gentian buds, so protect the plants with hardware cloth or screen. Germination of closed gentian requires stratification (3 months at 40°F) and is enhanced by exposure to the light, so lightly scatter the seeds just on the surface of a flat containing a mixture of loam and compost. Do not scratch the seeds into the soil, but moisten them and cover lightly with peat moss. Leave the flats out for the winter so the seeds can be chilled, or artificially refrigerate seeds stored in moist peat moss and then plant them in flats indoors in early spring, keeping the surface moist. The seeds will germinate in 1 to 4 weeks following spring temperatures above 65°F, but the process may be slow. The first year the seedling will form only a rosette of leaves, and should be provided with light shade and moisture. Leave seedlings in the flat for the first growing season, transplant them to a holding bed for the second year, and then move them to a permanent location the following year. Plants from seed will usually flower in the third or fourth year.

COMPANIONS   New England aster, nodding wild onion, false dragonhead, gayfeather, and meadow beauty.

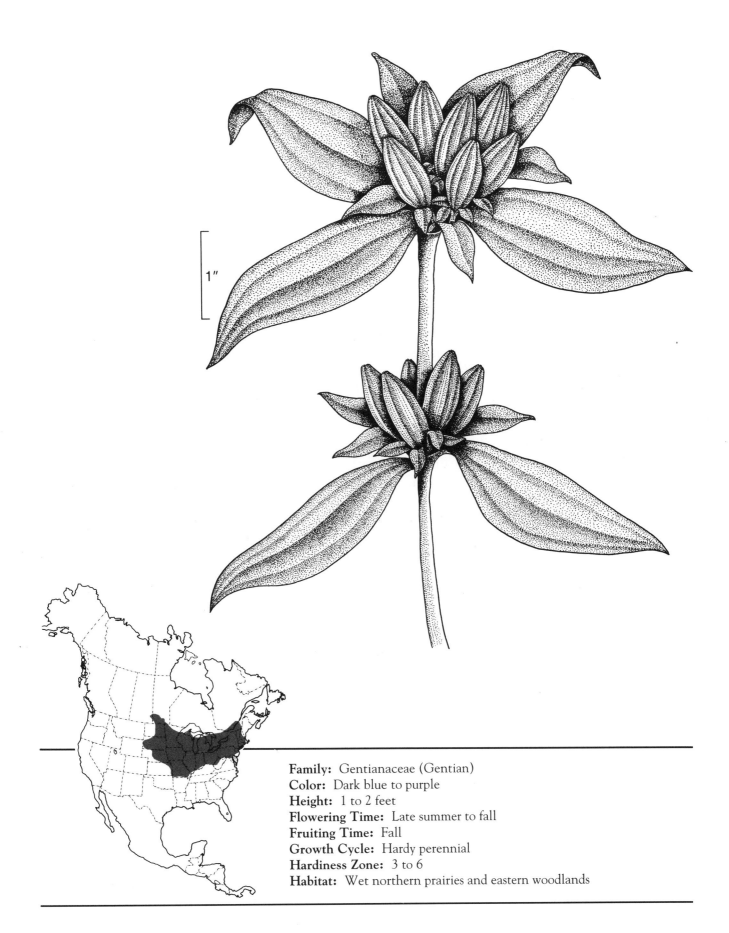

1"

Family: Gentianaceae (Gentian)
Color: Dark blue to purple
Height: 1 to 2 feet
Flowering Time: Late summer to fall
Fruiting Time: Fall
Growth Cycle: Hardy perennial
Hardiness Zone: 3 to 6
Habitat: Wet northern prairies and eastern woodlands

CLOSED GENTIAN (*Gentiana andrewsii*)

NEW ENGLAND ASTER

Aster novae-angliae

(Aster de la Nouvelle-Angleterre)

Why bother planting a common garden variety of aster when there is this stunning native species? New England asters hardly confine themselves to New England, for they can be found growing in fields from Colorado to Maine and from Kansas to North Carolina. The species can be cultivated as a perennial north of hardiness zone 3 and is the stock from which many of the horticultural varieties of hardy asters have been bred. Usually reaching a height of 2-4 feet, the New England aster has dense leaves covered with bristly hairs and bears clusters of flowers at the tips of leafy branches. The flower heads have violet-purple ray flowers surrounding the golden yellow disc flowers. New England asters attract bees and many species of butterflies, cross-pollination being necessary for it to produce seeds. It remains in flower until heavy frost, although the ray flowers close over the flower head at night and on cloudy days. The disc flowers develop into fuzzy ⅛- inch-long seeds that are carried away by the wind. Native Americans smoked the dried roots and made an infusion from the plant to treat intestinal disorders.

CULTURE   Grow New England asters in full sun to partial shade. They will not grow well if too densely shaded, but are easy to grow in fields and meadows. They grow nicely under a variety of soil acidity conditions from slightly acid to neutral (pH 5.5-7) and are best planted where soil moisture is ample throughout the summer. For a bushier form prune New England asters in the late spring. They make attractive cut flowers in the fall but wilt quickly, so take your vase to the garden when you cut them.

PROPAGATION   Although a perennial, New England asters can be grown as an annual. If the seeds are sown in the fall, plants usually flower the next fall. Seeds should be damp-stratified for 4 to 6 weeks prior to planting. Stratified seeds have three times the germination rate of non-stratified seeds and can be expected to germinate in 1 to 2 weeks. The seeds should be planted about ¼ inch deep in mineral soil with no mulch. The best time to propagate by root division is in the late fall. Roots should be divided every several years anyway, to keep the plants growing vigorously, so you might as well put the surplus material to good use. Space root divisions a couple of feet apart with the tops of the rhizomes just at the surface of the soil. Once established, New England asters will self-sow if bare mineral soil and sufficient moisture are available.

COMPANIONS   False dragonhead, queen-of-the-prairie, closed gentian, showy tick trefoil, and wild bergamot.

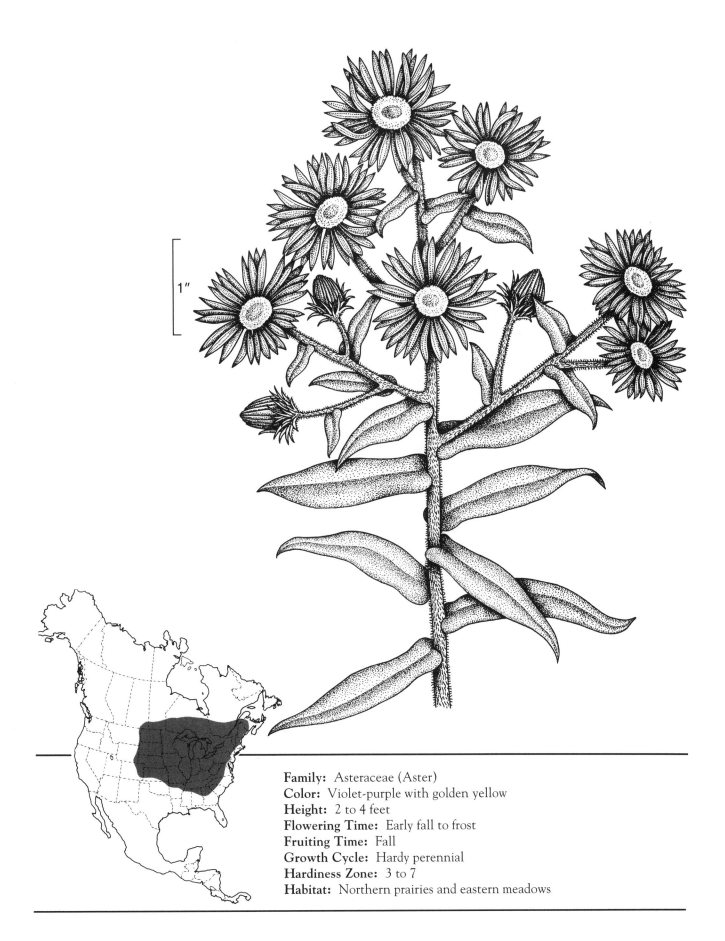

Family: Asteraceae (Aster)
Color: Violet-purple with golden yellow
Height: 2 to 4 feet
Flowering Time: Early fall to frost
Fruiting Time: Fall
Growth Cycle: Hardy perennial
Hardiness Zone: 3 to 7
Habitat: Northern prairies and eastern meadows

SILKY ASTER

Aster sericeus

(Western silvery aster, mouse-eared aster)

The silky aster gets its name from the hairy surfaces of its leaves. It is a hardy perennial of the dry prairies, yet is a pleasant addition to gardens for both its flowers and attractive foliage. The numerous 1-inch leaves are soft and silky as they emerge in the late spring, stiffen and become silvery during the summer, and frequently turn a bright red in the fall. Small clusters of ½-1½-inch flower heads are borne atop the smooth, branched, 1-2-foot-high stems. The deep lavender to light blue ray flowers surround the yellow disc flowers, a delightful contrast to the silver-green foliage. A large variety of butterflies and bees are attracted to this wildflower and ensure its pollination. Silky aster has been used as a remedy for arthritis.

CULTURE

Silky aster grows best in full sun although it can be planted in light shade. Its natural habitat is dry grasslands and woods, where it grows best, yet it can be successfully grown in moderately moist gardens as well. It thrives on soils that are rich in organic matter and slightly acidic (pH 5-6.5). Once established, silky aster competes well with native prairie grasses.

PROPAGATION

Silky aster is usually propagated by seeds, although its roots also can be divided in the fall or spring when the plant is dormant. Collect seed in the mid-fall when they are ripe. Plant them thickly on the surface of flats with a mixture of 2 parts sand, 1 part compost, and 1 part peat moss. Cover seeds with ⅛ inch of sand, keep moist, and leave outdoors for the winter. Silky aster seeds benefit from moist stratification (10 weeks at 40°F) and will germinate faster if given a cold treatment. They will germinate quickly as soon as spring has warmed the soil. Thin the seedlings when they are about 1 month old, and carefully transplant them to permanent locations a month later. Though some plants may flower the first year, most wait till their second year. Once established, silky aster tends both to form clumps and to self-seed.

COMPANIONS

Leadplant, purple prairie clover, butterfly weed, wild bergamot, and snow-on-the-mountain.

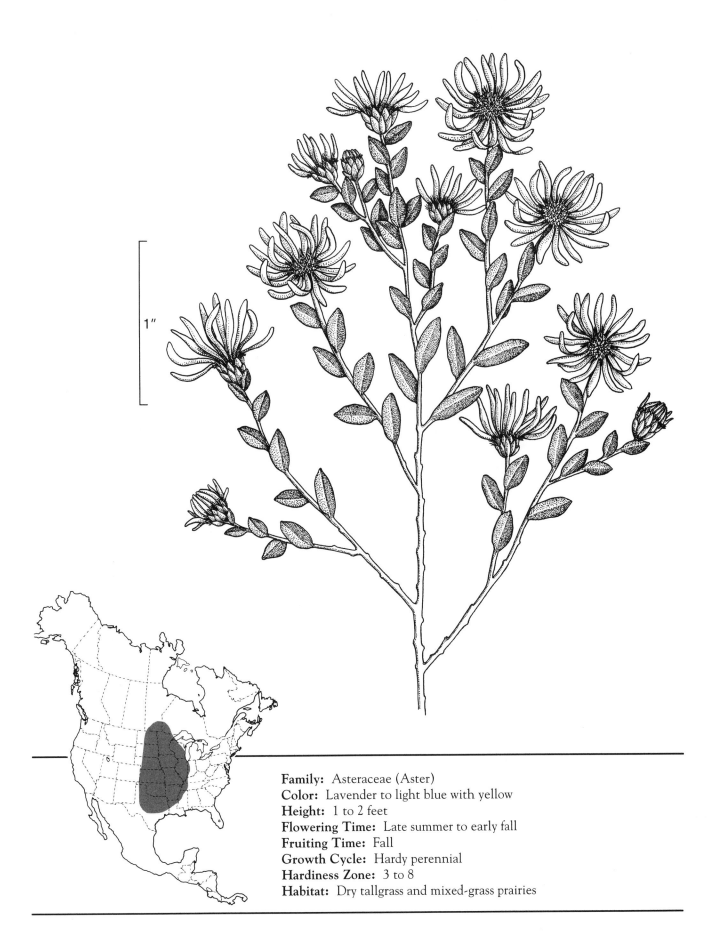

Family: Asteraceae (Aster)
Color: Lavender to light blue with yellow
Height: 1 to 2 feet
Flowering Time: Late summer to early fall
Fruiting Time: Fall
Growth Cycle: Hardy perennial
Hardiness Zone: 3 to 8
Habitat: Dry tallgrass and mixed-grass prairies

SILKY ASTER *(Aster sericeus)*

Appendixes

Suppliers

The following list of suppliers is provided as a service to the reader without any implication of endorsement of the business or products supplied. It is recommended that seeds and plants be purchased from a source as close as possible to the location where wildflowers and grasses will be planted. Some of the suppliers listed below sell retail, some sell only in large quantities as wholesalers, and still others sell both as wholesale and retail vendors. Please do not bother wholesale outlets if your orders are small. Payment should be in the appropriate currency, i.e. U.S. dollars to U.S. businesses and Canadian dollars to Canadian businesses.

California

J.L. Hudson, Seedsman
P.O. Box 1058
Redwood City, CA 94064

Sells seeds and books, retail and wholesale, by mail. Catalog $1.00. Many species of wildflowers, shrubs, and trees.

Redwood City Seed Company
P.O. Box 361
Redwood City, CA 94064
(415)325-7333

Sells seeds, books, and bunchgrass plants, retail and wholesale, by phone and mail order. Catalog $1.00. Specializes in California native wildflowers and grasses.

Clyde Robin Seed Company
P.O. Box 2366
Castro Valley, CA 94546
(415)785-0425

Sells seeds and books, retail and wholesale, by mail, phone order, and over the counter. Free catalog. Full range of wildflower seeds.

Wildflowers International, Inc.
P.O. Box 131
Elk, CA 95432
(707)877-3400

Sells seeds wholesale only, by phone. Brochure describes custom mixture design services.

Colorado

Applewood Seed Company
5380 Vivian Street
Arvada, CO 80002
(303)431-6283

Sells seeds, retail and wholesale, by mail and phone order. Specializes in wildflower, herb, and specialty seeds.

Dean Swift Seed
Company
P.O. Box B
Jaroso, CO 81138-0028
(719)672-3739

Sells seeds, wholesale, by mail and phone order. Free catalog. Specializes in native wildflowers, grasses, shrubs, and conifers.

Idaho

High Altitude Gardens
P.O. Box 4619
500 Bell Drive # 7
Ketchum, ID 83340
(800)874-7333

Sells seeds and live plants, retail and wholesale, by phone and mail order. Catalog $2.00. Specializes in wildflowers and native grasses for harsh montane climates.

Northplan/Mountain Seed
P.O. Box 9107
Moscow, ID 83843-1607
(208)882-8040
FAX (208)882-7446

Sells seeds and live plants, by mail and phone order. For free seed list, enclose a self-addressed, stamped, legal-size envelope.

Winterfeld Ranch Seed
Company
P.O. Box 97
Swan Valley, ID 83449
(208)483-3683

Sells seeds wholesale, by phone and mail order. Catalog available.

Illinois

Midwest Wildflowers
Box 64
Rockton, IL 61072

Sells wildflower seeds and books retail by mail order. Catalog $1.00. Specializes in regional wildflowers of tallgrass prairies.

The Natural Garden
38W443 Highway 64
St. Charles, IL 60175
(708)584-0150

Sells seeds, live plants, and books, retail and wholesale, over-the-counter, by mail, and phone order. Catalog $2.00. Specializes in native Illinois prairie grasses and wildflowers.

Kansas

Sharp Brothers Seed Co.
P.O. Box 140
Healy, KA 67850
(316)398-2231

Sells seeds retail and wholesale, by mail and phone order. Catalog $1.00. Native wildflowers and grass seed adapted to North American grasslands.

Minnesota

Prairie Moon Nursery
Route 3
Box 163
Winona, MN 55987
(507)452-1362

Sells books, seeds and live plants, retail and wholesale, by mail and phone order. Catalog $1.00. Specializes in native wildflowers and grasses of the upper Midwest and adjacent Canada.

Prairie Restorations, Inc.
P.O. Box 327
Princeton, MN 55371
(612)389-4342

Sells seeds and live plants, retail and wholesale, over-the-counter, by phone and mail order. Catalog available. Ships only within 200 miles of Princeton, MN. Specializes in native grasses and wildflowers.

Missouri

Sharp Brothers Seed Company
Route 4, Box 237A
Clinton, MO 64735
(816)885-7551

Sells seeds retail and wholesale, by mail and phone order. Catalog $1.00. Specializes in native wildflowers.

Montana

Lawyer Nursery, Inc.
950 Highway 200 West
Plains, MT 59859
(406)826-3881
FAX (406)826-5700

Sells seeds and live woody plant seedlings, wholesale, by phone and mail order. Free catalog.

Nebraska

Bluebird Nursery, Inc.
521 Linden
P.O. Box 460
Clarkson, NE 68629
(402)892-3457

Sells live plants and books, wholesale only, over-the-counter and by phone order. Specializes in wildflowers and grasses.

Miller Grass Seed Co., Inc.
1600 Corn Husker Highway
Lincoln, NE 68501
(402)475-1232

Sells seeds wholesale and retail, over-the-counter, by phone order and C.O.D. Catalog available. Specializes in grasses and some wildflowers.

Stock Seed Farms
Route 1
Box 112
Murdock, NE 68407
(800)759-1520

Sells seeds and books, retail and wholesale, over-the-counter, by phone and mail order. Catalog free. Specializes in prairie grasses and wildflowers.

New Jersey

Thompson & Morgan
P.O. Box 1308
Jackson, NJ 08527-0308
(201)363-2225
FAX (201)363-9356

Sells seeds, wholesale and retail, by phone and mail order. Free catalog.

New Mexico

Curtis & Curtis
Star Route Box 8A
Clovis, NM 88101
(505)762-4759

Sells seeds, wholesale and retail, over the counter and by phone. Specializes in native grasses.

Plants of the Southwest
930 Baca Street
Santa Fe, NM 87501
(505)983-1548

Sells seeds, live plants, and books, wholesale and retail, over the counter, by phone, and mail order. Catalog $2.00. Specializes in grasses, wildflowers, shrubs, vegetables, and biological controls for the West.

Pennsylvania

W. Atlee Burpee & Company
300 Park Avenue
Warminster, PA 18991-0003
(800)888-1447

Sells seeds, live plants, and books, retail and wholesale, by phone and mail order. Free catalog. Specializes in a wide variety of plant seeds and gardening aids.

Texas

Anton Seed Company, Inc.
P.O. Box 667
Lockhart, TX 78644
(512)398-2433

Sells seeds retail and wholesale, by mail order. Specializes in bluebonnet seed.

Bamert Seed Co.
Route 3, Box 1120
Muleshoe, TX 79347
(800)262-9892

Sells seeds retail and wholesale, over-the-counter, by phone and mail order. Free catalog. Specializes in native grasses.

Robinson Seed Co.
1113 Jefferson Drive
Plainview, TX 79072
(806)293-4959

Sells seeds retail and wholesale, by mail order. Specializes in buffalo grass and other native grasses.

J'Dons Seeds International
P.O. Box 10998-533
Austin, TX 78766
(512)343-6360

Sells seeds retail and wholesale, by phone and mail order. Free catalog. Specializes in native wildflower seeds and mixes.

Green Horizons
218 Quinlan #571
Kerrville, TX 78028
(512)257-5141

Sells seeds, books, and live plants, retail, over-the-counter, by phone and mail order. Free catalog for stamped, self-addressed envelope. Specializes in wildflower and grass seeds native to Texas.

Gunsight Mountain
Ranch and Nursery
P.O. Box 86
Tarpley, TX 78883

Sells live plants, retail and wholesale, over-the-counter. Free catalog. Specializes in container grown plants native to region.

Douglass W. King Co.
P.O. Box 200320
San Antonio, TX 78220
(512)661-4191

Sells seeds retail and wholesale, over-the-counter, by phone and mail order. Specializes in bluebonnet seed and wildflower mixtures.

Lone Star Growers
Route 9
Box 220
San Antonio, TX 78252

Sells live plants, WHOLESALE only. Specializes in annuals, perennials, and shrubs.

Native American Seed
3400 Long Prairie Road
Flower Mound, TX 75028
(214)539-0534

Sells seeds retail and wholesale, by phone and mail order. Catalog $1.00. Specializes in native wildflower and grass seeds as well as organic products for landscape restoration.

Wildseed, Inc.
1101 Campo Rosa Road
P.O. Box 308
Eagle Lake, TX 77434
(409)234-7353
FAX (409)234-7407

Sells seeds, books, and live plants, retail and wholesale, over-the-counter, by phone and mail order. Free Catalog. Specializes in native North American wildflower seeds.

Utah

Granite Seed Company
P.O. Box 177
Lehi, UT 84043
(801)531-1456

Sells seeds wholesale, by phone and mail order. Catalog $3.00. Specializes in western wildflowers, grasses, and shrubs for erosion control.

Wisconsin

Little Valley Farm
Route 3, Box 544
Spring Green, WI 53588
(608)935-3324

Sells seeds, books, and live plants, retail, over-the-counter, by phone and mail order. Catalog $0.25. Specializes in native plants of prairies and woodlands.

Prairie Nursery
P.O. Box 306
Westfield, WI 53964
(608)296-3679

Sells seeds, books, and live plants, retail and wholesale, by phone and mail order. Excellent catalog $2.00. Specializes in wildflowers and grasses native to North American tallgrass prairies.

Prairie Ridge Nursery
RR 2
9738 Overland Road
Mt. Horeb, WI 53572
(608)437-5245

Sells seeds and live plants, wholesale, by phone and mail order. Helpful catalog $1.00. Specializes in native wildflower seeds and plants; consulting services available.

Prairie Seed Source
P.O. Box 83
North Lake, WI 53064-0083

Sells seeds and books, retail by mail order. Well-organized catalog $1.00. Specializes in southeastern Wisconsin prairie seeds.

Wildlife Nurseries
P.O. Box 2724
Oshkosh, WI 54903
(414)231-3780

Sells seeds retail over-the-counter, by phone and mail order. Catalog $1.00. Specializes in grasses, upland and wetland plants for wildlife.

Botanical Gardens

Alberta

Devonian Botanic Garden
University of Alberta
Edmonton, Alberta T6G 2E1
(403)987-3054

Free. Open May-Sept 10 am-7 pm. Sells seeds to members, sells books. Collection of labeled native plants.

Colorado

Denver Botanic Gardens
1005 York Street
Denver, CO 80206
(303)331-4000

Entrance fee: $4.00 winter, $3.00 summer. Open daily 9:00 am-4:45 pm. Sells seeds, books, and has plant sale. Classes in native plant identification and use in landscaping. Large collection of western native plants, including Chatfield Arboretum and Mt. Goliath Alpine Units outside Denver.

Illinois

Chicago Botanic Garden
Lake-Cook Road
P.O. Box 400
Glencoe, IL 60022
(708)835-5440

Parking fee. Open daily 8:00 am to sunset, except Christmas. Sells books and has periodic plant sales. Conducts many courses.

Ladd Arboretum
2024 McCormick Blvd.
Evanston, IL 60201
(708)864-5181

Free. Open 9:00 am to 4:30 pm Tuesday to Saturday, grounds open daily sunrise to sunset. Sells books and has periodic plant sales. Environmental education courses for children and adults.

Kishwaukee College
Route 38
Malta, IL 60150
(815)825-2086

Free. Grounds open daylight hours, all year. Offers course on managing native prairies.

Lincoln Memorial Garden and Nature Center
2301 East Lake Drive
Springfield, IL 62707
(217)529-1111

Free. Open all year daylight hours. Sells books, seeds and live plants. Prairie propagation workshops.

Morton Arboretum
Route 53
Lisle, IL 60532
(708)968-0074

Entrance fee: $3.00 per car. Open 9 am - 7 pm (summer), 9 am - 5 pm (winter). Sells books. Large prairie restoration.

Edward L. Ryerson Conservation Area
21950 N. Riverwoods Road
Deerfield, IL 60015
(708)948-7750

Free. Open all year 8:30 am - 5 pm. Wide range of programs and native plant displays.

Severson Dells Environmental Education Center
8786 Montague Road
Rockford, IL 61102
(815)335-2915

Free. Open all year 8 am - 4:30 pm Mon. - Sat., 1 - 5 pm Sun. Sells books and live plants. Workshops on native plant gardening.

James Woodworth Prairie Preserve
Milwaukee Avenue (¼ mile north of Greenwood Ave.)
Niles, IL
(708) 965-3488

mailing address:
c/o Department of Biological Sciences
U. Illinois at Chicago
Box 4348
Chicago IL 60680
(312) 996-8673

Free. Open 10 am - 3 pm June -Sept. Remnant tallgrass prairie with interpretive center and native plant displays.

Indiana

Christy Woods of Ball State University
Riverside Avenue
Muncie, IN 43702
(317) 285-8838

Free. Open all year 7:30 am - 4:30 pm Mon.-Fri., 8 am-4:30 pm Sat.

Holcomb Gardens
Butler University
4600 Sunset Avenue
Indianapolis, IN 46208

Free. Open all year by appointment. Butler University Prairie established in 1987.

Gene Stratton Porter State Historic Site
Box 639
Rome City, IN 46784
(219)854-3790

Donation. Open all year. Sells books. Native wildflower areas on the grounds.

Iowa

Bickelhaupt Arboretum
340 S. 14th Street
Clinton, IA 52732
(319) 242-4771

Free. Open all year daylight hours. Prairie restoration started in 1977.

DesMoines Botanical Center
909 East River Drive
Des Moines, IA 50316
(515)283-4148

Entrance fee: $1.00. Open all year 10 am - 6 pm Mon.-Thurs., 10 am - 9 pm Fri., 10 am - 5 pm Sun. Sells books, seeds, and live plants. Flower shows and programs.

Iowa Arboretum
RR1 - Box 44A
Madrid, IA 50156

Free. Open all year sunrise to sunset. Educational tours and workshops. Bimonthly newsletter for members.

Kansas

Dyck Arboretum of the Plains
Hesston College
Box 3000
Hesston, KS 67062
(316) 327-8127

Free. Open all year daylight hours. Prairie restorations.

Michigan

Beall-Garfield Botanical Garden
412 Olds Hall
Michigan State University
East Lansing, MI 48824
(517) 355-9582

Free. Open all year daylight hours. Sells books, wildflower seeds, and live plants. .

Cranbrook House & Garden
380 Lone Pines Road
P.O. Box 801
Bloomfield Hills, MI 48303
(313) 645-3149

Entrance Fee $2.00. Open 1 - 5 pm daily May - Sept., weekends Oct.; 10 am - 5 pm Mon. - Sat. 1 - 5 pm Sun. summer. Small native plant garden.

Fernwood Garden and Nature Center
13988 Range Line Road
Niles, MI 49120
(616) 683-8653

Entrance Fee $2.00. Open all year 9 am - 5 pm Mon.-Sat., noon -5 pm Sun. Sells books, wildflower seeds, and live plants. Programs on native plant gardening.

For-Mar Nature Preserve and Arboretum
5360 E. Potter Road
Flint, MI 48506
(313) 789-8548

Free. Open all year 8 am - sunset.

Matthaei Botanical Garden
1800 N. Dixboro Road
University of Michigan
Ann Arbor, MI 48105
(313) 998-7061

Entrance fee $1.00 to conservatory, grounds are free. Grounds open all year daylight hours. Sells books, wildflower seeds, and live plants. Many educational programs.

Whitehouse Nature Center
Albion College
Albion, MI 49224
(517) 629-2030

Free. Open all year daylight hours. Variety of environmental programs.

Minnesota

Minnesota Landscape Arboretum
3675 Arboretum Drive
P.O. Box 39
Chanhassen, MN 55317
(612) 443-2460

Entrance Fee $3.00. Open all year 8 am - sunset, except major holidays. Sells books and wildflower seeds. Library and other information resources.

Sibley Park
Park Lane
Mankato, MN 56001

Free. Open all year daylight hours.

Missouri

Missouri Botanical Garden
4344 Shaw Boulevard
St. Louis, MO 63110
(314) 577-5125

Entrance fee: $2.00. Open all year 9 am - 5 pm. Sells books, seeds and live plants. Many educational programs and botanical information services.

Missouri Prairie Foundation
P.O. Box 200
Columbia, MO 65205

Manages a system of prairies scattered about the state. Write for locations. Conducted field trips available.

Shaw Arboretum of the Missouri Botanical Garden
I-44 & Route 100
P.O. Box 38
Gray Summit, MO 63039
(314) 577-5138 or 742-3512

Entrance Fee $2.00. Open all year 7 am - sunset, closed during deer hunting season. Sells books, wildflower seeds, and live plants. Prairie restoration area and woodlands.

Montana

Native Plant Gardens
University of Montana
University & Arthur Avenues
Missoula, MT 59801

Free. Open daylight hours. Native plant collection on campus of University of Montana.

Nebraska

Alice Abel Arboretum
5000 St. Paul
Nebraska Wesleyan University
Lincoln, NE 68504
(402) 465-2371

Free. Open all year daylight hours. Small native plant garden.

Chet Ager Nature Center
Pioneers Park
Lincoln, NE 68502

Free. Open 8:30 am - 8:30 pm (June-Aug.), 8:30 am - 5 pm (Sept.- May). Sells books. Wide variety of educational programs.

Earl G. Maxwell Arboretum
East Campus
University of Nebraska
Lincoln, NE 68583-0823
(402) 472-2971

Free. Open all year daylight hours.

Nebraska Statewide Arboretum
C.Y. Thompson Library
East Campus
University of Nebraska
Lincoln, NE 68583-0715
(402) 472-2971

System of over 40 arboreta in Nebraska. Write for details. Publishes newsletter.

North Dakota

USDA Soil Conservation Service
Plant Materials Center
3310 University Drive
P.O. Box 1458
Bismarck, ND 58502
(701) 223-8536

Free. Open all year 8 am - 4:30 pm, Mon. - Fri. Site of developing native grasses.

Ohio

Aullwood Audubon Center and Farm
900 Aullwood Road
Dayton, OH 45414
(513) 890-7360

Entrance Fee $2.00. Open all year 9 am - 5 pm Mon. - Sat., 1 - 5 pm Sun.; closed major holidays. Sells books and wildflower seeds. Many educational programs.

Cedar Bog State Memorial
980 Woodburn Road
Urbana, OH 43708

Entrance Fee $2.00. Open 1 - 3 pm Sat. - Sun. (Apr.-Sept.); otherwise by appointment.

Cincinnati Nature Center
4949 Tealtown Road
Milford, OH 45150-9752
(513) 831-1711

Entrance Fee $1.00. Open all year daylight hours Mon. - Fri. Sells books. Educational programs and workshops.

The Garden Center of Greater Cleveland
11030 East Boulevard
Cleveland, OH 44106
(216) 721-1600

Free. Grounds open all year daylight hours. Sells books. Library and other educational resources available.

Glen Helen
405 Corry Street
Antioch University
Yellow Springs, OH 45387
(513) 767-7375

Free. Open all year daylight hours. Sells books. Woodlands and restored prairie.

Holden Arboretum
9500 Sperry Road
Mentor, OH 44060
(216) 256-1110

Entrance fee $2.50. Open all year, except major holidays, 10 am - 5 pm, Tues-Sun. Sells books. Focus on native flora of Ohio and habitat displays modeled after plant communities. Participating regional Center for Plant Conservation.

Kingwood Center
900 Park Avenue West
Mansfield, OH 44906
(419) 522-0211

Free. Open all year 8 am - sunset. Woodland and tall grass prairie. Library and other information resources.

Toledo Botanical Garden
5403 Elmer Drive
Toledo, OH 43615
(419) 536-8365

Free. Open all year, daylight hours. Sells books.

Oklahoma

Oxley Nature Center
Mohawk Park
(mailing address: 200 Civic Center)
Tulsa, OK 74103
(918) 832-8112

Entrance fee $1.00 for parking on weekends. Open all year 8 am - 5 pm. Varied programs on native plants.

Tulsa Garden Center
Woodward Park
2435 S. Peoria Avenue
Tulsa, OK 74114
(918) 749-6401

Free. Open all year 9 am - 4 pm, Mon.-Fri. Woodward Park open daylight hours.

South Dakota

McCory Gardens
South Dakota State University
Box 2207-C
Brookings, SD 57007-0996
(605) 688-5136

Free. Open all year daylight hours. Prairie garden.

Texas

Dallas Arboretum and Botanic Garden
8525 Garland Road
Dallas, TX 75218
(214) 327-8263

Entrance Fee $5.00, free after 3 pm on Fridays. Open all year, Tues.- Sun., 10 am - sunset (summer), 10 am - 5 pm (winter). Sells books. Wildflower area, native plants used in garden settings, many programs and events.

Dallas Nature Center
Green Hills Foundation
7575 Wheatland Road
Dallas, TX 75249
(214) 296-1955

Free. Open all year daylight hours. Sells books, wildflower seeds, and live plants. Educational programs, wildflower festival, library, and more.

Fort Worth Botanic Garden
3220 Botanic Garden Drive
Fort Worth, TX 76107
(817) 870-7689 information
(817) 870-7686 office

Free. Open all year 8 am -11 pm Mon. - Sun. Sells books, wildflower seeds, and live plants. Many programs.

The Houston Arboretum & Nature Center
4501 Woodway Drive
Houston, TX 77024
(713) 681-8433

Free. Grounds open 8:30 am - 8 pm (May - Oct.), 8:30 am - 6 pm (Nov. - Apr.). Sells books. Many horticultural and environmental programs.

Mercer Arboretum and Botanic Gardens
22306 Aldine Westfield
Humble, TX 77338
(713) 443-8731

Free. Open all year 8 am - 7 pm (daylight savings time), 8 am - 5 pm (winter). Wide range of programs.

The National Wildflower Research Center
2600 FM 973 North
Austin, TX 78725
(512) 929-3600

Free. Open all year 9 am - 4 pm Mon. - Fri., weekends during spring. Sells books. Wildflower gardens and research plots, excellent source of information on native wildflowers, their ecology and culture.

San Antonio Botanical Center
555 Funston Place
San Antonio, TX 78209
(512) 821-5115

Entrance Fee $3.00. Open all year 9 am - 6 pm Tues. -Sun. Sells books, wildflower seeds, and some live plants. Extensive native plant gardens and programs on their cultivation.

South Texas Plant Materials Center
Caesar Kleberg Wildlife R.I.
P.O. Box 218
Kingville, TX 78363

Free. Open all year 8 am - 5 pm Mon. - Fri. Variety selection gardens for native wildflowers and grasses.

Wild Basin Wilderness Preserve
Capital of Texas Highway, Loop 360
P.O. Box 13445
Austin, TX 78711

Free. Open all year daylight hours. 220-acre nature preserve, programs featuring xeriscaping and other uses of native plants.

Wisconsin

Boerner Botanical Gardens
Whitnall Park
5879 S. 92nd Street
Hales Corners, WI 53130
(414) 425-1131

Entrance fee $2.00 for parking. Open all year 8 am - sunset. Sells books. Native plant gardens.

Paine Art Center and Arboretum
1410 Algoma Boulevard
Oshkosh, WI 54901
(414) 235-4530

Free. Open all year 10 am - 4:30 pm. Sells books and wildflower seeds. Offers seminars and workshops.

Schlitz-Audubon Nature Center
1111 E. Brown Deer Road
Milwaukee, WI 53217
(414) 352-2880

Entrance fee $1.50. Open all year, except holidays, 9 am - 5 pm. Programs and courses on native plants and landscaping.

University of Wisconsin Arboretum
1207 Seminole Highway
Madison, WI 53711
(608) 263-7888

Free. Open all year, dawn - 10 pm. Sells books. Extensive prairie restorations, native plant communities, and programs on native plants.

APPENDIX C
Native Plant and Horticultural Societies

Colorado

Colorado Native Plant Society
Box 200
Fort Collins, CO 80522

Publishes Aquilegia. *Regional chapters.*
Sponsors field trips, seminars, and work-
shops.

Colorado Natural Areas Inventory
Department of Natural Resources
1313 Sherman Street, Room 718
Denver, CO 80203
(303)866-3311

State Natural Heritage Program Office.

The Nature Conservancy
Colorado Field Office
1244 Pine Street
Boulder, CO 80302
(303)444-2950

Upper Colorado Environmental Plant
Center
P.O. Box 448
Meeker, CO 81641
(303)878-5003

Part of the network of plant material centers.

Illinois

Illinois Natural Heritage Inventory
Department of Conservation
524 S. 2nd Street
Springfield, IL 62706
(217) 785-8774

State Natural Heritage Program Office.

The Nature Conservancy
Illinois Field Office
79 West Monroe Street, Suite 708
Chicago, IL 60603
(312) 346-8166

Indiana

Indiana Heritage Program
Division of Nature Preserves
Indiana Department of Natural Resources
605b State Office Building
Indianapolis, IN 46204
(317) 232-4052

State Natural Heritage Program Office.

The Nature Conservancy
Indiana Field Office
4200 N. Michigan Road
Indianapolis, IN 46208
(317) 923-7547

Iowa

Iowa Natural Areas Inventory
Bureau of Preserves and Ecological Ser-
vices
Department of Natural Resources
Wallace State Office Building
Des Moines, IA 50319
(515) 281-8524

State Natural Heritage Program Office.

The Nature Conservancy
Iowa Field Office
431 E. Locust, Suite 200
Des Moines, IA 50309
(515) 244-5044

Kansas

Kansas Natural Heritage Program
Kansas State Biological Survey
University of Kansas
Raymond Nichols Hall
2291 Irving Hill Drive - Campus West
Lawrence, KS 66045-2969
(913) 864-3453

State Natural Heritage Program Office.

Kansas Wildflower Society
Mulvane Art Center
Washburne University
17th and Jewell
Topeka, KS 66621

Publishes The Kansas Wildflower Society Newsletter. *Field trips,*
workshops, tours, programs, and exhibits.

The Nature Conservancy
Kansas Field Office
Southwest Plaza Building
Suite 112B
3601 W. 29th Street
Topeka, KS 66614
(913) 272-5115

Michigan

Michigan Botanical Club
Matthaie Botanical Gardens
1800 Dixboro Road
Ann Arbor, MI 48105

Publishes The State Newsletter *and*
Michigan Botanist. *Has 5 regional*
chapters, programs on natural history and
native plants.

Michigan Natural Features Inventory
Mason Building, 5th floor
Box 30028
Lansing, MI 48909
(517) 373-1552

State Natural Heritage Program Office.

The Nature Conservancy
Michigan Field Office
2840 East Grand River, Suite 5
East Lansing, MI 48823
(517) 332-1741

Minnesota

Minnesota Natural Heritage Program
Department of Natural Resources
500 Lafayette Road
St. Paul, MN 55155
(612) 296-4284

State Natural Heritage Program Office.

Minnesota State Horticultural Society
1970 Folwell Avenue, # 161
St. Paul, MN 55108

*Publishes 3 newsletters and Minnesota
Horticulturalist magazine. Seminars, library, and educational programs.*

Minnesota Native Plant Society
220 Biological Science Center
University of Minnesota
1445 Gortner Avenue
St. Paul, MN 55108

*Publishes The Minnesota Plant Press.
Annual conference on native plants, field
trips, regional fairs and exhibits.*

The Nature Conservancy
Minnesota Field Office
1313 5th Street
Minneapolis, MN 55414
(612) 379-2134

Missouri

Missouri Native Plant Society
P.O. Box 6612
Jefferson City, MO 65102

*Publishes Missouriensis, a journal, and
The Petal Pusher newsletter. State and 6
chapter meetings, programs, and field trips.*

Missouri Natural Heritage Inventory
Missouri Department of Conservation
P.O. Box 180
Jefferson City, MO 65102
(314) 751-4115

State Natural Heritage Program Office.

The Missouri Prairie Foundation
P.O. Box 200
Columbia, MO 65205

*Dedicated to the acquisition and restoration
of prairie grasslands and wildlife. Educational programs.*

The Nature Conservancy
Missouri Field Office
2800 South Brentwood Boulevard
St. Louis, MO 63144
(314) 968-1105

Montana

Montana Natural Heritage Program
State Library Building
1515 E. 6th Avenue
Helena, MT 59620
(406) 444-3009

State Natural Heritage Program Office.

The Nature Conservancy
Montana Field Office
Last Chance Gulch and 6th
P.O. Box 258
Helena, MT 59624
(406) 443-0303

Nebraska

The Nature Conservancy
Nebraska Field Office
418 South 10th Street
Omaha, NE 68102
(402) 342-0282

Nebraska Natural Heritage Program
Game and Parks Commission
2200 N. 33rd Street
P.O. Box 30370
Lincoln, NE 68503
(402) 471-5421

State Natural Heritage Program Office.

New Mexico

Native Plant Society of New Mexico
P.O. Box 5917
Santa Fe, NM 87502

*Publishes a newsletter. Sells books on native plants. Has source list for native plant
suppliers. Five regional chapters.*

The Nature Conservancy
New Mexico Field Office
107 Cienega Street
Santa Fe, NM 87501
(505)988-3867

New Mexico Natural Resources Survey
  Section
Villagra Building
Santa Fe, NM 87503
(505)827-7862

State Natural Heritage Program Office.

Plant Materials Center
U.S.D.A. Soil Conservation Service
1036 Miller Street SW
Los Lunas, NM 87031

One of the network of plant material centers.

North Dakota

The Nature Conservancy
Dakotas Field Office
1014 East Central Avenue
Bismarck, ND 58501
(701) 222-8464

Ohio

Native Plant Society of Northeastern
  Ohio
6 Louise Drive
Chagrin Falls, OH 44022

Publishes On the Fringe. *Sponsors field trips and lectures.*

Ohio Natural Heritage Program
Ohio Department of Natural Resources
Division of Natural Areas and Preserves
Fountain Square Building
Columbus, OH 43224
(614) 265-6453

State Natural Heritage Program Office.

The Nature Conservancy
Ohio Field Office
1504 West 1st Avenue
Columbus, OH 43212
(614) 486-6789

Oklahoma

The Nature Conservancy
Oklahoma Field Office
320 South Boston, Suite 846
Tulsa, OK 74103
(918) 585-1117

Oklahoma Native Plant Society
c/o Tulsa Garden Center
2435 South Peoria
Tulsa, OK 74114

Publishes Gaillardia. *Sponsors workshops and field trips. Has 2 local chapters.*

Oklahoma Natural Heritage Inventory
Oklahoma Biological Survey
Sutton Hall, Room 303
625 Elm Street
Norman, OK 73019
(405) 325-1985

State Natural Heritage Program Office.

South Dakota

South Dakota Natural Heritage
South Dakota Department of Game,
Fish, and Parks Wildlife Division
445 E. Capitol Avenue
Pierre, SD 57501-3185
(605) 773-4277

State Natural Heritage Program Office.

Texas

Keep Texas Beautiful, Inc.
P.O. Box 2251
Austin, TX 78768

Encourages the beautification of Texas through planting native wildflowers and trees.

Native Plant Society of Texas
P.O. Box 891
Georgetown, TX 78627

Dedicated to education about, and promotion of preservation, conservation, and utilization of native plants. Regional chapters. Publishes newsletter.

The Native Prairies Association of
Texas
Green Hills Center
7575 Wheatland Road
Dallas, TX 75249

Organization dedicated to the study and preservation of Texas native prairies.

The Nature Conservancy
Texas Field Office
P.O. Box 1440
San Antonio, TX 78295-1440
(512) 224-8774

Texas Natural Heritage Program
Texas Parks and Wildlife Department
4200 Smith School Road
Austin, TX 78744
(512) 389-4586

State Natural Heritage Program Office.

Wisconsin

The Nature Conservancy
Wisconsin Field Office
333 West Mifflin, Suite 107
Madison, WI 53703
(608) 251-8140

Wisconsin Natural Heritage Program
Endangered Resources/4
Department of Natural Resources
101 S. Webster Street, Box 7921
Madison, WI 53707
(608) 266-0924

State Natural Heritage Program Office.

Wyoming

The Nature Conservancy
Wyoming Field Office
258 Main Street
P.O. Box 450
Lander, WY 82520
(307) 332-2971

Wyoming Native Plant Society
P.O. Box 1417
Cheyenne, WY 82003

Publishes WNPS Newsletter. *Sponsors annual field trip.*

Wyoming Natural Diversity Database
3165 University Station
Laramie, WY 82071
(307)766-3441

State Natural Heritage Program Office.

National Organizations

American Horticultural Society
7931 East Boulevard Drive
Alexandria, VA 22308
(707)768-5700

Publishes American Horticulturalist.

American Rock Garden Society
c/o Carole Wilder
221 Ninth Street
Hastings, MN 55033
(612) 437-4390

Publishes The Bulletin of the American Rock Garden Society. *Twenty-nine chapters in North America.*

Canada Wildflower Society
1220 Fieldstone Circle
Pickering, Ontario L1X 1B4

Publishes Wildflower. *Conducts a native plant seed exchange for members, supports wildflower conservation projects, has local chapters.*

Center for Plant Conservation
125 Arbor Way
Jamaica Plain, MA 02130
(617)524-6988

Conservation Foundation/World
 Wildlife Fund
1250 24th Street N.W.
Suite 500
Washington, DC 20037
(202)293-4800

Environmental Defense Fund
444 Park Avenue South
New York, NY 10016
(212)686-4191

National Wildflower Research Center
2600 FM 973 North
Austin, TX 78725
(512)929-3600

Publishes Wildflower. *Conducts research on native plants. Information clearing house. Phone hotline on Texas wildflowers in the spring.*

National Xeriscape Council, Inc.,
P.O. Box 163172
Austin, TX 78757

Publishes Xeriscape News. *State branches; 36 state educational programs.*

The Nature Conservancy
1815 North Lynn Street
Arlington, VA 22209
(703)841-5300

Operation Wildflower
National Council of State Garden Clubs
Mrs. Norman Collard, Chairman
P.O. Box 860
Pocasset, MA 02559

Publishes Columbine. *State and regional chapters. Works with Department of Transportation to plant wildflowers along highways.*

Soil and Water Conservation Society
7515 Northeast Ankeny Road
Ankeny, IA 50021
(515) 289-2331

Dedicated to the conservation of land and water resources, regional chapters, sponsors Managed Natural Areas Program.

U.S. Fish and Wildlife Service
Office of Endangered Species
Washington, D.C. 20240
(703) 235-2771

References

Andrews, J., 1986. *The Texas Bluebonnet.* U. Texas Press, Austin, TX. 64 pp.

A diverse look at the state flowers of Texas in a handsome small volume.

Art, H.W., 1986. *A Garden of Wildflowers.* Garden Way Publishing/ Storey Communications, Pownal, VT. 290 pp.

An illustrated guide to 101 native North American species and how to grow them.

Art, H.W., 1987. *The Wildflower Gardener's Guide: Northeast, Mid-Atlantic, Great Lakes, and Eastern Canada Edition.* Garden Way Publishing/ Storey Communications, Pownal, VT. 180 pp.

A guide on how to grow 32 species native to northeastern North America. Illustrated with color photographs and superb line drawings.

Art, H.W., 1988. *Creating a Wildflower Meadow.* Garden Way Publishing/ Storey Communications, Pownal, VT. 32 pp.

A Garden Way Publishing Bulletin on grasses and wildflowers suitable for North American meadows.

Art, H.W., 1990. *The Wildflower Gardener's Guide: California, Desert Southwest, and Northern Mexico Edition.* Garden Way Publishing/ Storey Communications, Pownal, VT. 176 pp.

A guide on how to grow 34 species native to the Southwest. Illustrated with color photographs and superb line drawings.

Art, H.W., 1990. *The Wildflower Gardener's Guide: Pacific Northwest, Rocky Mountain, and Western Canada Edition.* Garden Way Publishing/ Storey Communications, Pownal, VT. 179 pp.

A guide on how to grow 33 species native to the Northwest and Rockies. Illustrated with color photographs and superb line drawings.

Bailey, L.H., 1935. *The Standard Cyclopedia of Horticulture.* MacMillan, New York, NY. 3639 pp.

A classic gardening encyclopedia containing information on numerous native wildflowers as well as domesticated species.

Brown, L., 1979. *Grasses.* Houghton Mifflin, Co., Boston, MA. 240 pp.

A Peterson Nature Library identification guide to the native and exotic grasses of northeastern North America.

Brown, L., 1985. *Grasslands.* Knopf, New York, NY. 608 pp.

The Audubon Society Nature Guide to the North American prairies. Includes color photos and descriptions of major plants, animals, and fungi.

Collard, L.R., ed., 1985. *Wildflower Culture Guide.* National Council of State Garden Clubs, Inc., St. Louis, MO. 44 pp.

Articles on wildflower culture, wildflower gardens, and "Operation Wildflower."

Costello, D., 1969. *The Prairie World.* U. Minnesota Press, Minneapolis, MN. 244 pp.

A readable narrative about the biology of North American prairies and grasslands.

Crittenden, M. & D. Telfer, 1975., Wildflowers of the West. Celestial Arts Press, Milbrae, CA. 199 pp.

A useful field guide to western wildflowers organized by flower characteristics.

Crockett, J.U. & O.E. Allen, 1977. Wildflower Gardening. Time- Life Books, Alexandria, VA. 160 pp.

Coast-to-coast examples of natives for the garden, with color illustrations.

Currah, R., A. Smreciu & M. Van Dyk, 1983. Prairie Wildflowers. Friends of the Devonian Botanical Garden, U. Alberta, Edmonton, Alberta. 300 pp.

An illustrated manual with suggestions on propagation of species suitable for cultivation and grassland restoration.

Edsall, M.S., 1985. Roadside Plants and Flowers. U. Wisconsin Press, Madison, WI. 143 pp.

A guide to Midwestern and Great Lakes native and exotic wildflowers of open habitats. Organized by flower color illustrated with color photographs.

Enquist, M., 1987. *Wildflowers of the Texas Hill Country*. Lone Star Botanical, Austin, TX. 275 pp.

A full-color photographic guide to wildflowers of the mid-section of the Texas limestone belt, organized by plant family.

Foster, H.L., 1982. *Rock Gardening*. Timber Press, Portland, OR. 466 pp.

A reprint of the 1968 classic guide to growing alpine plants and other wildflowers in American gardens.

Fitzharris, 1986. *Wildflowers of Canada*. Oxford U. Press, Toronto, Ontario. 156 pp.

A handsome book with basic information about common wildflowers and superb color photographs.

Gould, F.W., 1951. *Grasses of the Southwestern United States*. U. Arizona Press, Tucson, AZ. 352 pp.

A somewhat technical, yet readable, guide to shortgrass and desert grassland grass species with excellent line drawings.

Hartmann, H.T. & D.E. Kester, 1975. *Plant Propagation*, 3rd Edition. Prentice-Hall, Englewood Cliffs, NJ. 662.pp

A standard text about plant propagation.

Hill, L., 1985. *Secrets of Plant Propagation*. Garden Way Publishing, Pownal, VT. 168 pp.

How to propagate woody and herbaceous plants.

Hull, H.S., ed., 1982. *Handbook on Gardening with Wildflowers*. Brooklyn Botanic Garden, Brooklyn, NY. [B.B.G. Plants & Gardens 18(1).] 85 pp.

A variety of articles about native plant gardening.

Jacob, W. & I. Jacob, 1985. *Gardens of North America and Hawaii*. Timber Press, Portland, OR. 368 pp.

A useful cross-continent guide to gardens and arboreta with short descriptions and helpful state maps.

Johnson, L.B. & C.B. Less, 1988. *Wildflowers Across America*. National Wildflower Research Center & Abbeyville Press, New York, NY. 309 pp.

A coffee-table book with exciting and elegant color photographs of native and exotic wildflowers.

Kirt, R.R., 1989. *Prairie Plants of Northern Illinois*. Stipes Publishing, Champaign, IL. 83 pp.

A guide to identification and ecology of common tallgrass prairie plants illustrated with line drawings, and organized by plant family.

Kucera, C.L., 1961. *The Grasses of Missouri*. U. Missouri Press, Columbia, MO. 241 pp.

A technical manual with keys to and illustrations of grasses of the central Midwest.

Loughmiller, C. & L. Loughmiller, 1984. *Texas Wildflowers*. U. Texas Press, Austin, TX. 271 pp.

A color photographic guide to Texas wildflowers organized by plant family.

Martin, A.C., H.S. Zim, & A.L. Nelson, 1951. *American Wildlife and Plants*. Dover, New York, NY. 500 pp.

While not a book about wildflower gardening, this book is quite helpful in planning gardens to attract various wildlife species.

Martin, L.C., 1986. *The Wildflower Meadow Book*. East Woods Press, Charlotte, NC. 303 pp.

A coast-to-coast treatment of native and exotic wildflowers that grow in fields and meadows.

McGourty, F., 1978. *Ground Covers and Vines*. Brooklyn Botanic Garden, Brooklyn, NY. [B.B.G. Plants & Gardens 32(3).] 80 pp.

A useful booklet with articles on both native and exotic plants used as ground covers.

Mohlenbrock, R.H., n.d. *Wildflowers of Fields, Roadsides, and Open Habitats of Illinois*. Illinois Department of Conservation, Springfield, IL. 226 pp.

A full-color guide to tallgrass prairie plants with detailed close-up photographs.

Moore, M., 1979. *Medicinal Plants of the Mountain West*. Museum of New Mexico Press, Santa Fe, NM. 200 pp.

An intriguing book detailing the medicinal properties of many wildflowers.

National Wildflower Research Center, 1989. *Wildflower Handbook*. Texas Monthly Press, Austin, TX pp 337.

A very useful reference on wildflowers, where to purchase them, and where to obtain further information about them.

Newcomb, L., 1977. *Newcomb's Wildflower Guide*. Little, Brown, Co., Boston, MA. 490 pp.

A field guide to wildflowers east of the Mississippi River and north of the Mason-Dixon Line.

Niehaus, T.F., C.L. Ripper, & V. Savage, 1984. *A Field Guide to Southwestern and Texas Wildflowers*. Houghton-Mifflin, Boston, MA. 449 pp.

A Peterson Field Guide Series edition for the area east of the Colorado River and south of the Red River.

Niering, W.A. & N.C. Olmstead, 1979. *The Audubon Society Field Guide to North American Wildflowers, Eastern Region*. Knopf, New York, NY. 887 pp.

A color photographic guide to wildflowers east of the Rocky Mountains.

Orr, R.T. & M.C. Orr, 1974. *Wildflowers of Western America*. Knopf, New York, NY. 270 pp.

A color photographic guide to western wildflowers with good written descriptions of plants and their ecology.

Owensby, C.E., 1980. *Kansas Prairie Wildflowers*. Iowa State U. Press, Ames, IA. 124 pp.

A color photographic guide, with maps, organized by flower color and season.

Peterson, R.T., 1968. *A Field Guide to Wildflowers of Northeastern and North-Central North America*. Houghton Mifflin, Boston, MA. 420 pp.

The Peterson Field Guide to wildflowers of the tallgrass prairies and northeastern deciduous forests.

Phillips, H.R., 1985. *Growing and Propagating Wildflowers*. U. North Carolina Press, Chapel Hill, NC. 331 pp.

An excellent book on eastern native plants, including many prairie species, giving information on seed collection and propagation.

Phillips, J., 1987. *Southwestern Landscaping with Native Plants*. Museum of New Mexico Press, Santa Fe, NM. 140 pp.

A helpful guide to planning and planting xeriscapes.

Phillips Petroleum Company, 1963. *Pasture and Range Plants*. Phillips Petroleum Company, Bartlesville, OK. 176 pp.

Range and forage plants of North American prairies illustrated with color drawings.

Ramaley, F., 1927. *Colorado Plant Life*. U. Colorado Press, Boulder, CO. 299 pp.

Out of print, but worth searching for this information-filled guide to many species of Rocky Mountain wildflowers.

Ray, M.H. & R.P. Nicholls, 1988. *The Traveller's Guide to American Gardens*. U. North Carolina Press, Chapel Hill, NC. 375 pp.

A state-by-state guide to gardens in the United States.

Rock, H.W., 1971, *Prairie Propagation Handbook*. Wher Nature Center, Whitnall Park, Hales Corners, WI. 80 pp.

An excellent compendium of information on propagation of prairie wildflowers organized alphabetically by species.

Runkel, S.T. and D.M. Roosa, 1989. *Wildflowers of the Tallgrass Prairie: The Upper Midwest*. Iowa State U. Press, Ames, IA. 279 pp.

A beautifully produced book, too large to fit in the pocket, with excellent color photos.

Sawyers, C.E., ed, 1989. *Gardening with Wildflowers & Native Plants*. Brooklyn Botanic Garden, Brooklyn, NY. [B.B.G. Plants & Gardens 18(1).] 104 pp.

A variety of articles about native plant gardening.

Smith, J.R. & B.S., 1980. *The Prairie Garden*. U. Wisconsin Press, Madison, WI. 219 pp.

A guide to gardening with 70 species of prairie plants with line drawings and some color photographs.

Snyder, L.C., 1978. *Gardening in the Upper Midwest*. U. Minnesota Press, Minneapolis, MN. 292 pp.

A horticultural guide to the states and provinces bordering Minnesota.

Steffek, E.F., 1983. *The New Wild Flowers and How to Grow Them*. Timber Press, Portland, OR. 186 pp.

A sampling of wildflowers from North America, with useful tables of species from various regions and habitats.

Stubbendieck, J., S.L. Hatch, & K.J. Hirsch, 1986. *North American Range Plants*. U. of Nebraska Press, Lincoln, NE. 465 pp.

An illustrated guide to wildflowers and forage plants of the Great Plains.

Sullivan, G.A. & R.H. Dailey, 1981. *Resources on Wildflower Propagation*. National Council of State Garden Clubs, Inc., St. Louis, MO. 331 pp.

Contains a wealth of technical information about plants native to various regions of North America.

Sunset Books, 1988. *Sunset Western Garden Book*. Lane Publishing, Menlo Park, CA. 592 pp.

An excellent resource book for gardeners from the Rocky Mountain foothills to the Pacific. Treats both native and exotic species with great care.

Vance, F.R., J.R. Jowsey, & J.S. McLean, 1984. *Wildflowers of the Northern Great Plains*. U. Minnesota Press, Minneapolis, MN. 336 pp. [also under the title of *Wildflowers Across the Prairie*. Western Producer Prairie Press, Saskatoon, SK].

Keys and color photos of wildflowers of the western Canadian prairie provinces and adjacent Great Plains.

Voigt, J.W. & R.H. Mohlenbrock, n.d. *Prairie Plants of Illinois*. Department of Conservation, State of Illinois, Springfield, IL. 272 pp.

An excellent pocket guidebook to plants of the tallgrass prairie, with attractive line drawings.

Wasowski, S. & J. Ryan, 1985. *Landscaping with Native Texas Plants.* Texas Monthly Press, Austin, TX. 233 pp.

More than just wildflowers, this book gives vignettes of native trees and shrubs as well, along with garden plans and color photographs.

Weaver, J.E. & F.W. Albertson, 1956. *Grasslands of the Great Plains, Their Nature and Use.* Johnsen Publishing Co., Lincoln, NE. 395 pp.

The classic work on shortgrass and mixed-grass prairie ecology is worth taking out of the library if it can't be found in used bookstores.

Webb, W.P., 1931., *The Great Plains.* Grosset & Dunlap, New York, NY. 525 pp.

The classic work exploring the geography, history, and culture of the Great Plains, laced with ecological observations.

Wilson, W.H.W., 1984. *Landscaping with Wildflowers and Native Plants.* Ortho Books, San Francisco, CA. 96 pp.

Listings of native plants for various regions and habitats.

Young, J.A. & C.G. Young, 1986. *Collecting, Processing, and Germinating Seeds of Wildland Plants.* Timber Press, Portland, OR. 236 pp.

Glossary

Annual. A plant whose life cycle from seed to mature plant, producing flowers, fruits and seeds, is completed in a single growing season. After seeds are produced, the plant usually dies.

Anther. A pollen-producing sac attached to the filament in the male portion of a flower.

Axil. The point of attachment between stem and leaf.

Basal rosette. An arrangement of leaves radiating from a short stem at the ground surface. Most biennials have a rosette form during their first growing season.

Biennial. A plant whose life cycle extends over two growing seasons. The first year the seed germinates, producing a seedling that usually remains short over the winter. The second growing season the seedling rapidly elongates, flowers, produces seeds, and then dies.

Bolting. The rapid elongation and flowering of biennials during their second growing season.

Boreal. Pertaining to regions of the northern hemisphere that have cold winters and forests dominated by coniferous species.

Bract. A modified leaflike structure, often resembling a petal, surrounding a flower or flower cluster.

Bulb. A fleshy rootstock composed of leaf bases or scaly leaves.

Bunch grasses. Species of grass that form distinct clumps or bunches as they grow, in contrast to the sod-forming grasses usually grown for lawns.

Calyx. The collective term for the sepals of a flower.

Capsule. A dry fruit that splits open to release its seeds.

Chaparral. Thickets of fire-adapted shrubs and small trees that develop in regions with hot dry summers and mild wet winters.

Coastal prairie. A natural grassland that develops near the Pacific Coast, usually on south-facing slopes that burn frequently.

Complete flowers. Flowers with sepals, petals, stamens, and a pistil all present.

Composite flower. A flower made up of many individual florets clustered into a common head, as is typical in members of the aster family.

Compound leaf. A leaf that is divided into two or more separate leaflets.

Corm. A fleshy rootstock formed by a short, thick, underground stem.

Corolla. The collective term for the petals of a flower.

Crest. A ridge of tissue.

Deciduous. Pertaining to plant parts, usually leaves, that are shed annually.

Desert. An ecosystem that develops in regions with annual precipitation of less than 10 inches, usually dominated by widely spaced shrubs and, where winters are mild, succulent species.

Disc flower (disc floret). One of the small, tubular flowers that form the central disc of flower heads in many members of the aster family.

Dissected. Deeply divided or split into lobes.

Dormancy. The resting or inactive phase of plants or seeds. Dormancy of shoots is usually in response to unfavorable environmental conditions. The breaking of seed dormancy requires moisture and sometimes cold tempertures and abrasion of the seed coat.

Elaiosome. An oily, starchy appendage on some seeds that attracts ants and other insects, which act as disperal agents.

Entire. A leaf margin that is smooth and lacking teeth.

Fibrous roots. A root system with many thin or branched root elements.

Filament. The anther-bearing stalk of a stamen.

Floret. One of the small flowers that is clustered together forming the composite flower head in members of the aster family. Florets may be either tubular disc florets or straplike ray florets.

Flowering shoot. A stem that produces flowers.

Flower head. A cluster of florets or small flowers gathered together on a common receptacle, typically found in members of the aster family.

Forcing. Inducing a perennial to flower out of season. Forcing often involves artificial chilling followed by warming the plant.

Germination. The breaking of dormancy in seeds or the sprouting of pollen grains deposited on a stigma.

Habitat. The kind of environment inhabited by a particular species.

Half-hardy. An annual plant that is sown in early spring and flowers in summer.

Hardiness zone. An index relating geographic regions to a plant's ability to withstand minimum winter temperatures. Hardiness zones developed by the U.S. Department of Agriculture range from zone 1, with a minimum temperature of -50°F, to zone 10, with minimum temperatures of 30 to 40°F.

Hardy annual. An annual plant whose seeds can withstand subfreezing winter temperatures and whose seedlings can withstand spring frosts.

Hardy perennial. A perennial plant that is not permanently injured or killed by subfreezing temperatures.

Herbaceous. Plants that lack woody tissues and therefore "die back" to the soil surface at the end of the growing season.

Humus. Soft brown or black amorphous substance formed through the decomposition of leaves, wood, and other organic materials.

Inoculant. A commercially formulated strain of rhizobium added to the soil to aid in the establishment of various members of the bean family.

Inoculation. The addition of rhizobia to the soil.

Involucre. A whorl of leafy bracts surrounding composite flower heads such as those in the aster family.

Keel. The lower, pouchlike lip of flowers of certain members of the bean family. The keel is formed by the fusion of two petals.

Leaflets. The individual segments of a compound leaf.

Legume. A dry, flattened pod fruit that splits open at both edges when mature, as is found in members of the bean family. The term is also applied to the species of the bean family.

Long-day plant. A plant that flowers in response to the short nights of late spring and early summer.

Moist chilling treatment. A means of enhancing the germination of some seeds by storing them under moist conditions at low temperatures prior to planting them.

Montane. Pertaining to mountain environments, usually below the timberline.

Nodules. Outgrowths on the roots of plants in the bean family that are inhabited by nitrogen-fixing microorganisms known as rhizobia.

Non-flowering shoot. A stem that does not produce flowers; a vegetative shoot.

Ovary. The swollen base of a pistil, containing ovules. The ripening ovary, which is sometimes fused to the receptacle, becomes the fruit.

Ovules. The female sex cells that become seeds following fertilization.

Palmate. A pattern of compound leaflets or leaf venation, with elements radiating from a central point.

Peduncle. The main flowering stalk of a plant.

Perennial. A plant whose life cycle extends for an indefinite period beyond two growing seasons. These plants generally do not die following flowering.

Perfect flowers. Flowers with both stamens and a pistil, but lacking either sepals and/or petals.

Petal. A modified leaf attached to the receptacle outside the stamens and inside the calyx. Petals are usually showy and serve to attract pollinators to the flower.

Petiole. The stalk that attaches a leaf to a stem.

pH. A measure of the acidity/alkalinity of a substance ranging from 0 (strongly acidic) to 14 (strongly alkaline), with 7 being neutral.

Pistil. The female sexual part of a flower, consisting of the stigma, style, and ovary.

Plugs. A method of propagation by planting individual seeds in specially designed trays with small indentations. The root system of the seedlings fills the hole, forming a plug that can be easily removed and planted where desired.

Pollen. The powdery material produced in anthers, containing the male sex cells of flowering plants.

Pollination. The transfer of pollen from an anther to a stigma.

Pollinia. A pair of sticky pollen masses produced by milkweeds.

Propagation. Increasing the numbers of plants through seeds, cuttings, or divisions.

Pulvinus. A small, bulbous organ at the base of a petiole that controls the sun-tracking movement of leaves.

Ray flower (ray floret). One of the small flowers with a straplike petal, usually arranged in rings around the margin of flower heads in members of the aster family.

Receptacle. The fleshy tissue at the tip of a flower stalk to which flower parts are attached. Different species may have receptacles that are positioned below the ovary, form a cup around the ovary, or completely enclose the ovary.

Rhizobia. Microorganisms that inhabit nodules on the roots of members of the bean family. These organisms have the ability to take nitrogen from the air and create nitrogen compounds, usable by their host plants.

Rhizome. A horizontal, usually branched, underground stem with buds and roots.

Root division. Propagating plants by cutting vertically between root segments.

Root rot. Plant diseases, usually caused by fungi, that lead to the degeneration of roots.

Rootstock. An underground stem of a perennial plant with its associated buds and roots.

Runner. A thin, creeping, horizontal stem that trails along the surface of the ground and gives rise to small plants.

Scape. A leafless stem bearing a cluster of flowers.

Scarification. Abrasion of the seed coat allowing the passage of water and oxygen into the seed, thereby enhancing germination in some species.

Seed coat. The outer protective covering of a seed.

Sepal. A modified leaf that forms the covering of a flower bud. Sepals are attached to the outer margin of the receptacle and are usually green. However, in some species the sepals are brightly colored and resemble petals.

Shoot. The aboveground or stem portion of a plant that bears leaves, buds, and flowers.

Shoot bud. A bud that develops into stem and leaf tissue.

Short-day plant. A plant that flowers in response to the long nights of fall or early spring.

Simple flower. A solitary flower borne on a single stem.

Slip. An old-fashioned name for a cutting used for propagation.

Sods. A method of propagation by densely planting seeds in flats or trays. The root systems of the seedlings intertwine, allowing the sod to be removed in a single piece and planted where desired.

Softwood cutting. A propagation technique of cutting green, rapidly growing portions of stems while they are pliable.

Spadix. A fleshy, spindle-shaped column bearing flowers in members of the arum family.

Spathe. A large, leafy bract that frequently envelops the spadix in members of the arum and other plant families.

Stamen. The male sexual part of a flower consisting of an anther and a filament.

Stigma. The top surface of a pistil upon which pollen grains are deposited.

Stolon. A thin, underground runner.

Stratification. Chilling seeds to enhance their germination.

Style. The portion of the pistil connecting the stigma and the ovary.

Taproot. A thick, strongly vertical root, usually extending to considerable depth, for example, the carrot.

Tender annual. An annual plant whose seedlings are killed by spring frosts.

Tender perennial. Perennial plants that are permanently damaged or killed by subfreezing temperatures.

True root. The descending, underground portion of a plant that is specialized to provide support and absorb water and nutrients. True roots usually lack buds.

Tuber. A rootstock formed by a fleshy, swollen tip of a stolon.

Tule meadow. Wetland vegetation interspersed in valley grasslands and dominated by tule (bulrush) and cattails.

Vernal pools. "Hog wallows" or depressions that collect water over the winter rainy season and form temporary pools. As pools dry out over the spring various wildflowers bloom at their edges.

Vernalization. The cold treatment needed by some fall-germinating plants to promote flowering the following spring.

Weed. Any plant that grows where it is not wanted.

Wetlands. An area of low-lying land with soils that are submerged or wet for a significant portion of each year.

Wildflower. An herbaceous plant capable of growing, reproducing, and becoming established without cultivation.

Winter annual. An annual plant that usually germinates in the fall, overwinters as a seedling, and flowers the following spring.

Woody. Having hard, tough tissues that persist from year to year and are capable of producing shoot or flower buds. Woody plants also have the capacity to increase in diameter from year to year.

Xeriscaping. A landscaping technique in which water consumption is reduced by planting drought-resistant species, matching water requirements of landscape plants to available soil moisture, using high-efficiency irrigation systems, and other water-conserving techniques.

Index

Boldface numbers, such as **55**, indicate that illustrations or tables appear on that page.

Oswego tea, 108
Ovary, **36**, 37
Ovules, 37
Ozark sundrops. *See* Missouri evening
  primrose

P

Panicum virgatum. See Switchgrass
Pansy violet. *See* Birdsfood violet
Parthenium integrifolium. See Wild
  quinine
Partridgeberry, **41, 64**
Pasqueflower, 13, **91**, 92-93, **93**
Pasture rose, **109**, 110-111, **111**
Peduncle, 36
Pests, 57-58
Petal, **36**
Petalostemum candidum. See White
  prairie clover
Petalostemum purpureum. See Purple
  prairie clover
Phlox pilosa. See Prairie phlox
Phlox pubescent. See Prairie phlox
pH of soil, 52-56, **53**
Physical characteristics of region, 3-6
Physostegia virginiana. See False
  dragonhead
Physostégie de Virginie. See False
  dragonhead
Pink evening primrose, 90
Pistil, **36**, 37
Plant descriptions, 36-41
Plant height, **39**
Planting stock, 15-18
  suppliers, 19, 168-179, 171, 172, 174
Planting techniques, 33-34, 61-63
Pleurisy root. *See* Butterfly weed
Plugs, 62
Pollination of butterfly weed, 12
Ponderosa pine, 27
Populus tremuloides. See Quaking aspen
Porcupine needlegrass, 8, **32, 91**
Post oak, 8
Potting soil, 62
Prairie avens. See Prairie smoke (*Geum
  triflorum*)
Prairie blazing star. *See* Gayfeather
Prairie coneflower. *See* Mexican hat
Prairie cordgrass, 6
Prairie dropseed, 8, **30, 32, 109**

Prairie grasses (native), **30-32.** *See also*
  Grass(es)
Prairie larkspur, 108
Prairie meadows, 27-29
  planting, 33-34
Prairie phlox, 13, **24, 91**, 102-103,
  103
Prairie rose. *See* Pasture rose
Prairie smoke (*Anemone patens*). *See*
  Pasqueflower
Prairie smoke (*Geum triflorum*), 13, **91**,
  98-99, **99**
Precipitation, 2
  annual, **68**
  geographic distribution of, 48
  tallgrass prairie region, 6
Propagation, 59-66
Purple coneflower, **24, 109**, 130-131,
  131
Purple poppy mallow. *See* Wine cup
Purple prairie clover, **24, 26, 133**,
  146-147, **147**

Q

Quaking aspen, 153
Queen-of-the-prairie, **109**, 120-121,
  121
Quercus macrocarpa. See Bur oak
Quercus stellata. See Post oak

R

Rainfall. *See* Precipitation
Ratibida columnaris. See Mexican hat
Ratibida columnifera. See Mexican hat
Rattlesnake master, **109**, 122-123, **123**
Ray flower, **36**, 37
Receptacle, 36, **36**
Redbud, 91
Red cedar, 109
Red Mexican hat. *See* Mexican hat
Red milkweed, 108
Red sunflower. *See* Purple coneflower
Red tassel flower. *See* Purple prairie
  clover
Reine des prés. See Queen-of-the-
  prairie
Rhexia virginica. See Meadow beauty
Rhexie de Virginie. See Meadow beauty
Rhizobia inoculants, 63
Rhizomes, 40, **41, 64**
Rhus aromatica. See Fragrant sumac

Rhus glabra. See Smooth sumac
Rhus trilobata. See Skunkbush sumac
Ribies aureum. See Golden currant
Ribies odoratum. See Golden currant
Rock gardens, 24
Rocky Mountain beeplant, 132
Roots, 40-41
Rootstock division, 63-65
Rosa carolina. See Pasture rose
Rosa woodsii. See Wood's rose
Rosier de Caroline. See Pasture rose
Rosinweed. *See* Compass plant
Rudbeckia hirta. See Black-eyed Susan
Rudbeckia serotina. See Black-eyed
  Susan
Rudbeckie hérissée. See Black-eyed
  Susan
Rudbeckie tardive. See Black-eyed Susan
Runners, 40
  division, 64, **64**

S

Sagebrush, 27, 133
Sand coreopsis. *See* Lance-leaved
  coreopsis
Scarification of seeds, 60-61
Scarlet globe mallow, 132
Scarlet paintbrush, 90
Schinia masoni. See Flower moth
Schizackyrium scoparium. See Little
  bluestem
Sedge, 8
Seedlings, care of, 61-62
Seeds, 40, 59-61
  collecting, 17, 59-60
  for prairie meadows, 27-28
  heat treatment, 61
  light or dark treatments, 61
  propagation by, 59-61
  scarification, 60-61
  sowing techniques, 33-35
  stratification, 60
  suppliers, 19, 168-170, 171, 172,
    173, 174
  wildflower mixtures, 17-18
Sepal, **36**
Shadbush, 91
Shade
  borders, 22
  wildflowers for, 24